Turkish

A ROUGH GUIDE
PHRASEBOOK

Compiled
by Lexus

Credits

Compiled by Lexus with Memduha Tee

Lexus Series Editor:	Sally Davies
Rough Guides Phrasebook Editor:	Jonathan Buckley
Rough Guides Series Editor:	Mark Ellingham

This first edition published in 1996 by Rough Guides Ltd, 1 Mercer Street, London WC2H 9QJ.

Distributed by the Penguin Group.

Penguin Books Ltd, 27 Wrights Lane, London W8 5TZ
Penguin Books USA Inc., 375 Hudson Street, New York 10014, USA
Penguin Books Australia Ltd, 487 Maroondah Highway, PO Box 257, Ringwood, Victoria 3134, Australia
Penguin Books Canada Ltd, Alcorn Avenue, Toronto, Ontario, Canada M4V 1E4
Penguin Book (NZ) Ltd, 182–190 Wairau Road, Auckland 10, New Zealand

Typeset in Rough Serif and Rough Sans to an original design by Henry Iles.
Printed by Cox & Wyman Ltd, Reading.

© Lexus Ltd 1996
256pp.

British Library Cataloguing in Publication Data
A catalogue for this book is available from the British Library.

ISBN 1-85828-173-3

CONTENTS

Introduction   v

The BASICS: Pronunciation (3); Abbreviations (4); The Turkish
    Alphabet (4); Suffixes (5); Vowel Harmony (5); Articles (6);
    Nouns (6); Cases (7); Adjectives (10); Possessive Suffixes
    (11); Demonstratives (14); Pronouns (14); Verbs (17);
    Questions (29); Also, Too (29); Can, To Be Able (30); Dates
    (30); Days (30); Months (31); Time (31); Numbers (31);
    Basic Phrases (33); Conversion Tables (35)

English - Turkish   39

Turkish - English   147

Menu Reader

    Food   227

    Drink   245

INTRODUCTION

The Rough Guide Turkish phrasebook is a highly practical introduction to the contemporary language. Laid out in clear A-Z style, it uses key-word referencing to lead you straight to the words and phrases you want – so if you need to book a room, just look up 'room'. The Rough Guide gets straight to the point in every situation, in bars and shops, on trains and buses, and in hotels and banks.

The main part of the Rough Guide is a double dictionary: English-Turkish then Turkish-English. Before that, there's a section called **The Basics**, which sets out the fundamental rules of the language and its pronunciation, with plenty of practical examples. You'll also find here other essentials like numbers, dates, telling the time and basic phrases.

Forming the heart of the guide, the **English-Turkish** section gives easy-to-use transliterations of the Turkish words wherever pronunciation might be a problem, and to get you involved quickly in two-way communication, the Rough Guide includes dialogues featuring typical responses on key topics – such as renting a car and asking directions. Feature boxes fill you in on cultural pitfalls as well as the simple mechanics of how to make a phone call, what to do in an emergency, where to change money, and more. Throughout this section, cross-references enable you to pinpoint key facts and phrases, while asterisked words indicate where further information can be found in the Basics.

In the **Turkish-English** dictionary, we've given not just the phrases you're likely to hear (starting with a selection of slang and colloquialisms), but also all the signs, labels, instructions and other basic words you might come across in print or in public places.

Finally the Rough Guide rounds off with an extensive **Menu Reader**. Consisting of food and drink sections (each starting with a list of essential terms), it's indispensable whether you're eating out, stopping for a quick drink, or browsing through a local food market.

iyi yolculuklar!
have a good trip!

The Basics

PRONUNCIATION

In this phrasebook, the Turkish has been written in a system of imitated pronunciation so that it can be read as though it were English, bearing in mind the notes on pronunciation given below:

a	as in f**a**r
ay	as in m**ay**
e/eh	as in g**e**t
ew	as in f**ew**
g	always hard as in **g**oat
H	a harsh 'ch' as in the Scottish way of pronouncing lo**ch**
ī	'i' as in m**i**ght
J	's' as in mea**s**ure
o	as in h**o**t
oh	'o' as in **o**pen
s	always 's' as in dre**ss** (never 'z')
uh	'u' as in b**u**t
y	as in **y**es

Letters given in bold type indicate the part of the word to be stressed (although the stress is not heavy). In most cases, the stress is on the end of a word.

As **i** and **u** are always pronounced 'ee' and 'oo' in Turkish, pronunciation has not been given for words containing these letters unless they present other problems for the learner.

Turkish Pronunciation

a	as in f**a**r
â	as in L**a**tin
ay	'i' as in m**i**ght
c	'j' as in **j**elly
ç	'ch' as in **ch**at
e	as in 'g**e**t'
ey	'ay' as in m**ay**
g	always hard as in '**g**oat'
ğ	generally silent, but lengthens the preceding vowel

h	sometimes pronounced 'h' as in **h**en; occasionally pronounced 'ch' as in the Scottish pronunciation of lo**ch**
ı	'u' as in b**u**t
i	'ee' as in 'n**ee**d'
j	's' as in 'mea**s**ure'
o	as in 'h**o**t'; sometimes 'o' as in **o**pen (usually when followed by ğ)
ö	'ur' as in b**ur**n (like German 'ö')
öy	'uh-i' run together quickly as one sound
s	's' as in dre**ss** (never 'z')
ş	'sh' as in **sh**ape
u	'u' as in p**u**ll, transcribed as 'oo' in the pronunciation
ü	'ew' as in f**ew** (like French 'u' and German 'ü')

When **e** occurs at the end of a Turkish word, it is always pronounced, for example **bile** (already) is pronounced [beel**eh**].

ABBREVIATIONS

abl	ablative	loc	locative
acc	accusative	nom	nominative
adj	adjective	pl	plural
dat	dative	pol	polite
fam	familiar	sing	singular
gen	genitive		

THE TURKISH ALPHABET

The Turkish-English section and Menu Reader are in Turkish alphabetical order which is as follows:

a, b, c, ç, d, e, f, g, ğ, h, ı, i, j, k, l, m, n, o, ö, p, r, s, ş, t, u, ü, v, y, z

SUFFIXES

One very special feature of Turkish is that endings or suffixes are added to words where in the equivalent English separate words would be used. In Turkish, for example, all prepositions and possessive adjectives are suffixes and some verbal structures are made up of a stem and suffixes. In the Turkish-English section of this book, suffixes have been listed as separate entries, for example: -den (from), -a (to).

For example:

oda-m-da
odamda
in my room
(literally: room-my-in)

ülke-miz-e
ewlkemeezeh
to our country
(literally: country-our-to)

şehir-de
sheh-heerdeh
in the city

VOWEL HARMONY

Vowels in Turkish fall into two categories: hard vowels (a ı o u) and soft vowels (e i ö and ü). Vowel harmony simply means that if the final vowel of a word is a hard vowel, any suffix added to the word will also contain hard vowels, and if the final vowel is a soft vowel, any suffix will contain only soft vowels:

final vowel in a word	can only be followed by
a or ı	a or ı
o or u	a or u
e or i	e or i
ö or ü	e or ü

For example:

dükkan
dewkkan
shop

İngiltere
eengeeltereh
England

dükkana
dewkkana
to the shop

İngiltere'den
eengeeltereh-den
from England

kapı
kapuh
door

gemi
gemee
ship

kapıya
kapuh-ya
to the door

gemiye
gemee-yeh
to the ship

havuz
havooz
pool

otobüs
otobews
bus

havuzda
havoozda
in the pool

otobüste
otobewsteh
in the bus

ARTICLES

The indefinite article (a, an) is the same as the word for 'one' bir:

> bir bardak çay
> beer bardak chī
> a glass of tea

> bir otel odası
> beer otel odasuh
> a hotel room

> balkonlu bir oda
> balkonloo beer oda
> a room with a balcony

> Türkiye hakkında bir film
> tewrkee-yeh hakkuhnda beer feelm
> a film about Turkey

In phrases with an adjective, bir usually comes between the adjective and the noun:

> büyük bir başarı
> bewyewk beer basharuh
> a great success

> bize başka bir oda verebilir misiniz?
> beezeh bashka beer oda verebeeleer meeseeneez
> can we have another room?

In Turkish, there is no separate word for the definite article (the):

> yönetici
> yurneteejee
> manager/the manager

> yemek listesi
> yemek leestesee
> menu/the menu

The context will indicate whether 'the' is meant in English:

> yöneticiyi görebilir miyim?
> yurneteejee-yee gurebeeleer mee-yeem
> can I see the manager?

> yemek listesini görebilir miyim?
> yemek leesteseenee gurebeeleer mee-yeem
> may I see the menu?

NOUNS

Gender

Turkish nouns do not have genders.

Plural Nouns

To make a noun plural, add the ending -ler or -lar depending on whether the final vowel of the noun is a soft or a hard vowel:

	after hard vowels a, ı, o, u	after soft vowels e, i, ö, ü
add	-lar	-ler

tren	trenler
train	trains
müze	müzeler
mewzeh	mewzeler
museum	museums

minare	minareler
meenare**h**	meenarel**er**
minaret	minarets
numara	numaralar
number	numbers
çarşı	çarşılar
charsh**uh**	charshuhl**ar**
market	markets
çocuk	çocuklar
choj**oo**k	chojookl**ar**
child	children

As a rule, plurals are used in Turkish only if there is no other indication of plurality such as a number or a word like 'a few', 'a lot' etc:

köpek	iki köpek
kurp**e**k	eek**ee** kurp**e**k
(the) dog	two dogs

birkaç köpek
beerk**a**ch kurp**e**k
some dogs,
a couple of dogs

köpekler havlıyor
kurpekl**e**r havl**uh**-yor
the dogs are barking

In greetings and expressions of good wishes a plural is used in Turkish when the singular is used in English:

iyi akşamlar
ee-y**ee** akshaml**ar**
good evening
(literally: good evenings)

iyi geceler
ee-y**ee** gejeler
good night
(literally: good nights)

CASES

Turkish has six cases: nominative, accusative, genitive, dative, locative and ablative. These cases are all formed using suffixes. The table on page 9 shows the endings for each case, examples of which are given below.

Nominative Case

The nominative is the case of the subject of the sentence. The nominative is the case in which nouns are given in the English-Turkish section of this book. In the following examples dükkan and Ahmed are in the nominative:

dükkan şimdi açık
dewkk**a**n sheemd**ee** ach**uh**k
the shop is open now

Ahmed bugün geldi
aHmed bewg**e**wn geld**ee**
Ahmed arrived today

Accusative Case

The object of most verbs takes the accusative. In the following examples the object (e.g. Topkapi Palace) is in the accusative:

Topkapı Sarayı'nı görmeye
gittik
topkapuh sarī-**uh** gurmay**eh**
geett**ee**k
we went to see the Topkapi
Palace

bavulumu gördünüz mü?
bavooloom**oo** gurdewn**ew**z
mew
did you see my suitcase?

telefonu kullanabilir miyim?
may I use the phone?

Genitive Case

The genitive is used to
indicate possession:

babamın evi
babam**uh**n ev**ee**
my father's house

Mustafa'nın annesi
moostafa-n**uh**n annes**ee**
Mustafa's mother

pilotun üniforması
peelot**oo**n ewneeformas**uh**
the pilot's uniform

There is no one word for 'of'
in Turkish. The genitive suffix
is used to translate of:

otelin adı
otel**ee**n ad**uh**
the name of the hotel

biletin fiyatı
beelet**ee**n fee-yat**uh**
the price of the ticket

Dative Case

The dative is used for indirect
objects with verbs like 'to
give' and 'to send'. It often
corresponds to 'to' (as in 'to
me') in English:

anneme biraz lokum aldım
annem**eh** beer**az** lok**oo**m
ald**uh**m
I've bought my mother
some Turkish delight

kitabı ona verdim
keetab**uh** on**a** verd**ee**m
I gave the book to him

Locative Case

The locative is used to
express position:

odada   Türkiye'de
odad**a**   te**w**rkee-yeh-deh
in the room   in Turkey

Ablative Case

The ablative is used to
indicate a point of origin in
space or time and
corresponds to the English
'from':

evden   istasyondan
from the   from the
house   station

dokuzdan beşe
dokoozd**a**n besh**eh**
from nine to five

The following table shows the endings for each case. The endings are regular apart from some consonant changes (see page 10). The rules of vowel harmony (see page 5) apply:

words ending in a consonant

final vowel	e or i	a or ı	o or u	ö or ü
nom	bez cloth	bar bar	koy cove	göz eye
acc	bez-i	bar-ı	koy-u	göz-ü
	bez**ee**	bar**uh**	koy-**oo**	gurz**ew**
gen	bez-in	bar-ın	koy-un	göz-ün
	bez**een**	bar**uh**n	koy-**oon**	gurz**ew**n
dat	bez-e	bar-a	koy-a	göz-e
	bez**eh**	bar**a**	koy-**a**	gurz**eh**
loc	bez-de	bar-da	koy-da	göz-de
	bezd**eh**	bard**a**	koyd**a**	gurzd**eh**
abl	bez-den	bar-dan	koy-dan	göz-den
	bezd**en**	bard**an**	koyd**an**	gurzd**en**

words ending in a vowel

final vowel	e or i	a or ı	o or u	ö or ü
nom	ülke country	masa table	boru pipe	ütü iron
acc	ülke-yi	masa-yı	boru-yu	ütü-yü
	ewlkeh-y**ee**	masī-**uh**	boroo-y**oo**	ewtewy**ew**
gen	ülke-nin	masa-nın	boru-nun	ütü-nün
	ewlken**een**	masanuhn	boroon**oon**	ewtewn**ew**n
dat	ülke-ye	masa-ya	boru-ya	ütü-ye
	ewlkeh-y**eh**	masī-**a**	boroo-y**a**	ewtew-y**eh**
loc	ülke-de	masa-da	boru-da	ütü-de
	ewlked**eh**	masad**a**	brood**a**	ewtewd**eh**
abl	ülke-den	masa-dan	boru-dan	ütü-den
	ewlked**en**	masad**an**	brood**an**	ewtewd**en**

nom	banka yakın mı?	dat	karım bankaya gitti
	banka yakuhn muh		karuhm bankī-**a** geett**ee**
	is the bank nearby?		my wife went to the bank
acc	bankayı arıyorum	loc	bankada
	bankī-**uh** aruh-yoroom		bankad**a**
	I am looking for the bank		in the bank
gen	bankanın kapısı	abl	bankadan aldım
	bankan**uh**n kapuhs**uh**		bankad**an** ald**uh**m
	the door of the bank		I got it from the bank

GRAMMAR

consonant changes

	k → ğ	p → b	ç → c	k → g	t → d
nom	köpek	dolap	amaç	kepenk	kurt
	dog	cupboard	purpose	shutter	wolf
acc	köpeğ-i	dolab-ı	amac-ı	kepeng-i	kurd-u
	kurpeh-**ee**	dolab**uh**	amaj**uh**	kepeng**ee**	koord**oo**
gen	köpeğ-in	dolab-ın	amac-ın	kepeng-in	kurd-un
	kurpeh-**een**	dolab**uhn**	amaj**uhn**	kepeng**een**	koord**oon**
dat	köpeğ-e	dolab-a	amac-a	kepeng-e	kurd-a
	kurpeh-**eh**	dolab**a**	amaj**a**	kepeng**eh**	koord**a**
loc	köpek-te	dolap-ta	amaç-ta	kepenk-te	kurt-ta
	kurpekt**eh**	dolapt**a**	amacht**a**	kepenkt**eh**	koortt**a**
abl	köpek-ten	dolap-tan	amaç-tan	kepenk-ten	kurt-tan
	kurpekt**en**	dolapt**an**	amacht**an**	kepenkt**en**	koortt**an**

However, if the final letter of a word is ç, f, h, k, p, d, ş, or t, the locative and ablative case endings will take t instead of d:

mutfakta	Sinop'tan	New York'tan
in the kitchen	from Sinop	from New York

Plural endings -lar and -ler are added to the word before case endings:

odalarda	çıkış kapılarına
in the rooms	to the exits

pencerelerden	yolcuların
from the windows	of the passengers

ADJECTIVES

Adjectives do not change according to case:

kırmızı otobüs dışarıda
kurmuhz**uh** otob**ews**
duhsharuhd**a**
the red bus is outside

kırmızı otobüsü gördün mü?
kuhrmuhz**uh** otobews**ew**
gurd**ew**n mew
did you see the red bus?

kırmızı otobüsten indi
kurmuhz**uh** otobewst**en** eend**ee**
he got out of the red bus

The indefinite article bir usually comes between the adjective and noun:

pahalı bir otel
pahal**uh** beer otel
an expensive hotel

güzel bir kadın
gewz**e**l beer kad**uh**n
a beautiful woman

uslu bir çocuk
oosl**oo** beer choj**oo**k
a well-behaved child

It is also acceptable for **bir** to precede the adjective, but this form is much less common:

bir uzun ağaç
beer ooz**oo**n a-**a**ch
a tall tree

Comparatives

To form the comparative, place **daha** 'more' before the adjective:

daha pahalı   daha yüksek
daha pahal**uh**   daha yewksek
more expensive   higher

To translate 'more... than' or '...-er than', add the ablative case suffixes (-den or -dan) to the noun (**daha** is optional):

İngiltere'den sıcak
eengeelter**e**h-den suhj**a**k
warmer than England

babamdan daha uzun
babamd**a**n daha ooz**oo**n
taller than my father

Superlatives

To translate the superlative, use the word **en**:

bu en ilginç
boo en eelg**ee**nch
this is the most interesting

en ucuz oda
en ooj**oo**z od**a**
the cheapest room,
the least expensive room

Adverbs

Most Turkish adjectives can be used as adverbs:

kötü   iyi
kurt**ew**   ee-y**ee**
bad/badly   good/well

iyi uyudunuz mu?
ee-y**ee** oo-yoodoon**oo**z moo
did you sleep well?

POSSESSIVE SUFFIXES

Instead of possessive adjectives, Turkish uses suffixes or endings which are added to nouns to indicate possession. There are also possessive adjectives (i.e. as separate words) in Turkish, but these are generally used for special emphasis. The possessive suffixes must also follow the rules of vowel harmony (see page 5).

GRAMMAR

12

words ending in a consonant
final vowel

e or i	a or ı	o or u	ö or ü	
el hand	baş head	boy height	göz eye	
el-im	baş-ım	boy-um	göz-üm	my
eleem	bashuhm	boy-oom	gurzewm	
el-in	baş-ın	boy-un	göz-ün	your (sing, fam)
eleen	bashuhn	boy-oon	gurzewn	
el-i	baş-ı	boy-u	göz-ü	his/her/its
elee	bashuh	boy-oo	gurzew	
el-imiz	baş-ımız	boy-umuz	göz-ümüz	our
eleemeez	bashuhmuhz	boy-oomooz	gurzewmewz	
el-iniz	baş-ınız	boy-unuz	göz-ünüz	your (pl or pol)
eleeneez	bashuhnuhz	boy-oonooz	gurzewnewz	
el-leri	baş-ları	boy-ları	göz-leri	their
elleree	bashlaruh	boylaruh	gurzleree	

words ending in a vowel
final vowel

e or i	a or ı	o or u	ö or ü	
dede grandfather	araba car	soru question	ütü iron	
dede-m	araba-m	soru-m	ütü-m	my
dedem	arabam	soroom	ewtewm	
dede-n	araba-n	soru-n	ütü-n	your (sing, fam)
deden	araban	soroon	ewtewn	
dede-si	araba-sı	soru-su	ütü-sü	his/her/its
dedesee	arabasuh	soroosoo	ewtewsew	
dede-miz	araba-mız	soru-muz	ütü-müz	our
dedemeez	arabamuhz	soroomooz	ewtewmewz	
dede-niz	araba-nız	soru-nuz	ütü-nüz	your (pl or pol)
dedeneez	arabanuhz	soroonooz	ewtewnewz	
dede-leri	araba-ları	soru-ları	ütü-leri	their
dedeleree	arabalaruh	soroolaruh	ewtewleree	

GRAMMAR

consonant changes

k → ğ	p → b	ç → c	
köpek dog	dolap cupboard	amaç purpose	
köpeğ-im	dolab-ım	amac-ım	my
kurpeh-**ee**m	dolab**uh**m	amaj**uh**m	
köpeğ-in	dolab-ın	amac-ın	your (sing, fam)
kurpeh-**ee**n	dolab**uh**n	amaj**uh**n	
köpeğ-i	dolab-ı	amac-ı	his/her/its
kurpeh-**ee**	dolab**uh**	amaj**uh**	
köpeğ-imiz	dolab-ımız	amac-ımız	our
kurpeh-eem**eez**	dolabuhm**uh**z	amajuhm**uh**z	
köpeğ-iniz	dolab-ınız	amac-ınız	your (pl or pol)
kurpeh-een**eez**	dolabuhn**uh**z	amajuhn**uh**z	
köpek-leri	dolapları	amaçları	their
kurpekler**ee**	dolaplar**uh**	amachlar**uh**	

k → g	t → d		
kepenk shutter	kurt wolf		
kepeng-im	kurd-um	my	
kepeng**ee**m	koord**oo**m		
kepeng-in	kurd-un	your (sing, fam)	
kepeng**ee**n	koord**oo**n		
kepeng-i	kurd-u	his/her/its	
kepeng**ee**	koord**oo**		
kepeng-imiz	kurd-umuz	our	
kepengeem**eez**	koordoom**oo**z		
kepeng-iniz	kurd-unuz	your (pl or pol)	
kepengeen**eez**	koordoon**oo**z		
kepenk-leri	kurt-ları	their	
kepenkler**ee**	koortlar**uh**		

sırt çantam	kız arkadaşım	odanız
suhrt chant**a**m	kuhz arkadash**uh**m	odan**uh**z
my backpack	my girlfriend	your room

defterim ve kalemim
defter**ee**m veh kalem**ee**m
my notebook and my pen

The possessive adjectives as follows are used for special
emphasis:

benim	[ben**ee**m]	my
senin	[sen**ee**n]	your (sing, fam)
onun	[on**oo**n]	his/her/its
bizim	[beez**ee**m]	our
sizin	[seez**ee**n]	your (pl or pol)
onların	[onlar**uh**n]	their

benim biletim ucuzdu   senin odan rahat
MY ticket was cheap   YOUR room is comfortable

The plural suffixes -ler and -lar precede the possessive suffix:

oda-lar-ınız bu katta   bilet-ler-imiz
odalaruhn**uh**z boo k**a**tta   beeletlereem**ee**z
your rooms are on this floor   our tickets

All other suffixes are added after the possessive suffixes:

otel-im-de   ad-ı-nı bilmiyorum
oteleemd**eh**   aduhn**uh** b**ee**lmee-yoroom
in my hotel   I don't know his name

çanta-nız-a koyabilirsiniz
chantanuhz**a** koy-abeeleerseen**ee**z
you can put it in your bag

DEMONSTRATIVES

Demonstrative adjectives and pronouns are as follows:

bu	[boo]	this (near the speaker)
şu	[shoo]	that (just over there)
o	[o]	that (over there, out of sight)

PRONOUNS

Personal Pronouns

nom	ben	[ben]	I
	sen	[sen]	you (sing, fam)
	o	[o]	he/she/it
	biz	[beez]	we
	siz	[seez]	you (pl or pol)
	onlar	[onl**ar**]	they

acc	beni	[ben**ee**]	me
	seni	[sen**ee**]	you (sing, fam)
	onu	[on**oo**]	him/her/it
	bizi	[beez**ee**]	us
	sizi	[seez**ee**]	you (pl or pol)
	onları	[onlar**uh**]	them

gen	benim	[ben**eem**]	of me
	senin	[sen**een**]	of you (sing, fam)
	onun	[on**oo**n]	of him/her/it
	bizim	[beez**eem**]	of us
	sizin	[seez**een**]	of you (pl or pol)
	onların	[onlar**uhn**]	of them

dat	bana	[ban**a**]	to me
	sana	[san**a**]	to you (sing, fam)
	ona	[on**a**]	to him/her/it
	bize	[beez**eh**]	to us
	size	[seez**eh**]	to you (pl or pol)
	onlara	[onlar**a**]	to them

loc	bende	[bend**eh**]	in me
	sende	[send**eh**]	in you (sing, fam)
	onda	[ond**a**]	in him/her/it
	bizde	[beezd**eh**]	in us
	sizde	[seezd**eh**]	in you (pl or pol)
	onlarda	[onlard**a**]	in them

abl	benden	[bend**en**]	from me
	senden	[send**en**]	from you (sing, fam)
	ondan	[ond**an**]	from him/her/it
	bizden	[beezd**en**]	from us
	sizden	[seezd**en**]	from you (pl or pol)
	onlardan	[onlard**an**]	from them

Personal pronouns are usually omitted as verb endings make it clear who is being referred to:

çok meşgul	Ankara'ya gidiyorum
chok meshg**oo**l	**a**nkara-ya geedee-yor**oo**m
he/she is very busy	I am going to Ankara

However, they can be retained for emphasis:

ben oradaydım, ama o yoktu
ben oradîd**uhm** am**a** o yokt**oo**
I was there, but HE/SHE wasn't

o haklı, sen haksızsın
o hakl**uh** sen haksuhzs**uhn**
HE/SHE is in the right, YOU are in the wrong

'You'

There are two ways of saying 'you' in Turkish. Sen is the singular, familiar form and it is used to address a relative, a close friend or a child; it is also used among young people, even if they don't know each other well. Siz is the singular, polite or plural form, and it is used to address someone the speaker doesn't know well or to address more than one person.

Emphatic Pronouns

kendim	myself
kendin	yourself (sing, fam)
kendi	himself/herself/itself
kendimiz	ourselves
kendiniz	yourselves (pl or pol)
kendileri	themselves

bavulumu kendim taşıyabilirim
bavooloom**oo** kend**ee**m tashuh-yabeeleer**ee**m
I can carry my suitcase myself

kendimiz yaptık
kendeem**eez** yapt**uh**k
we made it ourselves

Possessive Pronouns

benimki	[beneemk**ee**]	mine
seninki	[seneenk**ee**]	yours (sing, fam)
onunki	[onoonk**ee**]	his/hers/its
bizimki	[beezeemk**ee**]	ours
sizinki	[seezeenk**ee**]	yours (pl or pol)
onlarınki	[onlaruhnk**ee**]	theirs

onunki benimkinden iyi
onoonk**ee** beneemk**ee**nden ee-y**ee**
his is better than mine

oteliniz pahalı mı? Bizimki değil
oteleen**eez** pahal**uh** muh? beezeemk**ee** deh-**eel**
is your hotel expensive? Ours isn't

In English, questions like 'Does this belong to me/you etc?' can be reformulated as 'Is this mine/yours etc?', using possessive pronouns. In Turkish, however, possessive adjectives (without the suffix ki) are used in these cases:

bu bavul sizin mi?	hayır, onun
boo bav**ool** seez**ee**n mee	hı-**uhr** on**oo**n
is this suitcase yours?	no, it's his

VERBS

Verbs are always at the end of a sentence. All Turkish verbs are regular, except for the consonant change t → d (see page 10).

Present Progressive Tense

The present progressive tense corresponds to 'I am leaving' in English. To form the present progressive tense, remove the last three letters of the verb and add the appropriate endings.

The present progressive tense has four endings. First person singular endings are:

after verb stems with the final vowel

e or i	-iyorum
a or ı	-ıyorum
o or u	-uyorum
ö or ü	-üyorum

final vowel in stem

e or i	a or ı	o or u	ö or ü
gel-mek	kal-mak	koy-mak	düşün-mek
to come	to stay	to put	to think
gel-iyorum	kal-ıyorum	koy-uyorum	düşün-üyorum
gel-iyorsun	kal-ıyorsun	koy-uyorsun	düşün-üyorsun
gel-iyor	kal-ıyor	koy-uyor	düşün-üyor
gel-iyoruz	kal-ıyoruz	koy-uyoruz	düşün-üyoruz
gel-iyorsunuz	kal-ıyorsunuz	koy-uyorsunuz	düşün-üyorsunuz
gel-iyorlar	kal-ıyorlar	koy-uyorlar	düşün-üyorlar

G R A M M A R

| | verb stem ends in a vowel | | |
e or i	a or ı	o or u	ö or ü
elle-mek	atla-mak	oku-mak	yürü-mek
to touch	to jump	to read	to walk
ell-iyorum	atl-ıyorum	oku-yorum	yürü-yorum
ell-iyorsun	atl-ıyorsun	oku-yorsun	yürü-yorsun
ell-iyor	atl-ıyor	oku-yor	yürü-yor
ell-iyoruz	atl-ıyoruz	oku-yoruz	yürü-yoruz
ell-iyorsunuz	atl-ıyorsunuz	oku-yorsunuz	yürü-yorsunuz
ell-iyorlar	atl-ıyorlar	oku-yorlar	yürü-yorlar

Since two vowels together sound awkward in Turkish, in the case of stems ending in e or a the final vowel of the stem is omitted. In the case of stems ending in u or ü the first vowel of the ending is omitted.

In Turkish, the present progressive is also used for mental functions and emotions which in English are expressed in the simple present:

cevabı biliyorum
jevab**uh** beel**ee**-yoroom
I know the answer

Tanrı'ya inanıyorum
tanruh-**ya** eenan**uh**-yoroom
I believe in God

seni seviyorum
sen**ee** sev**ee**-yoroom
I love you

Simple Present Tense

The simple present tense corresponds to 'I leave'. It is used to describe actions carried out habitually and regularly and for general statements, requests and promises.

The simple present tense has six endings. First person singular endings are:

after verb stems with the final vowel

e or i	-irim or -erim
a or ı	-ırım or -arım
o or u	-arım or -urum
ö or ü	-erim or -ürüm

If the verb stem ends in a vowel, the first vowel of the ending is
omitted.

	final vowel in stem		
e or i	a or ı	o or u	ö or ü
gel-mek	kal-mak	koy-mak	düşün-mek
to come	to stay	to put	to think
gel-irim	kal-ırım	koy-arım	düşün-ürüm
gel-irsin	kal-ırsın	koy-arsın	düşün-ürsün
gel-ir	kal-ır	koy-ar	düşün-ür
gel-iriz	kal-ırız	koy-arız	düşün-ürüz
gel-irsiniz	kal-ırsınız	koy-arsınız	düşün-ürsünüz
gel-irler	kal-ırlar	koy-arlar	düşün-ürler

	verb stem ends in a vowel		
e or i	a or ı	o or u	ö or ü
dene-mek	atla-mak	koru-mak	yürü-mek
to try	to jump	to protect	to walk
dene-rim	atla-rım	koru-rum	yürü-rüm
dene-rsin	atla-rsın	koru-rsun	yürü-rsün
dene-r	atla-r	koru-r	yürü-r
dene-riz	atla-rız	koru-ruz	yürü-rüz
dene-rsiniz	atla-rsınız	koru-rsunuz	yürü-rsünüz
dene-rler	atla-rlar	koru-rlar	yürü-rler

babam çok okur
babam chok ok**oo**r
my father reads a lot

biraz daha alır mısınız?
bee**ra**z dah**a** al**u**hr muhsuhn**uh**z
would you like some more?

sonra öderim
sonra urder**ee**m
I'll pay later

Past Tense

The past tense has four endings. First person singular endings
are:

after verb stems with the final vowel

e or i	-dim	o or u	-dum
a or ı	-dım	ö or ü	-düm

final vowel in verb stem			
e or i	a or ı	o or u	ö or ü
gel-mek	kal-mak	oku-mak	düşün-mek
to come	to stay	to read	to think
gel-dim	kal-dım	oku-dum	düşün-düm
gel-din	kal-dın	oku-dun	düşün-dün
gel-di	kal-dı	oku-du	düşün-dü
gel-dik	kal-dık	oku-duk	düşün-dük
gel-diniz	kal-dınız	oku-dunuz	düşün-dünüz
gel-diler	kal-dılar	oku-dular	düşün-düler

Consonant Changes: Verbs

If the final consonant in the verb stem is ç, f, h, k, p, s, ş or t, then the d in the past tense changes to a t:

aç-tım	[achtuhm]	I opened or I have opened
çık-tı	[chuhktuh]	he went out or he has gone out
it-tim	[itteem]	I pushed or I have pushed

Imperfect Tense

This tense is used to describe an action that was taking place in the past or something that went on over a period of time (e.g. 'at that time I was living in Turkey'). To form the imperfect, take the verb stem and add the following endings:

iç-iyor-dum	I was drinking
iç-iyor-dun	you were drinking
iç-iyor-du	he/she/it was drinking
iç-iyor-duk	we were drinking
iç-iyor-dunuz	you were drinking
iç-iyor-lardı	they were drinking

Future Tense

The future tense has four endings. First person singular endings are:

after verb stems with the final vowel	
e or i, ö or ü	-yeceğim or -eceğim
a or ı, o or u	-acağım or -yacağım

	final vowel in verb stem		
ending in a consonant		ending in a vowel	
e, i, ö or ü	a, ı, o or u	e, i, ö or ü	a, ı, o or u
içmek	kalmak	denemek	okumak
to drink	to stay	to try	to read
iç-eceğim	kal-acağım	dene-yeceğim	oku-yacağım
iç-eceksin	kal-acaksın	dene-yeceksin	oku-yacaksın
iç-ecek	kal-acak	dene-yecek	oku-yacak
iç-eceğiz	kal-acağız	dene-yeceğiz	oku-yacağız
iç-eceksiniz	kal-acaksınız	dene-yeceksiniz	oku-yacaksınız
iç-ecekler	kal-acaklar	dene-yecekler	oku-yacaklar

If the final vowel of the verb stem is **e** it is sometimes changed into **i**:

de-mek to say   **di-yecek** he will say

Present Tense of 'To Be'

The Turkish equivalent of the present tense of the verb 'to be' is formed by using suffixes which are attached to the adjective or noun and which follow the rules of vowel harmony:

final vowel if word ends in a consonant				
e or i	a or ı	o or u	ö or ü	
İngiliz	Fransız	uzun	üzgün	
English	French	tall	sad/sorry	
-im	-ım	-um	-üm	I am
-sin	-sın	-sun	-sün	you are (sing, fam)
-dir*	-dır*	-dur*	-dür*	he/she/it is
-iz	-ız	-uz	-üz	we are
-siniz	-sınız	-sunuz	-sünüz	you are (pl or pol)
-ler	-lar	-lar	-ler	they are

* These endings are omitted in spoken Turkish.

final vowel if word ends in a vowel				
e or i	a or ı	o or u	ö or ü	
iyi	kısa	kuru	örtülü	
well	short	dry	covered	
-yim	-yım	-yum	-yüm	I am
-sin	-sın	-sun	-sün	you are (sing, fam)
-dir*	-dır*	-dur*	-dür*	he/she/it is
-yiz	-yız	-yuz	-yüz	we are
-siniz	-sınız	-sunuz	-sünüz	you are (pl or pol)
-ler	-lar	-lar	-ler	they are

* These endings are omitted in spoken Turkish.

İngilizim	çok naziksiniz	kırmızı
eengeel**ee**zeem	chok naz**ee**kseeneez	kuhrmuhz**uh**
I am English	you are very kind	(it's) red

The following consonant changes take place when a suffix beginning with a vowel is added:

words ending in	change to
k	ğ
p	b
ç	c
t	d

Past Tense of 'To Be'

The past tense of 'to be' is formed by adding one of the suffixes below to the adjective or noun, following the rules of vowel harmony:

final vowel if word ends in a consonant				
e or i	a or ı	o or u	ö or ü	
bitkin	kızgın	yorgun	üzgün	
exhausted	angry	tired	sad/sorry	
-dim	-dım	-dum	-düm	I was
-din	-dın	-dun	-dün	you were (sing, fam)
-di	-dı	-du	-dü	he/she/it was
-dik	-dık	-duk	-dük	we were
-diniz	-dınız	-dunuz	-dünüz	you were (pl or pol)
-diler	-dılar	-dular	-düler	they were

final vowel if word ends in a vowel

e or i	a or ı	o or u	ö or ü	
iyi	hasta	mutlu	açgözlü	
well	unwell	happy	greedy	
-ydim	-ydım	-ydum	-ydüm	I was
-ydin	-ydın	-ydun	-ydün	you were (sing, fam)
-ydi	-ydı	-ydu	-ydü	he/she/it was
-ydik	-ydık	-yduk	-ydük	we were
-ydiniz	-ydınız	-ydunuz	-ydünüz	you were (pl or pol)
-ydiler	-ydılar	-ydular	-ydüler	they were

kızgın-dım
kuhzguhnd**uh**m
I was angry

yeşil-di
yesh**ee**ldee
it was green

çekici-ydi
chekeejee-idee
she was attractive

heyecanlıydık
hayejanluh-id**uh**k
we were excited

If the final letter of an adjective is ç, f, h, k, p, s, ş or t, then the **d** of the past tense changes to **t**:

aç-tım
achtuhm
I was hungry

boş-tu
b**o**shtoo
it was empty

Present Tense of 'To Have'

The Turkish equivalent of the present tense of the verb 'to have' is formed by attaching possessive suffixes to the noun and adding **var** to the end of the sentence to mean 'have' and **yok** to mean 'have not':

(benim) biletim var
ben**ee**m beelet**ee**m var
I have a ticket

(onun) parası yok
on**oo**n paras**uh** yok
he has no money

(bizim) vaktimiz yok
beez**ee**m vakteem**ee**z yok
we don't have time

(sizin) rezervasyonunuz var mı?
seez**ee**n reservas-yonoon**oo**z var muh
do you have a reservation?

Past Tense of 'To Have'

This is formed in the same way as the present except that the past tense ending -dı is added to var and -tu is added to yok:

(benim) biletim vardı
ben**ee**m beelet**ee**m vard**uh**
I had a ticket

(onun) parası yoktu
on**oo**n paras**uh** yokt**oo**
he had no money

(bizim) vaktimiz yoktu
beez**ee**m vakt**ee**m**ee**z yokt**oo**
we didn't have time

In questions, -ydı is added to the question particle, in this case mı (see Questions page 29):

(sizin) rezervasyonunuz var mıydı?
seez**ee**n rezervas-yonoon**oo**z muh-id**uh**
did you have a reservation?

Regular Verbs

The following list shows some common verbs conjugated in the first person:

infinitive	present progressive	simple present	past	future
almak to take	alıyorum	alırım	aldım	alacağım
bakmak to look	bakıyorum	bakarım	baktım	bakacağım
başlamak to begin	başlıyorum	başlarım	başladım	başlayacağım
beklemek to wait	bekliyorum	beklerim	bekledim	bekleyeceğim
bırakmak to leave	bırakıyorum	bırakırım	bıraktım	bırakacağım
bilmek to know	biliyorum	bilirim	bildim	bileceğim
bulmak to find	buluyorum	bulurum	buldum	bulacağım
çalışmak to work	çalışıyorum	çalışırım	çalıştım	çalışacağım
çıkmak	çıkıyorum	çıkarım	çıktım	çıkacağım

infinitive	present progressive	simple present	past	future
to go out				
demek	diyorum	derim	dedim	diyeceğim
to say				
etmek	ediyorum	ederim	ettim	edeceğim
to do				
gelmek	geliyorum	gelirim	geldim	geleceğim
to come				
getirmek	getiriyorum	getiririm	getirdim	getireceğim
to bring				
girmek	giriyorum	girerim	girdim	gireceğim
to enter				
gitmek	gidiyorum	giderim	gittim	gideceğim
to go				
göndermek	gönderiyorum	gönderirim	gönderdim	göndereceğim
to send				
görmek	görüyorum	görürüm	gördüm	göreceğim
to see				
içmek	içiyorum	içerim	içtim	içeceğim
to drink				
istemek	istiyorum	isterim	istedim	isteyeceğim
to want				
kalmak	kalıyorum	kalırım	kaldım	kalacağım
to stay				
kaybetmek	kaybediyorum	kaybederim	kaybettim	kaybedeceğim
to lose				
koymak	koyuyorum	koyarım	koydum	koyacağım
to put				
konuşmak	konuşuyorum	konuşurum	konuştum	konuşacağım
to speak				
okumak	okuyorum	okurum	okudum	okuyacağım
to read				
oturmak	oturuyorum	otururum	oturdum	oturacağım
to live, to sit				
sevmek	seviyorum	severim	sevdim	seveceğim
to love				
sormak	soruyorum	sorarım	sordum	soracağım
to ask				

infinitive	present progressive	simple present	past	future
söylemek to say, to tell	söylüyorum	söylerim	söyledim	söyleyeceğim
taşımak to carry	taşıyorum	taşırım	taşıdım	taşıyacağım
unutmak to forget	unutuyorum	unuturum	unuttum	unutacağım
uyumak to sleep	uyuyorum	uyurum	uyudum	uyuyacağım
varmak to arrive	varıyorum	varırım	vardım	varacağım
vermek to give	veriyorum	veririm	verdim	vereceğim
yapmak to make, to do	yapıyorum	yaparım	yaptım	yapacağım
yazmak to write	yazıyorum	yazarım	yazdım	yazacağım
yemek to eat	yiyorum	yerim	yedim	yiyeceğim

Negatives

To form the negative of a verb, add the negative particle -me- or -ma- after the verb stem and before the other endings. If the tense ending starts with a vowel, the negative particle changes to -mi-, -mı-, -mü- or -mu- according to the rules of vowel harmony (see page 5) and a y is inserted after the particle to separate the two vowels.

The tables below show how to form the negative of the verb in the first person:

	final vowel in verb stem	
	e or i	a or ı
	gelmek to come	kalmak to stay
present progressive	gel-mi-yorum	kal-mı-yorum
	gelmee-yoroom	kalmuh-yoroom
past tense	gel-me-dim	kal-ma-dım
	gelmedeem	kalmaduhm

imperfect tense	gel-mi-yordum	kal-mı-yordum
	gelmee-yordoom	kalmuh-yordoom
future tense	gel-mi-yeceğim	kal-mı-yacağım
	gelmee-yejeh-eem	kalmuh-yaja-uhm

final vowel in verb stem

	o or u	ö or ü
	sormak to ask	düşünmek to think
present progressive	sor-mu-yorum	düşün-mü-yorum
	sormoo-yoroom	dewshewnmew-yoroom
past tense	sor-ma-dım	düşün-me-dim
	sormaduhm	dewshewnmedeem
imperfect tense	sor-mu-yordum	düşün-mü-yordum
	sormoo-yordoom	dewshewnmew-yordoom
future tense	sor-ma-yacağım	düşün-mi-yeceğim
	sorma-yaja-uhm	dewshewnmee-yejeh-eem

The negative of the simple present tense is irregular:

verb stems ending in

e, i, ö or ü	a, ı, o or u
gelmek to come	kalmak to stay
gel-me-m	kal-mam
gelmem	kalmam
gel-mez-sin	kal-maz-sın
gelmezseen	kalmazsuhn
gel-mez	kal-maz
gelmez	kalmaz
gel-me-yiz	kal-mayız
gelmeh-yeez	kalmī-uhz
gel-mez-siniz	kal-maz-sınız
gelmezseeneez	kalmazsuhnuhz
gel-mez-ler	kal-maz-lar
gelmezler	kalmazlar

okuyorum	kalıyorum	söylemem
okoo-yoroom	kaluh-yoroom	suh-ilemem
I am reading	I am staying	I won't say
okumuyorum	kalmıyorum	sormaz
okoomoo-yoroom	kalmuh-yoroom	sormaz
I am not reading	I am not staying	he/she doesn't/won't ask

Negative of 'To Be'

The negative of the verb 'to be' is formed by using the
following words which are placed after the adjective

değil-im	[deh-eel**eem**]	I am not
değil-sin	[deh-eel**seen**]	you are not (sing, fam)
değil	[deh-**eel**]	he/she/it is not
değil-iz	[deh-eel**eez**]	we are not
değil-siniz	[deh-eelseen**eez**]	you are not (pol or pl)
değil-ler	[deh-eell**er**]	they are not

emin değilim
em**ee**n deh-eel**eem**
I am not sure

Türk değil
tewrk deh-**eel**
he/she is not Turkish

orada rahat değilsiniz
orad**a** rah**a**t deh-eelseen**eez**
you are not comfortable there

evde değiller
evd**eh** deh-eeller
they are not at home

Imperative

To form the polite form of the imperative, take the verb stem
and add the following suffixes:

final vowel of verb stem if ending in a consonant

e or i	a or ı	o or u	ö or ü
-in	-ın	-un	-ün

final vowel of verb stem if ending in a vowel

-yin	-yın	-yun	-yün

gelin!	durun!	dinleyin!
gel**ee**n	d**oo**roon	deenl**ay**een
come!	stop!	listen!

The negative imperative is formed by taking the verb stem and
adding -me- or -ma- according to the rules of vowel harmony;
then onto this are added the endings as in the table above:

gelmeyin!	durmayın!	dinlemeyin!
gelmay**ee**n	d**oo**rmı-uhn	deenlemay**ee**n
don't come!	don't stop!	don't listen!

QUESTIONS

Questions are formed by using one of the particles mi-, mı-, mü- or mu-; the particle used depends on the preceding vowel and follows the rules of vowel harmony. To create a question, split the person ending of the verb as given in the tables earlier and add one of these particles as follows:

okumak to read

present progressive	**okuyor musunuz?** are you reading?
	okoo-**yor** moosoon**oo**z
simple present	**okur musunuz?** would you read?, do you read?
	ok**oo**r moosoon**oo**z
past tense	**okudunuz mu?** did you read?
	okoodoon**oo**z moo
imperfect tense	**okuyor muydunuz?** were you reading?
	okoo-yor moo-idoon**oo**z
future tense	**okuyacak mısınız?** will you read?
	okoo-yaj**a**k muhsuhn**uh**z

okuyorsunuz
okoo-yorsoon**oo**z
you are reading

okuyor musunuz?
okoo-**yor** moosoon**oo**z
are you reading?

okuyor
okoo-y**or**
he/she is reading

okuyor mu?
okoo-y**or** moo
is he/she reading?

ALSO, TOO

Turkish has two words for 'also' and 'too': **de** and **da**.

The one you use depends on the final vowel of the preceding word:

final vowel of preceding word	
a ı o u	e i ö ü
da	**de**

Ahmed de
Ahmed too

ben de
me too

onlar da
they too

Da and **de** should not be confused with the suffixes -da and -de meaning 'at (the)', 'in (the)' or 'on (the)'.

CAN, TO BE ABLE

To translate this, take the stem of the relevant verb (e.g. kal- 'stay', gel- 'come'), add -a- or -e- according to the final vowel in the stem, then add the appropriate conjugation of bilmek 'to know':

final vowel in verb stem

a ı o u	e i ö ü
-a-	-e-

kal-a-bilmek
kalabeelm**e**k
to be able to stay

gel-e-bilmek
gelebeelm**e**k
to be able to come

girebilir miyim?
geerebeel**ee**r mee-y**ee**m
can I come in?

If the verb stem (e.g. taşı-) ends in a vowel, a y is inserted in front of the -a- or -e-:

bavulumu taşıyabilir misiniz?
bavooloom**oo** tashuh-yabeel**ee**r
  meeseen**ee**z
can you carry my suitcase?

DATES

The formation of dates is similar to English, except that, both in speech and writing, only cardinal numbers are used (e.g. 1 November, not 1st November) and years are also referred to by simple cardinal numbers (e.g. the year 1996 is referred to not as 'nineteen ninety-six' but 'one thousand nine hundred and ninety-six'):

1 Ocak (Bir Ocak)
beer oj**a**k
1 January

10 Nisan 1996 (On Nisan bin
  dokuz yüz doksan altı)
on neesa**n** been dok**oo**z yewz
  dok**sa**n alt**uh**
10 April 1996

1 Eylül, Cuma (Bir Eylül, Cuma)
beer ayl**ew**l joom**a**
Friday, 1 September

DAYS

Sunday Pazar
Monday Pazartesi
Tuesday Salı [sal**uh**]
Wednesday Çarşamba
  [charshamb**a**]
Thursday Perşembe
  [pershemb**eh**]
Friday Cuma [joom**a**]
Saturday Cumartesi
  [joom**a**rtesee]

MONTHS

January Ocak [ojak]
February Şubat [shoobat]
March Mart
April Nisan
May Mayıs [mī-uhs]
June Haziran
July Temmuz
August Ağustos [a-oostos]
September Eylül [aylewl]
October Ekim
November Kasım [kasuhm]
December Aralık [araluhk]

TIME

what time is it? saat kaç? [sa-at
    kach]
(it's) one o'clock saat bir
(it's) two o'clock saat iki
(it's) ten o'clock saat on
five past one biri beş geçiyor
    [besh gechee-yor]
ten past two ikiyi on geçiyor
quarter past one biri çeyrek
    geçiyor [chayrek]
quarter past two ikiyi çeyrek
    geçiyor
half past one bir buçuk
    [boochook]
half past ten on buçuk
twenty to ten ona yirmi var
quarter to one bire çeyrek var
    [beereh chayrek]
quarter to ten ona çeyrek var
at quarter to ten ona çeyrek
    kala
at quarter past one biri çeyrek
    geçe [gecheh]

at eight o'clock (saat) sekizde
    [sa-at sekeezdeh]
at half past four (saat) dört
    buçukta [durt boochookta]
2 a.m. gece iki [gejeh]
2 p.m. öğledensonra iki [ur-
    ledensonra]
6 a.m. sabah altı [sabaH altuh]
6 p.m. akşam altı [aksham]
10 a.m. sabah on [sabaH]
10 p.m. gece on [gejeh]
18.00 on sekiz
14.30 on dört otuz [durt]
noon öğle [urleh]
at noon öğleyin [urlayeen]
midnight gece yarısı [gejeh
    yaruhsuh]
hour saat [sa-at]
minute dakika
two minutes iki dakika
second saniye [sanee-yeh]
quarter of an hour çeyrek saat
    [chayrek sa-at]
half an hour yarım saat
    [yaruhm]
three quarters of an hour kırk
    beş dakika [kuhrk besh], üç
    çeyrek saat [ewch chayrek
    sa-at]

NUMBERS

0	sıfır [suhfuhr]
1	bir
2	iki
3	üç [ewch]
4	dört [durt]
5	beş [besh]
6	altı [altuh]
7	yedi

8	sekiz	
9	dokuz	
10	on	
11	on bir	
12	on iki	
13	on üç [ewch]	
14	on dört [durt]	
15	on beş [besh]	
16	on altı [altuh]	
17	on yedi	
18	on sekiz	
19	on dokuz	
20	yirmi	
21	yirmi bir	
22	yirmi iki	
30	otuz	
31	otuz bir	
32	otuz iki	
33	otuz üç [ewch]	
40	kırk [kuhrk]	
50	elli	
60	altmış [altmuhsh]	
70	yetmiş [yetmeesh]	
80	seksen	
90	doksan	
100	yüz [yewz]	
101	yüz bir	
102	yüz iki	
200	iki yüz	
300	üç yüz [ewch]	
500	beş yüz [besh]	
1,000	bin	
2,000	iki bin	
3,000	üç bin [ewch]	
5,000	beş bin [besh]	
10,000	on bin	
1,000,000	bir milyon	

Ordinals

1st	birinci [beereenjee]	
2nd	ikinci [eekeenjee]	
3rd	üçüncü [ewchewnjew]	
4th	dördüncü [durdewnjew]	
5th	beşinci [besheenjee]	
6th	altıncı [altuhnjuh]	
7th	yedinci [yedeenjee]	
8th	sekizinci [sekeezeenjee]	
9th	dokuzuncu [dokoozoonjoo]	
10th	onuncu [onoonjoo]	

BASIC PHRASES

yes
evet

no
hayır
hī-**uhr**

OK
tam**am**

please
lütfen
le**w**tfen

thank you
teşekkür ederi**m**
teshekke**wr**

thanks
teşekkürler
teshekkewrl**er**

don't mention it
bir şey değil
shay deh-**eel**

yes, please
(evet) lütfen
le**w**tfen

no thank you
hayır, teşekkür ederim
hī-**uhr** teshekke**wr**

hello
m**er**haba

good morning
günaydın
gewnid**uhn**

good evening
iyi akşamlar
akshaml**ar**

good night
iy**i** geceler
gejel**er**

goodbye (general use)
hoşça kalın
hosh-ch**a** kal**uhn**

(said by person leaving)
Allahaısmarladık
al**a**ha-uhsmarladuhk

(said to person leaving) güle güle
ge**w**leh

hi! (hello)
m**er**haba!

see you!
görüşürüz!
gu**r**ewshewrewz

see you later
görüşmek üzere
gurewshm**ek** ewzer**eh**

how are you?/how do you do?
nasılsınız?
nasuhl-suhn**uhz**

I'm fine, thanks
iyiyi**m**, teşekkür ederim
teshekke**wr**

nice to meet you
memn**u**n old**u**m

excuse me (to get past)
pardon

(to get attention) affe**d**ersiniz

(to say sorry) özür dile**r**im
urz**ew**r

(I'm) sorry
özür dile**r**im
urz**ew**r

sorry?/pardon (me)?
(didn't understand/hear) ef**en**dim?

what?
ne?
neh

what did you say?
ne dedin**iz**?

I see/I understand
anl**ı**yorum
anl**uh**-yoroom

I don't understand
anlam**ı**yorum
anl**a**muh-yoroom

do you speak English?
İngilizce biliy**or** musun**uz**?
eengeel**ee**zjeh

I don't speak Turkish
Türkçe b**i**lmiyorum
tewrkch**eh**

could you speak more slowly?
lütfen daha yavaş konuşur
musun**uz**?
le**w**tfen – yava**sh** konoosh**oo**r

could you repeat that?
tek**r**ar söyler misin**iz**?
s**uh**-iler

please write it down
lütfen yaz**ar** mısınız?
le**w**tfen – muhsuhn**uh**z

I'd like ...
... isti**y**orum

can I have ...?
b**a**na ... verebi**l**ir misiniz?

how much is it?
ka**ç**a?
kach**a**

(at) what time?
ka**ç**ta?
kacht**a**

cheers! (toast)
şerefe!
sheref**eh**

where is/are the ...?
... nerede?
n**e**redeh

CONVERSION TABLES

1 centimetre = 0.39 inches	1 inch = 2.54 cm

1 metre = 39.37 inches = 1.09 yards

1 foot = 30.48 cm

1 yard = 0.91 m

1 kilometre = 0.62 miles = 5/8 mile

1 mile = 1.61 km

km	1	2	3	4	5	10	20	30	40	50	100
miles	0.6	1.2	1.9	2.5	3.1	6.2	12.4	18.6	24.8	31.0	62.1

miles	1	2	3	4	5	10	20	30	40	50	100
km	1.6	3.2	4.8	6.4	8.0	16.1	32.2	48.3	64.4	80.5	161

1 gram = 0.035 ounces

1 kilo = 1000 g = 2.2 pounds

g	100	250	500
oz	3.5	8.75	17.5

1 oz = 28.35 g

1 lb = 0.45 kg

kg	0.5	1	2	3	4	5	6	7	8	9	10
lb	1.1	2.2	4.4	6.6	8.8	11.0	13.2	15.4	17.6	19.8	22.0

kg	20	30	40	50	60	70	80	90	100
lb	44	66	88	110	132	154	176	198	220

lb	0.5	1	2	3	4	5	6	7	8	9	10	20
kg	0.2	0.5	0.9	1.4	1.8	2.3	2.7	3.2	3.6	4.1	4.5	9.0

1 litre = 1.75 UK pints / 2.13 US pints

1 UK pint = 0.57 l	1 UK gallon = 4.55 l
1 US pint = 0.47 l	1 US gallon = 3.79 l

centigrade / Celsius $C = (F - 32) \times 5/9$

C	-5	0	5	10	15	18	20	25	30	36.8	38
F	23	32	41	50	59	65	68	77	86	98.4	100.4

Fahrenheit $F = (C \times 9/5) + 32$

F	23	32	40	50	60	65	70	80	85	98.4	101
C	-5	0	4	10	16	18	21	27	29	36.8	38.3

English-Turkish

A

a, an* bir
about: about 20 yirmi
 civarında [jeevaruhnd**a**]
 at about 5 o'clock saat beş
 civarında [sa-**a**t]
 a film about Turkey Türkiye
 hakkında bir film
 [t**e**wrkee-yeh hakk**uh**nda]
above: above the ... ...-in
 üstünde [ewstewnd**eh**]
abroad yurt dışında
 [duh-shuhnd**a**]
absolutely! (I agree) kesinlikle!
 [keseenl**ee**kleh]
absorbent cotton hidrofil
 pam**u**k
accelerator gaz pedalı [pedal**uh**]
accept kab**u**l etmek
accident ka**z**a
 there's been an accident bir
 kaza old**u**
accommodation kalacak yer
 [kalaj**a**k]
 see room, hotel and guesthouse
accurate doğru [doh-r**oo**]
ache ağrı [a-r**uh**]
 my back aches sırtım ağrıyor
 [suhrt**uh**m a-r**uh**-yor]
across: across the ... (road
 etc) ...-un karşı tarafında
 [karsh**uh** tarafuhnd**a**]
adapter adaptör [adapt**ur**]
address adres
 what's your address?
 _adresiniz nedir?

In Turkish addresses, street
names precede the number; if
the address is on a minor alley,
this will be included after the
main thoroughfare it leads off.
If you see a right-hand slash
between two numbers, the first
is the building number, the
second the apartment or office
number. A letter following a
right-hand slash can mean
either the shop or unit number,
or be part of the general
building number. For example:
 Halil Güner
 Kıbrıs Şehitleri Cad.
 Poyraz Sok.
 Ulus Apartmanı 36/2, Kat 1
 Delikliçınar
 34800 Direkköy
which means that Halil Güner
lives on Poyraz Sokak No. 36,
just off Kıbrıs Şehitleri Caddesi,
on the first floor, Apartment 2,
of the Ulus apartments, in the
Delikliçınar area of a larger
postal district known as
.Direkköy.

address book adres defteri
admission charge giriş ücreti
 [geer**ee**sh ewjret**ee**]
adult yetişkin [yeteesh-k**ee**n]
advance: in advance önceden
 [urnjed**e**n]
Aegean Ege [eg**eh**]
aeroplane uçak [oochak]
after: after the ... ...-den sonra

after you siz buyrun
[b**oo**-iroon]
after lunch öğle yemeğinden
sonra
afternoon öğleden sonra
[ur-led**en**]
in the afternoon öğleden
sonra
this afternoon bugün öğleden
sonra [b**oo**gewn]
aftershave tıraş losyon**u**
[tuhr**a**sh]
aftersun cream güneş sonrası
krem**i** [gewn**e**sh sonras**uh**]
afterwards sonra
again yine [y**ee**neh]
against: against the ... ...-e
karş**ı** [-eh karsh**uh**]
age yaş [yash]
ago: a week ago bir haft**a** önce
[**u**rnjeh]
an hour ago bir saat önce
agree: I agree ol**ur**
AIDS Aids
air hava
by air uçakla [ooch**a**kla]
air-conditioning klima,
havalandırma [–d**u**hrm**a**]
airmail: by airmail uçak
postasıyla [ooch**a**k postas**uh**la]
airmail envelope uçak zarf**ı**
[zarf**uh**]
airport havaalanı [hava-alan**uh**]
to the airport, please
havaalanına, lütfen
[–alan**uh**na l**e**wtfen]
airport bus havaalanı otobüsü
[otob**ew**sew]
aisle seat koridor yanı [yan**uh**]

alarm clock çalar saat [chal**ar**
sa-**a**t]
alcohol alkol
alcoholic alkollü [alkoll**ew**]
all: all the boys bütün oğlanlar
[bewt**ewn**]
all the girls bütün kızlar
all of it hepsi
all of them onların hepsi
[onlar**uh**n]
that's all, thanks hepsi bu
kadar, teşekkür eder**i**m
[teshekk**ewr**]
allergic: I'm allergic to ... ...-a
alerjim var [aler**J**eem]
allowed: is it allowed? serbest
mi?
all right peki
I'm all right ben iyiyim
are you all right? iyi misin?
almond badem
almost neredeyse [n**e**redayseh]
alone yalnız [y**a**lnuhz]
alphabet alfabe [**a**lfabeh]

a a	m meh
b beh	n neh
c jeh	o o
ç cheh	ö ur
d deh	p peh
e eh	r reh
f feh	s seh
g geh	ş sheh
ğ yoomoosh**a**k geh	t teh
h ha	u oo
ı uh	ü ew
i ee	v veh
j Jeh	y yeh
k ka	z zeh
l leh	

already bile [beel**eh**]
  the film has already started
  film başladı bile [bashl**a**duh]
also de [deh], da
although halde [h**a**ldeh]
altogether tümüyle
  [tewm**ew**leh]
always hep
am*: I am ... (ben) ...-im
a.m. (from midnight to 4 a.m.) gece
  [gej**eh**]
  (from 4 a.m. to noon) sabah
  [sab**a**H]
amazing (surprising) şaşılacak
  [shashuhlaj**ak**]
  (very good) şahane [shah**a**neh]
ambulance cankurtaran
  [jankoortar**a**n]
  call an ambulance! bir
  cankurtaran çağırın!
  [cha-**u**Hruhn]

> Dial 112 for an ambulance. This
> call costs one small **jeton** or one
> phonecard unit.

America Amerika
American (adj) Amerikan
  I'm American Amerikalıyım
  [–luh-y**uh**m]
among: among the ... ...-in
  arasında [arasuhnd**a**]
amount miktar
  (money) tut**a**r
amp: a 13-amp fuse on üç
  amperlik sigorta
amphitheatre amfiteatr
Anatolia Anadolu
and ve [veh]

angry kızgın [kuhzg**uh**n]
animal hayvan [h**ī**van]
ankle ayak bileği [**ī**-ak
  beeleh-**ee**]
anniversary (wedding) evlenme
  yıldönümü [evlenm**eh**
  y**uh**l-durnewmew]
annoy: this man's annoying me
  bu adam beni rahatsız
  ediyor [rahats**uh**z]
annoying can sıkıcı [jan
  suhkuhj**uh**]
another başka bir [bashk**a**]
  can we have another room?
  bize başka bir oda verebilir
  misiniz? [beez**eh**]
  another beer, please bir bira
  daha, lütfen [l**ew**tfen]
antibiotics **a**ntibiyotik
antifreeze **a**ntifriz
antihistamine **a**ntihistamin
antique: is it an antique? bu
  antika mı? [muh]
antique shop antikacı
  [**a**nteekajuh]
antiseptic **a**ntiseptik
any: do you have any ...?
  sizde ... var mı? [seezd**eh** –
  muh]
  sorry, I don't have any
  üzgünüm, hiç yok
  [**ew**zgewnewm heech]
anybody kimse [k**ee**mseh]
  does anybody speak English?
  İngilizce bilen var mı?
  [**ee**ngeeleezjeh – muh]
  there wasn't anybody there
  orada kimse yoktu
  [k**ee**mseh]

anything bir şey [shay]

•••••• DIALOGUES ••••••

anything else? başka bir şey? [bashka]

nothing else, thanks hepsi bu kadar, teşekkür ederim [teshekkewr]

would you like anything to drink? bir şey içmek ister misiniz? [eechmek]

I don't want anything, thanks hiç bir şey istemiyorum, teşekkür ederim [heech]

apart from ... ...-den başka [bashka]

apartment apartman dairesi [da-eeresee], daire [da-eereh]

apartment block apartman

aperitif aperetif

apology özür [urzewr]

appendicitis apandisit

appetizer ordövr [ordurvr], meze [mezeh]

apple elma

appointment randevu

•••••• DIALOGUE ••••••

good morning, how can I help you? günaydın, buyrun? [gewnīduhn boo-iroon]

I'd like to make an appointment randevu almak istiyorum

what time would you like? saat kaç için istersiniz? [sa-at kach eecheen]

three o'clock üç için

I'm afraid that's not possible, is four o'clock all right? korkarım o mümkün değil, saat dörtte olur mu? [korkaruhm o mewmkewn deh-eel sa-at durtteh]

yes, that will be fine evet, o çok iyi [chok]

the name was? isim neydi? [naydee]

apricot kayısı [kī-uhsuh]

April nisan

are*: we are ... biz ...-iz
you are ... siz ...-siniz
they are ... onlar ...-dırlar [duhrlar]

area (place) semt
(space) alan

area code şehir kodu [sheh-heer]

arm kol

Armenia Ermenistan

Armenian (adj, person) Ermeni

arrange: will you arrange it for us? bunu bizim için ayarlar mısınız? [icheen ī-arlar muhsuhnuhz]

arrival varış [varuhsh]

arrive varmak
when do we arrive? ne zaman varacağız? [neh – varaja-uhz]
has my fax arrived yet? faksım geldi mi?
we arrived today bugün geldik

art sanat

art gallery sanat galerisi

artist sanatçı [sanatchuh]

as: as big/small as ... ... kadar
büyük/küçük
  as soon as possible en kısa
  zamanda [kuhsa]
ashtray kül tablası [kewl
tablasuh]
Asia Asya
ask (question etc) sormak
  I didn't ask for this ben bunu
  istemedim
  could you ask him/her to ...?
  ondan ...-mesini isteyebilir
  misiniz?
asleep: he/she's asleep uyuyor
[oo-yoo-yor]
aspirin aspirin
asthma astım [astuhm]
astonishing şaşırtıcı
[shashuhr-tuhjuh]
at: at the hotel otelde [oteldeh]
  at the station istasyonda
  at six o'clock saat altıda [sa-at
  altuhda]
  at Ali's Ali'de [alee-deh]
Athens Atina
athletics atletizm
attractive çekici [chekeejee]
aubergine patlıcan [patluhjan]
August ağustos [a-oostos]
aunt (maternal) teyze [tayzeh]
  (paternal) hala
Australia Avustralya
Australian (adj) Avustralya
  I'm Australian Avustralyalıyım
  [–yaluh-yuhm]
automatic otomatik
automatic teller bankamatik
autumn sonbahar
  in the autumn sonbaharda

avenue cadde [jaddeh]
average (ordinary) sıradan
  [suhradan]
  (not good) orta
  on average ortalama olarak
awake: is he/she awake?
  uyanık mı? [oo-yanuhk muh]
away: go away! çekil git!
  [chekeel geet]
  is it far away? uzakta mı?
  [muh]
awful berbat
axle aks

B

baby bebek
baby food mama
baby's bottle biberon
baby-sitter çocuk bakıcısı
  [chojook bakuhjuhsuh]
back (of body) sırt [suhrt]
  (back part) arka
  at the back arkada
  can I have my money back?
  paramı geri alabilir miyim?
  [paramuh]
  to come back geri gelmek
  to go back dönmek [durnmek]
backache sırt ağrısı [suhrt
  a-ruhsuh]
bacon beykın [baykuhn]
bad kötü [kurtew]
  not bad fena değil [deh-eel]
badly kötü [kurtew]
bag çanta [chanta]
  (handbag) el çantası
  [chantasuh]
  (suitcase) bavul

baggage bagaj [baga**J**]
baggage check emanet
baggage claim bagaj alım
  [baga**J** al**uh**m]
bakery fırın [fuhr**uh**n]
balcony balk**o**n
  a room with a balcony
  balkonl**u** bir oda
bald kel
ball top
ballet bale [bal**eh**]
ballpoint pen tükenmez kalem
  [tewkenm**ez**]
banana muz
band (musical) ork**e**stra
bandage sargı [sarg**uh**]
Bandaids® flast**e**r, y**a**ra bandı
  [band**uh**]
bank (money) b**a**nka

Banks are open Monday to
Friday, 8.30 to noon and 1.30
to 5 p.m. Between April and
October most coastal resorts
between Çanakkale and Alanya
have **nöbetçi** (duty banks)
which are open at the weekend
and in the evening; a list is
posted in the window or door
of each branch telling you
who's open that week. Banks
charge around three per cent
commission; the PTT (post and
telephone office) charges one
per cent; and free transactions
and the best rates are to be had
at the new **döviz** or exchange
houses all over western Turkey
→

– though they rarely deal with
travellers' cheques. Because of
the Turkish lira's constant
devaluation you should only
change money every few days
as you need it, unless you're
going east.

bank account b**a**nka hesabı
  [hesab**uh**]
bar bar

Turkey is primarily a Muslim
country and bars are not social
places for most people. In large
cities and resorts, Western-style
bars are found in areas
frequented by foreign visitors.
You might also come across
traditional drinking places
called **meyhane** (literally:
wine house), whose customers
are usually regulars enjoying
their drinks (**rakı** or wine)
with the traditional accom-
paniment of various **mezes**
(snacks). Women should avoid
meyhanes and **birahanes**
(beer halls) as they are
exclusively male drinking
preserves.

a bar of chocolate bir paket
çikolata [cheekol**a**ta]
barber's berber
bargain (verb) pazarlık etmek
  [pazarl**uh**k]

bargaining

It is customary to bargain in Turkish bazaars. Begin at a figure rather lower than whatever you are prepared to pay, usually around half of your shopkeeper's starting price. Once a price has been agreed on, you are ethically committed to buy, so don't commence haggling unless you are reasonably sure you want the item. You can haggle for souvenir purchases, minor repair services, rural taxis, car rental, hotels out of season, and meals – especially seafood ones – at eateries where a menu is absent.

•••••• DIALOGUE ••••••

how much do you want for this?
bunun için ne kadar
istiyorsunuz? [eecheen neh]
300,000 lira üç yüz bin lira
that's too much – I'll give you
200,000 lira o çok fazla – size iki
yüz bin lira veririm [chok –
seezeh]
I'll let you have it for 250,000 lira
size iki yüz elli bin liraya
bırakırım [buhrakuhruhm]
can't you make it cheaper?/OK it's a
deal
daha ucuza olmaz mı?/tamam,
anlaştık [oojooza – muh/anlaştuhk]

basket sepet
bath banyo

can I have a bath? banyo
yapabilir miyim?
bathroom banyo
with a private bathroom
banyolu oda
bath towel havlu
bathtub küvet [kewvet]
battery pil
bay koy
(large) körfez [kurfez]
bazaar çarşı [charshuh], pazar

There are several kinds of bazaar in Turkey. Covered bazaars are found in large towns like İstanbul, Bursa and Kayseri. Surrounding these covered bazaars are large areas of small shops, essentially open-air extensions of the covered areas and governed by the same rules. Prices on the street are often a bit lower than in the covered areas, owing to lower rents. In addition there are weekly or twice-weekly street markets in most towns selling everyday household products.

be* olmak
beach plaj [plaʒ]
on the beach plajda

Pollution and over-crowding are not yet as problematic as in the Western Mediterranean, though beaches close to big cities are often polluted. Look out for
→

signs: **denize girmek tehlikeli ve yasaktır** (it is dangerous and prohibited to go in the sea) and **yüzmek tehlikelidir** (swimming is dangerous). While most beaches do not have lifeguards, a line of buoys indicate the safe distance from the shore. Most large hotels have their own beach facilities within an enclosed area: topless sunbathing and swimming should be confined to these areas.

two beers, please iki bira, lütfen [**lew**tfen]

Beer is sold principally in bottles but also in cans (expensive) and on draught (cheaper). There are three main brands, **Efes Pilsen**, **Tuborg**, and **Venus**, also produced by Tuborg. The **birahane**, an imitation-German beer hall, has cropped up in many tourist towns but often has a distinctly aggressive atmosphere.

beach mat plaj yaygısı [plaʃ yīguhs**uh**]
beach umbrella plaj şemsiyesi [shemsee-yes**ee**]
beans fasulye [fahs**ool**-yeh]
 French beans ayşekadın fasulyesi [īsh**e**kaduhn]
 broad beans bakl**a**
bear ayı [ī-**uh**]
beard sakal
beautiful güzel [gewz**el**]
because çünkü [ch**ew**nkew]
 because of ... ... nedeniyle [neden**ee**leh]
bed yatak
 I'm going to bed now ben artık yatıyorum [art**uh**k yatuh-y**o**room]
bed and breakfast pansiyon see guesthouse
bedroom yatak odası [odas**uh**]
beef sığır eti [suh-**uhr**]
beer bira

before önce [**u**rnjeh]
begin başlamak [bashlam**ak**]
 when does it begin? ne zaman başlıyor? [neh – bashluh-**yo**r]
beginner acemi [ajem**ee**]
beginning: at the beginning başlangıçta [bashlanguhcht**a**]
behind: behind the ... ...-in arkasında [arkasuhnd**a**]
 behind me arkamd**a**
beige bej [be**ʃ**]
Belgian (adj) Belçika [b**e**lcheeka]
Belgium Belçika
believe inanmak
below: below the ... ...-in altında [altuhnd**a**]
belt kemer
bend (in road) viraj [veera**ʃ**]
berth (on ship) ranza, yatak
beside: beside the ... ...-in yanında [yanuhnd**a**]
best en iyi
better daha iyi
 are you feeling better?

kendini**z** daha iyi hissediyor
musun**uz**?
between: between the ...
...-lerin arasında [arasuhnd**a**]
beyond: beyond the ... ...-in
ötesinde [urteseend**eh**]
bicycle bisiklet
big büyük [bew-y**ew**k]
too big fazla büyük
it's not big enough yeterince
büyük değil [yetereenj**eh** –
deh-**ee**l]
bike bisiklet
(motorbike) motosiklet
bikini bikini
bill hes**ap**
(US) kâğıt para [ka-**uh**t]
could I have the bill, please?
hesap, lütfen [l**ew**tfen]

Apart from self-service cafés
and cafeterias etc, where you
pay in advance, you normally
pay in cafés and restaurants
when you are ready to leave.
Turks enjoy treating their
friends and guests and often
insist on paying for your drink
or meal even if no special
invitation was made to take you
out.

bin çöp kutus**u** [churp]
bin liners çöp torbası
[torbas**uh**]
bird kuş [koosh]
birthday doğum günü [doh-**oo**m
gewn**ew**]
happy birthday! doğum

gününüz kutl**u** olsun!
[gewnewn**ew**z]
biscuit bisküvi [beesk**ew**-
vee]
bit: a little bit birazcık
[beerazj**uh**k]
a big bit büyük bir parça
[bew-y**ew**k beer parch**a**]
a bit of ... bir parça ...
a bit expensive/small biraz
pahalı/küçük
bite (by insect) sokm**a**
(by dog) ısırma [uhs**uh**rma]
bitter (taste etc) acı [aj**uh**]
black siyah [see-ya**H**], kara
Black Sea Karadeniz
blanket battaniye [batt**a**nee-
yeh]
bleach (for toilet) tuvalet
temizleyicisi [temeezlay-eejee-
s**ee**]
bless you! çok yaşa! [chok
yash**a**]
blind kör [kur]
blinds jaluzi [Jalooz**ee**]
blister su toplaması
[toplamas**uh**]
I have a blister on my heel
topuğum su topladı [topoo-
oom soo toplad**uh**]
blocked (road) kapalı [kapal**uh**]
(sink, pipe) tıkalı [tuhkal**uh**]
blond (adj) sarışın
[saruh-sh**uh**n]
blood kan
high blood pressure yüksek
tansiyon [yewks**e**k]
blouse bluz
blow-dry (noun) fön [furn]

I'd like a cut and blow-dry
lütfen kesip fönleyin
[**lew**tfen – f**ur**nlayeen]
blue mavi
blusher allık [all**uh**k]
boarding house pansiyon
boarding pass biniş kartı
[ben**ee**sh kart**uh**]
boat gemi
(small) kayık [kī-**uh**k]
body vücut [vewj**oot**]
boiled egg haşlanmış yumurta
[hashlanm**uh**sh]
boiler kazan
bone kemik
bonnet (of car) motor kapağı
[kapa-**uh**], kap**ut**
book (noun) kit**a**p
(verb: seat etc) ayırtmak
[ī-uhrtm**ak**]
can I book a seat? bir yer
ayırtabilir miy**im**?
[ī-uhrtabeel**eer**]

•••••• DIALOGUE ••••••

I'd like to book a table for two iki
kişilik bir masa ayırtmak
istiyorum [keeshe el**eek**]
what time would you like it booked
for? saat kaç için ayırtmak
istiyorsunuz? [sa-**at** kach eech**een**]
half past seven yedi buçuk
that's fine tamam, olur
and your name? isminiz?

bookshop, bookstore kitapçı
[keet**a**p-chuh]
boot (footwear) çizme
[cheezm**eh**]
(of car) bagaj [baga**J**]

border (of country) sınır
[suhn**uhr**]
bored: I'm bored canım
sıkılıyor [jahn**uh**m suhkuhluh-
yor]
boring sıkıcı [suhkuh-j**uh**]
born: I was born in Manchester
Manchester'de doğdum
[–d**eh** doh-do**om**]
I was born in 1960 bin dokuz
yüz altmış'da doğdum
borrow ödünç alm**ak**
[urd**ew**nch]
may I borrow ...? ...-i ödünç
alabilir miy**im**?
Bosphorus İstanbul Boğazı
[eest**a**nbool bo-**a**zuh]
both ikisi de [eekees**ee** deh]
bother: sorry to bother you
rahatsız ettiğim için özür
dilerim [rahats**uh**z ett**ee**-eem
eech**ee**n urz**ewr**]
bottle şişe [sheesh**eh**]
bottle-opener şişe açacağı
[achaj**a**-uh]
bottom (of person) pop**o**
at the bottom of the hill
tepenin eteğinde
[eteh-eend**eh**]
at the bottom of the street
yol**un** alt kısmında
[kuhsm**uh**nda]
box kut**u**
(large) sandık [sand**uh**k]
box office bilet gişesi
[geeshes**ee**]
boy oğlan [oh-l**an**]
boyfriend erkek arkadaş
[arkad**a**sh]

bra sütyen [sewt-yen]
bracelet bilezik
brake fren
brandy konyak
brass pirinç [peereench]
bread ekmek
　white bread beyaz ekmek
　[bayaz]
　brown bread kara ekmek
　wholemeal bread kepekli
　ekmek
break (verb) kırmak [kuhrmak]
　I've broken the ... ...'i kırdım
　[kuhrduhm]
　I think I've broken my wrist
　sanırım bileğimi kırdım
　[sanuh-ruhm]
break down arıza yapmak
　[aruhza]
　I've broken down arabam
　arıza yaptı [yaptuh]
breakdown (mechanical) arıza

The Turkish motoring organ-
ization, the TTOK (Turkish
Touring and Automobile
Association) can advise on
Turkish insurance and related
matters, especially if you are
planning on staying several
months. They have branches in
a number of cities. You will
have to pay for their breakdown
service unless you've equipped
yourself with vouchers or an
insurance policy prior to arrival.

breakdown service araç
　kurtarma [arach]

breakfast kahvaltı [kaHvaltuh]

The Turkish breakfast served at
hotels and pansiyons is almost
invariably a pile of day-old
bread slices with a pat of
margarine, a slice of cheese, a
dab of jam and a couple of
olives. Only tea is likely to be
available in quantity; seconds
are likely to be charged for.

break-in: I've had a break-in
　evime hırsız girdi [eveemeh
　huhrsuhz]
breast göğüs [gur-ews]
breathe nefes almak
breeze esinti
bridge köprü [kurprew]
brief kısa [kuhsa]
briefcase evrak çantası
　[chantasuh]
bright (light etc) aydınlık
　[iduhnluhk]
　(colour) canlı [janluh]
　bright red ateş kırmızısı
　[atesh kuhrmuhzuhsuh]
brilliant (person) çok zeki [chok]
　(idea) parlak
bring getirmek
　I'll bring it back later sonra
　geri getiririm
Britain Büyük Britanya [bew-
　yewk]
British İngiliz [eengeeleez]
brochure broşür [broshewr]
broken bozuk
　(leg etc) kırık [kuhruhk]
bronchitis bronşit [bronsheet]

50

brooch broş [brosh]
broom süpürge [sewrpewrgeh]
brother erkek kardeş [kardesh]
brother-in-law (husband's/wife's
brother) kayınbirader
[kī-uhn-beerader]
(sister's husband) enişte
[eneeshteh]
brown kahverengi
[kaHverengee]
bruise çürük [chewrewk]
brush (for cleaning) fırça [fuhrcha]
(for hair) saç fırçası [sach
fuhrchasuh]
(artist's) resim fırçası
bucket kova
buffet car yemekli vagon
buggy (for child) puset
building bina
bulb (light bulb) ampul
Bulgaria Bulgaristan
Bulgarian (adj, person) Bulgar
bumper tampon
bunk ranza
bureau de change kambiyo
see bank
burglary hırsızlık [huhrsuhzluhk]
burn (noun) yanık [yanuhk]
(verb) yanmak
burnt: this is burnt bu yanmış
[yahnmuhsh]
burst: a burst pipe patlamış
boru [patlamuhsh]
bus otobüs [otobews]
what number bus is it to ...?
...-'a kaç numaralı otobüs
gidiyor? [kach noomaraluh]
when is the next bus
to ...? ...-'a bundan sonraki

otobüs ne zaman? [neh]
what time is the last bus? son
otobüs saat kaçta? [sa-at
kachta]

The Turkish long-distance bus
is an immensely popular form
of transport. There is no
national bus company in
Turkey. Most routes are covered
by several firms, with ticket
booths both at the otogar (bus
terminal) from which they
operate, and also in the city
centre. When you buy your
ticket at a yazıhane, or sales
office in a town centre, you
should ask about free service
buses to the otogar, especially
if it's located a few miles out.
Most companies provide small
minibuses even for a single
passenger; the question to ask
is 'servis arabası var mı?'.
In larger towns the main means
of transport are the red and
white city buses, which take
pre-purchased tickets available
from kiosks near the main
terminals, newsagents, or from
touts (at slightly inflated
prices). The only exceptions are
the orange buses in İstanbul,
whose drivers have been known
to take cash in place of tickets.
On public transport there is a
tendency to act protectively
towards women travelling on
→

ENGLISH ◆ TURKISH | Br

51

their own: when a lone woman buys a seat ticket, it is customary to arrange things so that she does not sit next to a man. The bus steward (**yardımcı** or **muavin**) may well intervene if you try to contravene the convention.
see **taxi**

•••••• DIALOGUE ••••••

does this bus go to ...?
bu ... otobüsü mü? [boo – mew]
no, you need a number ... hayır,
onun için ... nolu otobüse
binmeniz lazım [hī-**uh**r –
eech**ee**n ... nol**oo** otob**ew**seh –
laz**uh**m]

business iş [eesh]
bus station otobüs garajı
[otob**ew**s garaJ**uh**l], oto**gar**
bus stop otobüs durağı
[doora-**uh**]
bust göğüs [gur-**ew**s]
bus terminal oto**gar**
busy (restaurant etc) kalabalık
[kalabal**uh**k]
I'm busy tomorrow yarın
meşgulüm [meshg**oo**lewm]
but ama
butcher's kasap
butter tereyağı [ter**ay**a-uh]
button düğme [dewm**eh**]
buy satın almak [sat**uh**n]
where can I buy ...?
nerede ... bulabilirim?
[n**e**redeh]
by: by bus/car otobüs/

otomobil ile [eel**eh**]
written by ... ... tarafından
yazılan [tarafuhnd**an** yazuhl**an**]
by the window pencere
yanında [yan**uh**nda]
by the sea deniz kenarında
[kenar**uh**nda]
by Thursday Perşembeye
kad**ar**
bye (general use) hoşça kalın
[hosh-ch**a** kal**uh**n]
(said by person leaving) hoşça kal
[h**o**sh-cha]
(said to person leaving) güle güle
[gewl**eh**]
Byzantine Bizans

C

cabbage lahana [laH**a**na]
cabin (on ship) kamara
cable car teleferik
café (for men) kahve [kaH**ve**h],
kahvehane [kaH**ve**h-H**a**neh],
çayhane [chīH**a**neh]
(for families) pastane
[past**a**neh], cafe [kaf**eh**]

Cafés serve hot drinks, soft
drinks, snacks, cakes and ice
cream. Hot drinks include tea,
coffee and **salep**, a hot
sweetened milk drink. You can
also get these at a **pastane**
(pastry shop), where they make
and sell cakes as well as serving
them. Some cafés also serve
alcoholic drinks but a pastane
does not.

cagoule naylon yağmurluk
[nilon ya-moorlook]

cake pasta

cake shop pastane [pastaneh]

call (verb) çağırmak
[cha-uhrmak]
(verb: to phone) telefon etmek
what's it called? ona ne
denir? [neh]
he/she is called ... adı ...
[aduh]
please call the doctor lütfen
doktoru çağırın [lewtfen –
cha-uhruhn]
please give me a call at 7.30
a.m. tomorrow lütfen yarın
sabah yedi buçukta bana bir
telefon edin
please ask him/her to call me
lütfen beni aramasını
söyleyin [aramasuhnuh
suh-ilay-een]

call back: I'll call back later
sonra tekrar uğrarım
[oo-raruhm]
(phone back) sonra tekrar
ararım [araruhm]

call round: I'll call round
tomorrow yarın uğrarım
[oo-raruhm]

camcorder video kamera

camel deve [deveh]

camera fotoğraf makinesi
[foto-raf]

camera shop fotoğrafçı
[foto-rafchuh]

camp (verb) kamp yapmak
can we camp here? burada
kamp yapabilir miyiz?

camping gas tüpgaz [tewpgaz]

> Camping gas is mostly imported
> from Greece and impossible to
> find away from the west coast.

campsite kamping, kamp yeri

> Wherever a pansiyon (guest-
> house) is found, there will also
> be a campsite – often run by
> the same people, who in the
> absence of a proper site may
> simply allow you to crash out in
> the garden. Campsites often
> rent out tents or provide A-
> frame chalet accommodation,
> which can be anything from a
> stuffy garden hut with a bed
> inside to a fairly luxurious affair
> with a bathroom. Campsites are
> open from April or May until
> October. Camping rough is not
> illegal, but hardly anybody does
> it except when trekking in the
> mountains.

can teneke kutu [tenekeh]
a can of beer bir kutu bira
can*: can you ...? ...-ebilir
misiniz?
can I have ...?
bana ... verebilir misiniz?
I can't ... ...-emem

Canada Kanada

Canadian (adj) Kanada
I'm Canadian Kanadalıyım
[kanadaluh-yuhm]

canal kanal

cancel iptal etmek
candies şeker [sheker]
candle mum [moom]
canoe kano
canoeing kano kullanmak
can-opener konserve açacağı
 [konserveh achaja-uh]
cap (hat) kasket
 (of bottle) kapak
car otomobil, araba
 by car otomobil ile [eeleh]
carafe sürahi [sewrahee]
 a carafe of house white, please
 bir sürahi beyaz
 şarabınızdan, lütfen [bayaz
 sharabuhnuhzdan lewtfen]
caravan karavan
caravan site kamping
carburettor karbüratör
 [karbewratur]
card (birthday etc) kart
 here's my (business) card
 buyrun, kartvizitim
 [boo-iroon]
cardigan hırka [huhrka]
cardphone kartlı telefon
 [kartluh]
careful dikkatli
 be careful! dikkatli olun!
caretaker kapıcı [kapuhjuh]
car ferry feribot
car hire kiralık otomobil
 [keeraluhk]
 see car rental
carnival karnaval
car park otopark
car rental kiralık otomobil
 [keeraluhk]

Car rental in Turkey is usually exorbitant, with rates equalling or exceeding any in Europe but there's often considerable scope for bargaining. Unlimited mileage is invariably a better deal than any time-plus-distance rate.
To rent a car you need to be at least 21 years of age, with a driver's licence held for at least one year. An International Driving Permit, from the RAC or AA in Britain or the AAA in the US, is not essential but very helpful. You'll also need to flash a credit card or leave a substantial cash deposit to cover the estimated rental total. see **bargaining** and **rent**

carpet halı [haluh]
carriage (of train) vagon
carrier bag naylon torba [nilon]
carrot havuç [havooch]
carry taşımak [tashuhmak]
carry-cot portbebe [portbebeh]
carton kutu
carwash (place) otomobil
 yıkama yeri [yuhkama]
case (suitcase) valiz, bavul
cash (noun) nakit para
 (verb) paraya çevirmek
 [parī-a cheveermek]
 will you cash this cheque for
 me? benim için bu çeki
 bozar mısınız? [eecheen –
 muhsuhnuhz]

It's wise to carry a fair wad of overseas cash with you in Turkey as you can often pay for souvenirs or accommodation with foreign currency directly (prices for both are often quoted in dollars, sterling or Deutschmarks) and it allows you to take advantage of the **döviz** brokers' convenient service and excellent rates.

cash desk k**a**sa
cash dispenser bank**a**matik
cashier kasi**y**er
cassette kas**e**t
cassette recorder kasetl**i** teyp
  [tayp]
castle kale [kal**eh**]
casualty department acil serv**i**s
  [**a**jeel]
cat kedi [ked**ee**]
catacomb yeralt**ı** mezarlar**ı**
  [yeralt**uh** mezarlar**uh**]
catch (verb: ball etc) yakal**a**mak
  where do we catch the bus to
  İzmir? İzmir otobüs**ü**ne
  nereden binebil**i**riz?
  [**ee**zmeer]
cathedral katedr**a**l
Catholic Kat**o**lik
cauliflower karnab**a**har
cave mağ**a**ra [ma-ar**a**]
ceiling tav**a**n
celery sap keriv**i**zi
cemetery mezarl**ı**k [mezarl**uh**k]
centigrade* santigr**a**t
centimetre* santim**e**tre

[santeem**e**treh]
central merkez**i**
central heating kalor**i**fer
centre merk**e**z
  how do we get to the city
  centre? şehir merkezine nasıl
  gidil**i**r? [sheh-h**ee**r
  merkezeen**eh** nas**uh**l]
certainly kesinl**i**kle
  [keseenl**ee**kleh]
  certainly not kesinlikle hay**ı**r
  [h**ı**-**uh**r]
chair iskemle [eesk**e**mleh]
champagne şamp**a**nya
  [shamp**a**nya]
change (noun: money) boz**u**k
  par**a**
  (verb: money) bozm**a**k
  can I change this for ...?
  bunu ... ile değiştirebil**i**r
  miy**i**m? [eel**eh**
  deh-eeshteereh-beel**ee**r]
  I don't have any change hiç
  boz**u**k par**a**m yok [heech]
  can you give me change for a
  100,000 lira note? ban**a**
  yüzbin lira bozabil**i**r
  misin**i**z? [yewzb**ee**n]
•••••• D I A L O G U E ••••••
  do we have to change (trains)?
  aktarma yapmamız lazım mı?
  [yapmam**uh**z laz**uh**m muh]
  yes, change at Bursa/no, it's a
  direct train evet, Bursa'da
  değiştirin [b**oo**rsa-da
  deh-eeshteer**ee**n]/hayır, bu tren
  direkt gider [h**ı**-**uh**r]

changed: to get changed üstünü

değiştirmek [ewstewn**ew**
deh-eeshteerm**ek**]
chapel kilise [keeleese**h**]
charge (noun) alınan p**a**ra
[aluhn**a**n]
(verb) p**a**ra alm**a**k
charge card kre**d**i kartı [kart**uh**]
see credit card
cheap ucuz [ooj**oo**z]
do you have anything cheaper?
da**h**a ucuz bir şey var mı?
[shay var muh]
check (verb) kontr**o**l etm**e**k
(US: noun) çek [chek]
see cheque
(US: bill) hes**a**p
see bill
could you check the ...,
please? ...-i kontr**o**l ed**e**r
misin**i**z, lütf**e**n? [l**e**wtfen]
checkbook çek defter**i** [chek]
check card çek kartı [kart**uh**]
check-in bag**a**j kay**ı**t [bag**a**ɟ
kĩ-**uh**t], check-in
check in (at hotel) yerleşm**e**k
[yerleshm**e**k]
(at airport) check-in
yaptırm**a**k [yaptuhrm**a**k]
where do we have to check in?
nerede check-in
yaptırm**a**mız laz**ı**m? [n**e**redeh
– yaptuhrm**a**m**uh**z laz**uh**m]
cheek yan**a**k
cheerio! eyvall**a**h! [ayvall**a**н]
cheers! (toast) şeref**e**! [sheref**eh**]
cheese peyn**i**r [payn**ee**r]
chemist's eczan**e** [ejz**a**neh]
see pharmacy
cheque çek [chek]

do you take cheques? çek
kab**u**l edi**y**or musun**uz**?

Travellers' cheques are not
always accepted – most **döviz
gişesi** won't take them at the
moment, and the bank must
have a specimen for the brand
you carry, or they'll refuse to
serve you. This is less of a
problem with Thomas Cook and
American Express cheques. For
both cash and travellers'
cheques transactions, sterling,
Deutschmarks or US dollars are
the preferred currencies.

cheque book çek defter**i** [chek]
cheque card çek kartı [kart**uh**]
cherry kir**a**z
chess satr**a**nç [satr**a**nch]
chest göğüs [gur-**ew**s]
chewing gum çiklet [cheekl**e**t]
chicken tav**u**k
chickenpox suçiçe**ği**
[sooch**e**ch**eh**-ee]
child çocuk [ch**o**j**oo**k]
children çocukl**a**r [chojookl**a**r]

Children are adored in Turkey;
childless couples will be asked
when they plan to have
some, and bringing children
along guarantees red carpet
treatment almost everywhere.
Three- or four-bedded hotel
rooms are easy to find, and
airlines, ships and trains offer
substantial discounts. Baby→

formulas are cheap and readily
available; disposable nappies
aren't.

child minder çocuk bakıcısı
  [chojook bakuhjuhsuh]
children's pool çocuk havuzu
children's portion çocuk
  porsiyonu
chin çene [cheneh]
china porselen
Chinese (adj) Çin [cheen]
chips patates kızartması
  [kuhzartmasuh]
  (US) çips [cheeps]
chocolate çikolata [cheekolata]
  milk chocolate sütlü çikolata
  [sewtlew]
  plain chocolate sade çikolata
  [sa-deh]
  a hot chocolate kakao
choose seçmek [sechmek]
Christian Hıristiyan
  [huhreestee-yan]
Christian name ad
Christmas Noel
  Christmas Eve Noel Gecesi
  [gejesee]
  merry Christmas! İyi Noeller!
  [ee-yee]
church kilise [keeleeseh]
cider elma şırası [shuhrasuh]
cigar puro
cigarette sigara

Turkish cigarettes can be rough,
but if you're keen to try them,
İkibin are the mildest followed →

by **Maltepe**. Better are the
cigarettes made in Turkey
under licence from foreign
brands, notably Marlboro.

cigarette lighter çakmak
  [chakmak]
cinema sinema

There are fewer than thirty
cinemas remaining in all
of Turkey, concentrated in
İstanbul, Ankara and İzmir.
Most foreign films are dubbed,
but you may find a film in
English in İstanbul, Ankara or
İzmir. Examine the posters
outside: **orijinal** means 'original
voice' and **alt yazılı** means 'sub-
titles'.

circle daire [da-eereh]
  (in theatre) balkon
citadel iç kale [eech kaleh]
city şehir [sheh-heer]
city centre şehir merkezi
clean (adj) temiz
  can you clean these for me?
  lütfen bana bunları temizler
  misiniz? [lewtfen – bunlaruh]
cleaning solution (for contact
  lenses) temizleme sıvısı
  [temeezlemeh suhvuhsuh]
cleansing lotion temizleme
  losyonu
clear duru
  (obvious) açık [achuhk]
clever akıllı [akuhlluh]

cliff yar
climbing dağcılık [da-juhl**uh**k]
cling film jelatin [Jelat**een**]
clinic klinik
cloakroom vestiyer
clock saat [sa-**at**]
close (verb) kapatmak

•••••• D I A L O G U E ••••••

what time do you close? saat
kaçta kapatıyorsunuz? [sa-**at**
k**a**chta kapatuh-y**or**–]
we close at 8 p.m. on weekdays
and 6 p.m. on Saturdays hafta
içinde akşam sekizde,
cumartesileri akşam altıda
kapatıyoruz [eecheend**eh** aksh**am**
sek**ee**zdeh joomarteseeler**ee** –
alt**uh**da kapatuh-yor**ooz**]
do you close for lunch? öğlenleri
kapatıyor musunuz? [ur-lenler**ee**
kapatuh-y**or**]
yes, between 1 and 3.30 p.m. evet,
saat birle üçbuçuk arasında
[sa-**at** beerl**eh** ewchbooch**ook**
aras**uh**nda]

closed kapalı [kapal**uh**]
cloth (fabric) kumaş [koom**ash**]
(for cleaning etc) bez
clothes giysiler [gee-is**ee**ler]
clothes line çamaşır ipi
[chamash**uhr**]
clothes peg çamaşır mandalı
[mandal**uh**]
cloud bulut
cloudy bulutlu
clutch (in car) debriyaj
[debree-y**a**ʒ]
coach (bus) yolcu otobüsü

[yolj**oo** otobews**ew**]
(on train) vag**o**n
see bus
coach station otobüs garajı
[garaʒ**uh**]
coach terminal otog**a**r
coach trip otobüsle gezi
[otob**ew**sleh]
coast sahil [sa**Heel**]
on the coast sahilde
[sa**Heel**d**eh**]
coat (long coat) p**a**lto
(jacket) ceket [jek**e**t]
coathanger askı [ask**uh**]
cockroach hamam böceği
[burj**e**h-ee]
cocoa kak**a**o
coconut hindistancevizi
[–jeveez**ee**]
code (for phoning) kod numarası
[noomaras**uh**]
what's the (dialling) code for
İzmir? İzmir'**i**n kodu nedir?
coffee kahve [ka**Hveh**]
two coffees, please iki kahve,
lütfen [l**ew**tfen]

Coffee is not as commonly
drunk in Turkey as tea. Instant
coffee (nescafe [neskaf**eh**]) is
relatively costly but increasingly
popular; much better is the
traditional, fine-ground Turkish
coffee, which is usually served
with a glass of water – a little
cold water added to the coffee
will help the grounds settle. For
an extended session of drinking →

either tea or coffee, you retire to a **çay bahçesi** (tea garden), which often will also serve ice cream and soft drinks. Useful terms are as follows:

Türk kahvesi [tewrk kaHvesee]
Turkish coffee
sade [sa-deh] without sugar
orta şekerli [orta shekerlee]
medium sweet
çok şekerli [chok] very sweet

coin **madeni para**
Coke® **Koka Kola**
cold **soğuk** [so-**ook**]
I'm cold **üşüyorum**
[ewsh**ew**-yoroom]
I have a cold **soğuk aldım**
[ald**uhm**]
collapse: he's collapsed
yığılıverdi [yuh-uhl**uh**yerdee]
collar **yaka**
collect **toplamak, biriktirmek**
I've come to collect ... ...-**ı**
almaya geldim [-uh alm**ī**-a]
collect call **ödemeli konuşma**
[urdemel**ee** konooshma]
college **kolej** [koleJ]
colour **renk**
do you have this in other colours? **bunun başka renkleri de bulunur mu sizde?** [b**a**shka – deh – seezd**eh**]
colour film **renkli film**
comb **tarak**
come (arrive) **gelmek**

•••••• DIALOGUE ••••••
where do you come from? **siz nerelisiniz?**
I come from Edinburgh **ben Edinburgluyum**

come back **dönmek** [durnmek]
I'll come back tomorrow **yarın tekrar gelirim**
come in **girmek**
comfortable **rahat**
compact disc **Compact Disc, CD** [see dee]
company (business) **şirket** [sheerk**et**]
compartment (on train) **kompartıman** [kompartuhm**an**]
compass **pusula**
complain **şikayet etmek** [sheekī-**et**]
complaint **şikayet**
I have a complaint **bir şikayetim var**
completely **tamamen**
computer **bilgisayar** [beelgeesī-**ar**]
concert **konser**
concussion **beyin sarsıntısı** [bay**ee**n sarsuhn-tuhs**uh**]
conditioner (for hair) **saç kremi** [sach]
condom **prezervatif**
conference **konferans**
confirm **doğrulamak** [doh-roolam**ak**]
congratulations! **tebrikler!**
connecting flight **aktarmalı sefer** [aktarmal**uh**]

connection bağlantı [ba-lant**uh**]

conscious şuuru yerinde [shoo-oo**roo** yereend**eh**]

constipation kabızlık [kabuhzl**uhk**]

consulate konsolos**l**uk

contact (verb) ilişki kurm**ak** [eeleeshk**ee**]

contact lenses kont**ak** lens**l**eri

contraceptive prezervatif, kor**u**yucu [koroo-yoo**joo**]

convenient uygun [oo-ig**oo**n] that's not convenient o pek uygun değil [deh-**eel**]

cook (verb) pişirmek [peesheerm**ek**] not cooked pişmemiş [**pee**shmemeesh]

cooker ocak [oj**ak**]

cookie bisküvi [beesk**ew**vee]

cooking utensils mutfak aletleri

cool serin

copper bakır [bak**uhr**]

cork mant**ar**

corkscrew tirbuşon [teerboosh**o**n]

corner: on the corner köşe başında [kursh**eh** bash**uh**nda] in the corner köşede [kursh**ed**eh]

cornflakes mısır gevreği [muhs**uhr** gevreh-**ee**]

correct (right) doğru [doh-**roo**]

corridor koridor

cosmetics makyaj malzemesi

cost (verb) mal olmak how much does it cost? fiyatı nedir? [fee-yat**uh**]

cot çocuk yatağı [choj**oo**k yat**a**-uh]

cotton pamuk

cotton wool hidrofil pamuk

couch (sofa) kanape [kan**a**peh]

couchette yatak, kuşet

cough (noun) öksürük [urksew-**rewk**]

cough medicine öksürük şurubu [shooroob**oo**]

could: could you give ...? ... verebilir misiniz? could I have ...? ... alabilir miyim? I couldn't ... ...-amadım [-**a**maduhm]

country (nation) ülke [ewlk**eh**] (countryside) kırsal alanlar [kuhrs**al**]

countryside kırlar [kuhrl**ar**], şehir dışı [sheh-h**eer** duhsh**uh**]

couple (two people) çift [cheeft] a couple of ... (two) bir çift ... (a few) bir iki tane ... [t**a**neh]

courgette kabak

courier kurye [koor-y**eh**]

course (main course etc) yemek çeşidi [chesheed**ee**] of course elbette [elbetteh] of course not tabii değil [tabee-ee deh-**eel**]

courtyard avlu

cousin (male) kuzen (female) kuzin

cow inek

crab yengeç [yengech]

cracker (biscuit) kraker

craft shop el sanatları dükkanı [sanatlar**uh** dewk-kan**uh**]

crash (noun) çarpışma
  [charpuhshma]
  I've had a crash kaza yaptım
  [yaptuhm]
crazy deli
cream (in cake etc) krema
  (lotion) krem
  (colour) krem rengi
creche kreş [kresh]
credit card kredi kartı [kartuh]
  do you take credit cards? kredi
  kartı kabul ediyor musunuz?

A major credit card is
invaluable for domestic ferry
and plane tickets, and also as a
waiver for a huge cash deposit
when renting a car. You can also
normally get cash advances at
any bank displaying the
appropriate sign, either over
the counter or from the
in-creasingly common ATMs.
Visa and Mastercard/Access are
widely accepted for fuel
purchases in much of Turkey.

•••••• DIALOGUE ••••••

can I pay by credit card? kredi
kartıyla ödeyebilir miyim?
[kartuh-ila urdayebeeleer]
which card do you want to use?
hangi kartla ödemek istersiniz?
[urdemek]
Access/Visa Access'le/Visa'yla
yes, sir peki efendim
what's the number? numarası
nedir? [noomarasuh]
and the expiry date? ve ne zamana

kadar geçerli? [veh neh –
gecherlee]

Crete Girit [geereet]
crisps çips [cheeps]
crockery tabak takımları
  [takuhmlaruh]
crossing (by sea) geçiş
  [gecheesh]
crossroads kavşak [kavshak]
crowd kalabalık [kalabaluhk]
crowded kalabalık
crown (on tooth) kuron
cruise vapur gezisi
crutches koltuk değnekleri
  [deh-nekleree]
cry (verb) ağlamak [a-lamak]
cucumber salatalık [salataluhk]
cup fincan [feenjan]
  a cup of ..., please lütfen bir
  fincan ... [lewtfen]
cupboard dolap
cure (verb) tedavi etmek
curly kıvırcık [kuhvuhrjuhk]
current (electrical) akım [akuhm]
  (in water) akıntı [akuhntuh]
curtains perdeler
cushion yastık [yastuhk]
custom gelenek
Customs Gümrük [gewmrewk]

Entering Turkey usually entails
a cursory Customs inspection: a
record of laptop computers,
video cameras etc, may be
made in your passport to ensure
that you take them out with you
when you leave. Checks on the
way out may be more thorough,
→

and you should arrive at the airport or ferry dock in good time. Only an idiot would try to take drugs through Turkish Customs.

cut (noun) kesik
  (verb) kesmek
  I've cut my finger parmağımı
  kestim [parma-uhmuh]
cutlery çatal bıçak [chatal
  buhchak]
cycling bisiklete binmek
  [beeseekleteh]
cyclist bisikletli
Cypriot (adj) Kıbrıs [kuhbruhs]
  (person) Kıbrıslı [kuhbruhsluh]
Cyprus Kıbrıs

D

dad baba
daily her gün [gewn]
  (adj) günlük [gewnlewk]
damage (verb) zarar vermek
damaged hasar görmüş
  [gurmewsh]
  I'm sorry, I've damaged this
  özür dilerim, bunu bozdum
  [urzewr]
damn! Allah kahretsin!
damp (adj) nemli
dance (noun) dans
  (verb) dans etmek
  would you like to dance? dans
  etmek ister misiniz?
dangerous tehlikeli
Danish (adj) Danimarka

(language) Danimarkaca
  [–markaja]
Dardanelles Çanakkale Boğazı
  [chanakkaleh bo-azuh]
dark (adj: colour) koyu
  (skin, hair) esmer
  it's getting dark hava
  kararıyor [kararuh-yor]
date*: what's the date today?
  bugün ayın kaçı? [boogewn
  ī-uhn kachuh]
  let's make a date for next
  Monday gelecek pazartesi
  için randevulaşalım [gelejek –
  eecheen randevoolashaluhm]
dates (fruit) hurma
daughter kız evlat [kuhz]
daughter-in-law gelin
dawn (noun) şafak [shafak]
  at dawn gün ağarırken [gewn
  a-aruhrken]
day gün [gewn]
  the day after ertesi gün
  the day after tomorrow öbür
  gün [urbewr]
  the day before bir gün önce
  [urnjeh]
  the day before yesterday
  evvelki gün
  every day her gün
  all day bütün gün [bewtewn]
  in two days' time iki gün
  içinde [gewn eecheendeh]
  have a nice day! iyi günler!
day trip günlük gezi
  [gewnlewk]
dead ölü [urlew]
deaf sağır [sa-uhr]
deal (business) iş [eesh]

it's a deal anlaştık
[anlasht**uh**k]
death ölüm [url**ew**m]
decaffeinated coffee kafeinsiz
kahve [kafeh-eens**eez** ka**H**ve**h**]
December aralık [aral**uh**k]
decide karar vermek
we haven't decided yet henüz
karar vermedik [hen**ew**z]
decision karar
deck (on ship) güverte
[g**ew**verteh]
deckchair şezlong [shezl**o**ng]
deep derin
definitely kesinlikle
[keseenl**ee**kleh]
definitely not kesinlikle değil
[deh-**ee**l]
degree (qualification) diploma
delay (noun) gecikme
[gejeekm**eh**]
deliberately kasten
delicatessen şarküteri
[sharkewter**ee**]
delicious nefis
deliver teslim etmek
delivery (of mail) dağıtım
[da-uht**uh**m]
Denmark Danimarka
dental floss diş ipi [deesh]
dentist dişçi [deesh-ch**ee**]

Turkish dentists are called **diş
doktoru, diş tabibi** or **hekimi**
and are well qualified and
experienced. Foreign visitors
usually have to pay for
medication and treatment by
→

private dentists. However the
cost of treatment is low and can
be claimed against insurance if
receipts are obtained.

•••••• DIALOGUE ••••••

it's this one here işte buradaki
[eesht**eh**]
this one? bu mu?
no, that one hayır, şu [hī-**uh**r shoo]
here? buradaki mi?
yes evet

dentures takma diş [deesh]
deodorant deodoran
department bölüm [burl**ew**m]
department store büyük
mağaza [bew-y**ew**k ma-**a**za]
departure kalkış [kalk**uh**sh]
departure lounge giden
yolcular salonu
depend: it depends duruma
göre [gur-**reh**]
it depends on ... ...-a bağlı
[ba-l**uh**]
deposit (noun) depozito
dervish derviş [derv**ee**sh]
description tanım [tan**uh**m]
dessert tatlı [tatl**uh**]
destination gidilecek yer
[geedeelej**ek**]
develop (film) banyo etmek

•••••• DIALOGUE ••••••

could you develop these films? bu
filmleri banyo edebilir misiniz?
yes, certainly evet, tabi
when will they be ready? ne
zaman hazır olurlar? [neh –

hazuhr]
tomorrow afternoon yarın öğleden
sonra
how much is the four-hour service?
dört saatlik servisin ücreti
nedir? [durt sa-atleek – ewjretee]

diabetic (noun) şeker hastası
[sheker hastasuh]
diabetic foods şeker hastaları
için diyet yemeği [–laruh
eecheen – yemeh-ee]
dial (verb) çevirmek
[cheveermek]
dialling code telefon kodu
dialling tone çevir sesi [cheveer]

For direct international calls
from Turkey, dial 00, then the
country code (given below), the
area code minus the first 0, and
finally the subscriber number:

USA and Canada 1
Britain 44   Ireland 353
Australia 63   New Zealand 64

diamond elmas
diaper çocuk bezi [chojook]
diarrhoea ishal
do you have something for
diarrhoea? sizde ishale karşı
bir ilaç var mı? [seezdeh
eeshaleh karshuh beer eelach
var muh]
diary (business etc) ajanda
[aJanda]
(for personal experiences) günce
[gewnjeh]
dictionary sözlük [surzlewk]

didn't* see not
Didyma Didim
die ölmek [urlmek]
diesel mazot
diet perhiz [perheez]
I'm on a diet perhiz
yapıyorum [yapuh-yoroom]
I have to follow a special diet
özel bir rejim izlemem
gerekiyor [urzel beer reJeem]
difference fark
what's the difference? ne fark
var? [neh]
different başka [bashka]
this one is different bu farklı
[farkluh]
a different table başka bir
masa
difficult zor
difficulty zorluk
dinghy sandal
dining room yemek salonu
dinner (evening meal) akşam
yemeği [aksham yemeh-ee]
(midday meal) öğle yemeği
[urleh]
to have dinner akşam yemeği
yemek
direct (adj) direkt
is there a direct train? direkt
giden bir tren var mı? [muh]
direction yön [yurn]
which direction is it? hangi
yönde? [yurndeh]
is it in this direction? bu yönde
mi?
directory enquiries bilinmeyen
numaralar [beeleenmayen]

64

Directory assistance 118
Inter-city operator 131
International operator 115

dirt pislik, kir
dirty kirli
disabled özürlü [urzewrl**ew**]
  is there access for the
  disabled? özürlüler için giriş
  var mı? [urzewrlewler eech**ee**n
  geer**ee**sh var muh]
disappear kaybolmak
  [kībolm**a**k]
  it's disappeared ortad**a**n
  kayboldu [kībold**oo**]
disappointed hayal kırıklığına
  uğramış [hī-**a**l kuhruhkluh-
  uhn**a** oo-ram**uh**sh]
disappointing düş kırıcı [dewsh
  kuhruhj**uh**]
disaster felak**e**t
disco disk**o**
discount i̇ndirim
  is there a discount? indirim
  var mı? [muh]
disease hastalık [hastal**uh**k]
disgusting iğrenç [eer**e**nch]
dish (meal) yem**e**k
  (bowl) tab**a**k
dishcloth bulaşık bezi
  [boolash**uh**k]
disinfectant (noun) dezenfekt**a**n
disk (for computer) disk**e**t
disposable diapers/nappies
  kâğıt çocuk bezi [ka-**uh**t
  choj**oo**k]
distance uzaklık [oozakl**uh**k]
  in the distance uzakt**a**

distilled water arı su [ar**uh** soo]
district semt
disturb rahatsız etmek
  [rahats**uh**z]
diversion (detour) geçici
  güzergah [gecheej**ee**
  gewzerg**a**H]
diving board tramplen
divorced boşanmış
  [boshanm**uh**sh]
dizzy: I feel dizzy başım
  dönüyor [bash**uh**m
  durnew-y**o**r]
do (verb) yapm**a**k
  what shall we do? ne
  yapalım? [neh yapal**uh**m]
  how do you do it? onu nasıl
  yapıyorsunuz? [nas**uh**l
  yap**uh**–]
  will you do it for me? benim
  için bunu yap**a**r mısınız?
  [eech**ee**n – muhsuhn**uh**]

•••••• DIALOGUES ••••••

how do you do? nasılsınız?
[nas**uh**l-suhnuhz]
nice to meet you tanıştığımıza
memnun oldum
[tanuhshtuh-uhmuh**z**a]
what do you do? (work) ne iş
yapıyorsunuz? [neh eesh]
I'm a teacher, and you?
öğretmenim, ya siz?
[ur-retmen**ee**m]
I'm a student öğrenciyim
[ur-renjee-y**ee**m]
what are you doing this evening?
bu akşam ne yapıyorsunuz?
we're going out for a drink, do you
want to join us? bir şey içmeye

ENGLISH ◆ TURKISH   Di

gidiyor**uz**, bize katılmak ister misiniz? [shay eechmay**eh** – beez**eh** katuhlm**a**k]

do you want cream? krema ister misiniz?

I do, but she doesn't ben isteri**m ama** o istemiy**or**

doctor dokt**or**

we need a doctor bize bir doktor lazım [beez**eh** – laz**uh**m]

please call a doctor lütfen bir doktor çağırın [l**ew**tfen – cha-uhr**uh**n]

You'll find well-trained doctors in larger towns and cities. Most of these are specialists, advertising themselves by means of signs outside their premises. Look for the words **dahiliye mütehassısı** or **iç hastalıkları mütehassısı**: both mean 'specialist in internal diseases' and are the nearest to a general doctor.

If you're not sure what's wrong with you, it's best to go instead to one of the free state clinics (who can give diagnoses and prescriptions) or a hospital. Hospitals are either public (**Devlet Hastanesi** or **SSK Hastanesi**) or private (**Özel Hastane**); the latter are vastly preferable in terms of cleanliness, shortness of queues and standard of care, and since all →

foreigners must pay for any attention anyway, you may as well get the best available. You should take out an insurance policy to cover against illness or injury before travelling to Turkey.

•••••• D I A L O G U E ••••••

where does it hurt? neresi acıyor? [ajuh-y**or**]

right here tam burası [booras**uh**]

does that hurt now? şimdi acıyor mu? [sheemd**ee**]

yes evet

take this to the chemist alın bunu, eczaneye götürün [al**uh**n – ejzanay**eh** gurtewr**ew**n]

document belge [belg**eh**]
dog köpek [kurp**e**k]
doll bebek
dome kubbe [koobb**eh**]
domestic flight iç hat seferi [eech]
donkey eşek [esh**e**k]
don't!* yapma!
   don't do that! onu yapma!
   see not
door kapı [kap**uh**]
doorman kapıcı [kapuhj**uh**]
double çift [cheeft]
double bed iki kişilik yatak [keeshee**lee**k]
double room iki kişilik oda
down (direction) aşağı [asha-**uh**]
   down here burda aşağıda
   put it down over there onu şuraya bırakın [shoorī-**a**

buhrak**uhn**]
it's down there on the right
şurada, aşağıda sağda
[shoor**a**da – s**a**-da]
it's further down the road
yolun daha aşağısında
[asha-uhsuhnd**a**]
downmarket (restaurant etc)
gösterişsiz [gurstereesh-s**eez**]
downstairs alt kat
dozen düzine [dewz**ee**neh]
half a dozen yarım düzine
[yar**uh**m]
drain (in sink) pis su boru**su**
(in street) kanalizasy**on**
draught beer fıçı birası
[fuhch**uh** beeras**uh**]
draughty: it's draughty cereyan
yapıyor [jerayan yapuh-y**or**]
drawer çekmece [chekmej**eh**]
drawing çizim [cheez**eem**]
dreadful berb**at**
dream (noun) rüya [rew-**ya**]
dress (noun) elbise [elbis**eh**]
dressed: to get dressed
giyin**mek**
dressing (for cut) pansum**an**
salad dressing sos
dressing gown (for women)
sabahlık [sabaH**luh**k]
(for men) robdöşambr
[robdursh**a**mbr]
drink (alcoholic) içki [eechk**ee**]
(non-alcoholic) içecek
[eechej**ek**], meşrubat
[meshroob**at**]
(verb) içmek [eechm**ek**]
a cold drink soğuk meşrubat
[so-**ook**]

can I get you a drink? içecek
bir şey ister misiniz? [shay]
what would you like (to drink)?
ne içki alırsınız? [neh eechk**ee**
aluhrsuhn**uh**z]
no thanks, I don't drink hayır
teşekkür, ederim alkol
almıyorum [hī-**uh**r
teshekk**ew**r – **a**lmuh-yoroom]
I'll just have a drink of water
sadece bir**az** su istiyorum
[sa-dej**eh**]
see **bar**
drinking water içme su**yu**
[eechm**eh**]
is this drinking water? bu içme
suyu mu?

> It's probably best to avoid
> drinking tap water, heavily
> chlorinated though it is, and
> with bottled water widely
> available you shouldn't need to.

drive (verb) sürmek [sewrm**ek**]
we drove here buraya
arabayla geldik [boor**ī**-a
arab**ī**la]
I'll drive you home ben sizi
arabayla evinize götürürüm
[eveeneez**eh** gurtewr-ewr**ew**m]

> You drive on the right, and
> always yield to those approach-
> ing from the right. Speed limits
> are 50km/hr within towns,
> 90km/hr on the open road for
> saloon cars and 80km/hr for →

lorries and vans. Major
violations such as jumping
red lights, speeding or drink
driving carry very heavy on-the-
spot fines. Breathalyzers
(**üfleme cihazı**) are widely
used by the traffic police.
The legal limit for blood
alcohol level when driving a car
is .05% but do not drink and
drive.

driver (of car) sürücü
[sewrewj**ew**]
(of bus) şoför [shof**ur**]
driving licence şoför ehliyet**i**
drop: just a drop, please (of
drink) yalnız bir damla, lütfen
[yaln**uh**z – lew**t**fen]
drugs (narcotics) uyuşturucu
[oo-yooshtooroojoo]
drunk (adj) sarhoş [sarh**osh**]
drunken driving içkili arab**a**
kullanma**k** [eechkeel**ee**]
dry (adj) kur**u**
(wine) sek
dry-cleaner kuru temizleyici
[temeez**lay**eejee]
duck ördek [urd**ek**]
due: he/she was due to arrive
yesterday dün gelmes**i**
gerekiyord**u** [dewn]
when is the train due? tren
kaçta gelecek? [k**a**chta
gelej**ek**]
dull (pain) don**uk**
(weather) sıkıntılı
[suhkuhntuhl**uh**]

dummy (baby's) emz**ik**
during sırasında [suhra-
s**uh**nda]
dust toz
dustbin çöp tenekes**i** [churp]
dusty tozlu
Dutch (adj) Hollanda
(language) Hollandaca
[holl**a**ndaja]
duty-free (goods) gümrüksüz
eşya [gewmr**ew**ksewz esh-y**a**]
duty-free shop duty-free
duvet yorgan

E

each (every) her
how much are they each?
tanes**i** kaça? [kach**a**]
ear kulak
earache: I have earache
kulağım ağrıyor [koola-**uh**m
a-ruh-yor]
early erken
early in the morning sabah
erkenden [sab**a**н]
I called by earlier daha önce
uğramıştım [**u**rnjeh
oo-ramuhshtuhm]
earring(s) küpe [kewp**eh**]
east doğu [doh-**oo**]
in the east doğu**da**
Easter Paskalya
easy kolay [ko-l**ī**]
eat yemek
we've already eaten, thanks
biz yedik, teşekkür ederi**z**
[teshekk**ew**r]

eating habits
Breakfasts usually consist of well-brewed tea (without milk), bread or toast, butter, jam or honey, olives and sheep's cheese. Sometimes sliced tomatoes, cucumber and boiled eggs are also available, as is soup. Tripe soup for early starters is also appreciated by many after a late night out.
Lunch (**öğle yemeği**) can be a simple toasted sandwich or **börek** (flaky, layered pastry containing cheese, spinach or minced meat) washed down with **ayran** (yoghurt drink). Otherwise it is very similar to dinner (**akşam yemeği**) which is usually the main meal of the day. They both start with soup followed by a meat dish served with rice or potatoes and a salad. Turkish cuisine is rich in vegetable dishes – some of which are cooked with meat. A vegetable dish follows the meat dish. Some vegetable dishes are cooked with olive oil (**zeytinyağlı**) and are served cold. The meal ends with dessert (**tatlı**) or fruit (**meyva**). The most famous desserts are **baklava** (layers of filo pastry filled with pistachio nuts or walnuts and soaked in syrup), **sütlaç** (rice pudding) and **tavuk** →

göğsü (milk pudding).
Most Turks, being Muslim, either do not drink alcohol or drink very little. Turkish men sometimes drink **rakı** and water when out in restaurants but in general and when at home most people drink water with meals. If Turks do drink in the evening, they will usually accompany the alcohol with **mezes** (hors d'œuvres). There are lots of different mezes and a typical selection might include **sigara böreği** (cigarette-shaped filo pastry with cheese and parsley filling), **cacık** (yoghurt, cucumber and garlic dip), **patlıcan salatası** (aubergine purée salad), **zeytinyağlı dolma** (stuffed vine leaves or green peppers), **imam bayıldı** (an aubergine dish cooked with olive oil), sheep's cheese and olives. Sometimes mezes form a starter to a main meal.

eau de toilette kolonya
EC AT [a teh]
economy class ekonomi sınıfı [suhnuhfuh]
Edinburgh Edinburg
egg yumurta
eggplant patlıcan [patluhjan]
either: either ... or ... ya ... ya ...
    either of them ikisinden biri
elastic (noun) lastik
elastic band lastik bant

elbow dirsek
electric elektrik**li**
electrical appliances elektrikli
aletler
electric fire elektrik sobası
[sobas**uh**]
electrician elektrikçi
[elektreekch**ee**]
electricity elektrik
see voltage
elevator asansör [asans**ur**]
else: something else başka bir
şey [b**a**shka beer shay]
somewhere else başka bir yer

•••••• DIALOGUE ••••••

would you like anything else?
başka bir şey ister misiniz?
no, nothing else, thanks hayır,
hepsi bu kad**a**r, teşekkür ederim
[hï-**uh**r – teshekke**w**r]

embassy elçilik [elchee**lee**k]
emergency acil durum [**a**jeel]
this is an emergency! bu
acildir! [ajeeld**ee**r]
emergency exit tehlike çıkışı
[tehleek**eh** chukuhsh**uh**]
empty boş [bosh]
end (noun) son
(verb) bitm**ek**
at the end of the ... (street etc)
...-**u**n son**u**nda
when does it end? ne zam**a**n
biti**yor**?
engaged (toilet, telephone) meşgul
[meshg**ool**]
(to be married) nişanlı
[neeshanl**uh**]
engine (car) mot**or**

England İngiltere [eengeelt**ereh**]
English (adj) İngiliz [**ee**ngeeleez]
(language) İngilizce
[eengeel**ee**zjeh]
I'm English ben İngilizim
do you speak English?
İngilizce bili**yor** musun**uz**?
enjoy: to enjoy oneself
eğlenmek [eh-lenm**ek**]

•••••• DIALOGUE ••••••

how did you like the film? film**i**
nasıl buldunuz? [nâs**uh**l]
I enjoyed it very much, did you
enjoy it? benim çok hoşuma gitti,
ya sizin? [chok hoshoom**a**]

enjoyable zevkl**i**
enlargement (of photo) büyültme
[bew-yewltm**eh**]
enormous dev
enough yet**er**
there's not enough yetm**ez**
it's not big enough yeterince
büyük değil [yeter**ee**njeh bew-
y**ew**k deh-**eel**]
that's enough bu kad**a**r yet**er**
entrance giriş [geer**ee**sh]
envelope zarf
Ephesus Efes
epileptic (adj) saralı [saral**uh**]
equipment donatım [donat**uh**m]
error hat**a**
especially özellikle
[urzelleekl**eh**]
essential şart [shart]
it is essential that ... ...-sı
şarttır [-shuh sh**a**rttuhr]
EU AB [a beh]
Eurocheque **Eu**rocheque

Eurocheque card Eurocheque
kardı [kard**uh**]
Europe Avrupa
European (adj) Avrupa
(person) Avrupalı [avroopal**uh**]
even ... ... bile [beel**eh**]
even if ... ...-se bile [-seh]
evening akşam [aksh**a**m]
this evening bu akşam
in the evening akşamleyin
[aksh**a**mlayeen]
evening meal akşam yemeği
[yemeh-**ee**]
eventually son**u**nda
ever hiç [heech]

•••••• D I A L O G U E ••••••

have you ever been to Antalya? hiç
Antalya'**ya** gittiniz mi?
yes, I was there two years ago
evet, iki yıl önce ordaydım [yuhl
urnjeh ordïd**uh**m]

every her
every day her gün [gewn]
everyone herkes
everything her şey [shay]
everywhere her yer
exactly! çok doğru! [chok d**oh**-
roo]
exam sınav [suhn**a**v]
example örnek [**u**rnek]
for example örneğin
[**u**rn**eh**-een]
excellent mükemmel
[mewkemm**e**l]
(food) nefis
(hotel) çok güzel [chok gewz**e**l]
excellent! mükemmel!
except ... ... hariç [h**a**reech]

excess baggage fazla bagaj
[bag**a**ɹ]
exchange rate döviz kuru
[durve**e**z]
exciting heyecan verici [hayej**a**n
vereej**ee**]
excuse me (to get past) pardon
(to get attention) affed**e**rsiniz
(to say sorry) özür dilerim
[urz**e**wr]
exhaust (pipe) egzos borusu
exhausted (tired) bitk**i**n
exhibition serg**i**
exit çıkış [chuhk**uh**sh]
where's the nearest exit? en
yakın çıkış nerede? [yak**uh**n
– neredeh]
expect beklemek
expensive pahalı [paHal**uh**]
experienced tecrübeli
[tejrewbel**ee**]
explain açıklamak
[achuhklam**a**k]
can you explain that? onu
açıklar mısınız? [achuhkl**a**r
muhsuhn**uh**z]
express (mail, train) ekspres
extension (telephone) dahili
numara [daHeel**ee**]
what is your extension? dahili
numaranız nedir?
[noomar**a**nuhz]
extension 221, please iki yüz
yirmi bir numara, lütfen
[yewz – l**e**wtfen]
extension lead uzatma kablosu
extra: can we have an extra
one? lütfen bir tane daha
[l**e**wtfen – tan**eh**]

do you charge extra for that?
bunun için ayrıca para
alıyor musunuz? [eecheen
īruhja para aluh-yor]
extraordinary çok garip [chok
gareep]
extremely son derece [derejeh]
eye göz [gurz]
  will you keep an eye on my
  suitcase for me? benim için
  bavuluma göz kulak olur
  musunuz? [eecheen]
eyebrow pencil kaş kalemi
  [kash]

---

eye contact
Local people often stare
blatantly at foreigners, and such
attention should not be
interpreted as rudeness.
However, staring back is likely
to be interpreted as hostility or
– if you're a woman – an
invitation to further interaction.
Scrupulously avoiding eye
contact is one of the best
defences against sexual
harassment.

---

eye drops göz damlası [gurz
damlasuh]
eyeglasses (US) gözlük
  [gurzlewk]
eyeliner eyeliner
eye make-up remover göz
  makyajı çıkarıcısı [gurz
  makyaJuh chuhkaruh-juhsuh]
eye shadow far

F

face yüz [yewz]
factory fabrika
Fahrenheit* Fahrenhayt [–hīt]
faint (verb) bayılmak [bī-uhlmak]
  she's fainted bayıldı
  [bī-uhlduh]
  I feel faint kendimi çok halsiz
  hissediyorum [chok]
fair (funfair) panayır [panī-uhr]
  (trade) fuar [fwar]
  (adj: just) adil, haklı [hakluh]
fairly oldukça [oldookcha]
fake taklit
fall (verb) düşmek [dewshmek]
  she's had a fall düştü
  [dewshtew]
  (US: noun) sonbahar
  in the fall sonbaharda
false sahte [saHteh]
Famagusta Magosa
family aile [a-eeleh]
famous ünlü [ewnlew]
fan (electrical) vantilatör
  [vanteelatur]
  (handheld) yelpaze [yelpazeh]
  (sports) taraftar
  (of pop star etc) hayran [hīran]
fanbelt vantilatör kayışı
  [vanteelatur kī-uhshuh]
fantastic fantastik, hayali
far uzak

•••••• DIALOGUE ••••••

is it far from here? buradan uzak
mı? [muh]
no, not very far hayır, pek uzak
değil [hī-uhr – deh-eel]

well how far? peki ne kadar
uzak? [neh]
it's about 20 kilometres yaklaşık
yirmi kilometre [yaklash**uhk** –
keelometr**eh**]

fare yol parası [paras**uh**]
farm çiftlik [cheeftl**eek**]
fashionable moda
fast hızlı [huhzl**uh**]
fat (person) şişman [sheeshm**an**]
   (on meat) yağ [ya]
father baba
father-in-law kayınpeder
   [kī-**uh**npeder]
faucet musluk
fault hata
   sorry, it was my fault özür
   dilerim, hata bendeydi
   [urz**ew**r – bend**ay**dee]
   it's not my fault hata bende
   değil [bend**eh** deh-**eel**]
faulty arızalı [aruhzal**uh**]
favourite gözde [gurzd**eh**]
fax faks
fax (verb: person) -a faks çekmek
   [chekm**ek**]
   (document) fakslamak
February şubat [shoob**at**]
feel hissetmek
   I feel hot sıcak bastı [suhj**ak**
   bast**uh**]
   I feel unwell kendimi kötü
   hissediyorum [kurt**ew**]
   I feel like going for a walk
   canım yürüyüşe çıkmak
   istiyor [jan**uh**m yewrew-
   yewsheh ch**uh**kmak]
   how are you feeling?

kendinizi nasıl
hissediyorsunuz? [nas**uhl**]
I'm feeling better kendimi
daha iyi hissediyorum
felt-tip (pen) keçe uçlu kalem
   [kech**eh** oochl**oo**]
fence parmaklık [parmakl**uhk**]
fender tampon
ferry feribot

City ferries, mainly serving foot
passengers and connecting
points within places like
İstanbul and İzmir, are
frequent, cheap and efficient,
running to very tight schedules.
In addition to these are short-
hop ferries, some of which serve
foot passengers only, while
others have provision for
vehicles.
Long-haul domestic ferries
are now restricted to the
coastal stretches where the
road network is substandard,
specifically between İstanbul
and Trabzon – with inter-
mediate stops – and direct from
İstanbul to İzmir. All long-haul
services are very popular, and
reservations must be made well
in advance through one of the
authorized TML agencies in the
appropriate ports.

festival festival
fetch gidip getirmek
   I'll fetch him/her gidip onu
   çağırayım [cha-uhrī-**uhm**]

will you come and fetch me
later? sonra gelip beni alır
mısınız? [aluhr muhsuhnuhz]
feverish ateşli [ateshlee]
few: a few birkaç [beerkach]
a few days birkaç gün [gewn]
fiancé(e) nişanlı [neeshanluh]
field tarla
fight (noun) kavga
figs incir [eenjeer]
fill in doldurmak
do I have to fill this in? bunu
doldurmam gerekli mi?
fill up doldurmak
fill it up, please lütfen depoyu
doldurun [lewtfen depo-yoo]
filling (in cake, sandwich) iç [eech]
(in tooth) dolgu
film film

•••••• DIALOGUE ••••••

do you have this kind of film? sizde
bu tip film var mı? [seezdeh boo
teep – muh]
yes, how many exposures? evet,
kaç pozluk? [kach pozlook]
36 otuz altı

film processing film banyosu
filter coffee süzme kahve
[sewzmeh kaHveh]
filter papers filtre kağıdı
[feeltreh ka-uhduh]
filthy pis [pees]
find (verb) bulmak
I can't find it bulamıyorum
[boolamuh-yoroom]
I've found it buldum
find out sorup öğrenmek
[ur-renmek]

could you find out for me?
benim için öğrenir misiniz?
[eecheen ur-reneer]
fine (weather) güzel [gewzel]
(punishment) ceza [jeza]

•••••• DIALOGUES ••••••

how are you? nasılsınız? [nasuhl-
suhnuhz]
I'm fine, thanks iyiyim, teşekkür
ederim [teshekkewr]

is that OK? nasıl, olur mu?
that's fine, thanks tamam,
teşekkür ederim

finger parmak
finish (verb) bitirmek
I haven't finished yet henüz
bitirmedim [henewz]
when does it finish? ne zaman
bitiyor? [neh]
fire (in hearth, campfire etc) ateş
[atesh]
(blaze) yangın [yanguhn]
fire! yangın var!
can we light a fire here?
burada ateş yakabilir miyiz?
it's on fire yanıyor [yanuh-yor]
fire alarm yangın alarmı
[yanguhn alarmuh]
fire brigade itfaiye [eetfa-ee-yeh]

ENGLISH ❖ TURKISH Fi

Dial 110 for the fire brigade.
This call costs one small jeton,
or one phonecard unit.

fire escape yangın merdiveni
[yanguhn]
fire extinguisher yangın

söndürücü [surndewrew-**jew**]
first ilk, birinci [beer**ee**njee]
  I was first ilk bend**im**
  at first ilk önce [**u**rnjeh]
  the first time ilk kez
  first on the left sold**an** birinci
first aid ilk yardım [yard**uh**m]
first aid kit ilk yardım çantası
  [chantas**uh**]
first class (travel etc) birinci sınıf
  [beer**ee**njee suhn**uh**f]
first floor birinci kat
  (US) zem**in** kat
first name ad
fish (noun) balık [bal**uh**k]
fish restaurant balık lokantası
  [bal**uh**k lokantas**uh**]
fishing village balıkçı köyü
  [bal**uh**kchuh kur-y**ew**]
fishmonger's balıkçı
fit (attack) nöbet [nurb**e**t]
fit: it doesn't fit me bana
  uymuyor [oo-imoo-y**o**r]
fitting room soy**u**nma odası
  [odas**uh**]
fix (arrange) hallet**me**k
  can you fix this? (repair) bun**u**
  tamir edebilir misin**iz**?
fizzy gazlı [gazl**uh**]
flag bayrak [b**ī**rak]
flannel el havlus**u**
flash (for camera) flaş [flash]
flat (noun: apartment) apart**man**
  dairesi [da-**ee**resee], daire
  [da-**ee**reh]
  (adj) düz [dewz]
  I've got a flat tyre lastiğim
  patladı [lastee-**ee**m patlad**uh**]
flavour tat

flea pire [peer**eh**]
flight uçak seferi [ooch**a**k]
flight number sefer sayısı
  [s**ī**-uhs**uh**]
flippers paletler
flood sel
floor (of room) yer
  (storey) kat
  on the floor yerde [yerd**eh**]
florist çiçekçi [cheech**e**kchee]
flour un
flower çiçek [cheech**e**k]
flu grip [greep]
fluent: he speaks fluent Turkish
  akıcı bir Türkçesi var
  [akuhj**uh** beer t**e**wrkchesee]
fly (noun) sinek
  (verb) uçmak [ooch**ma**k]
fly in inmek
fly out uçmak [ooch**ma**k]
fog sis
foggy: it's foggy sisl**i**
folk dancing halk oyunları
  [oyunlar**uh**]
folk music halk müziği
  [mewz**ee**-ee]
follow takip etmek
  follow me beni takip ed**in**
food yiyecek [yee-yej**e**k]
food poisoning gıda
  zehirlenmesi [guhd**a**]
food shop/store bakk**a**l
foot* (of person, measurement) ayak
  [**ī**-ak]
  on foot yayan [y**ī**-an]
football (game) futb**o**l
  (ball) top
football match futbol maçı
  [mach**uh**]

for için [eecheen]
do you have something for ...?
(headache/diarrhoea etc) ... için
bir şeyiniz var mı?
[shayeeneez var muh]

•••••• DIALOGUES ••••••

who's the imam bayıldı for? imam
bayıldı kim için? [bī-uhld**uh**]
that's for me o benim için
and this one? ya bu?
that's for her o, bayanın [bī-an**uh**n]

where do I get the bus for İzmir?
İzmir otobüsüne nereden
binebilirim? [**ee**zmeer
otob**ew**sewneh]
the bus for İzmir leaves from İstiklal
Caddesi İzmir otobüsü İstiklal
Caddesi'nden kalkıyor [kalk**uh**-
yor]

how long have you been here for?
ne zamandan beri buradasınız?
[neh – b**oo**radasuhnuhz]
I've been here for two days, how
about you? ben iki gündür
buradayım, ya siz? [gewnd**ewr**
b**oo**radī-uhm]
I've been here for a week bir
haftadır buradayım [haftad**uh**r
b**oo**radī-uhm]

forehead alın [al**uh**n]
foreign yabancı [yabanj**uh**]
foreigner yabancı
forest orman
forget unutmak
I forget, I've forgotten unutt**um**
fork çatal [chat**al**]
(in road) iki yol ağzı [**a**-zuh]

form (document) form, formüler
[formewl**er**]
formal (dress) resm**i**
fortnight on beş gün [besh gewn]
fortress kale [kal**eh**]
fortunately bereket versin
forward: could you forward my
mail? mektuplarımı yeni
adresime gönderir misiniz?
[–laruhm**uh** – **a**dreseemeh
gurnder**eer**]
forwarding address
gönderilecek adres
[gurndereelej**ek**]
foundation cream fondöten
[fondurt**en**]
fountain çeşme [cheshm**eh**]
foyer giriş holü [geer**ee**sh
hol**ew**], fuaye [fwī-eh]
fracture (noun) kırık [kuhr**uh**k]
France Fransa
free serbest
(no charge) bedava
is it free (of charge)? ücretsiz
mi? [ewjr**e**ts**ee**z]
freeway otoyol
see road
freezer buzluk
French (adj) Fransız [fransuhz]
(language) Fransızca
[fransuhzja]
French fries patates kızartması
[kuhzartmas**uh**]
frequent sık [suhk]
how frequent is the bus to
Edirne? Edirne'ye kaç saatte
bir otobüs var? [edeern**eh**-yeh
kach sa-att**eh**]
fresh (breeze) serin

(fruit etc) taze [taz**eh**]
fresh orange juice taze portakal
suy**u**
Friday cuma [joom**a**]
fridge buzdolabı [b**oo**zdolabuh]
fried kızarmış [kuhzarm**uh**sh]
fried egg yağda yumurt**a**
[ya-d**a**]
friend arkadaş [arkad**ash**]
friendly (person, animal) sokulg**an**
(behaviour) dostça [d**o**stcha]
from -den
when does the next train from
Eskişehir arrive? Eskişehir'den
bir son**ra**ki tren ne zam**an**
geliy**or**? [eskisheheer-d**en** –
neh]
from Monday to Friday
Pazartesiden Cumay**a**
from next Thursday bir dah**a**ki
Perşembeden itibar**en**

•••••• DIALOGUE ••••••

where are you from? nerelisini**z**?
I'm from Slough ben Slough'lıyım
[–luh-y**uh**m]

front ön [urn]
in front önde [urnd**eh**]
in front of the hotel otelin
önünde [urnewnd**eh**]
at the front ön taraft**a**
frost don
frozen donmuş [donm**oo**sh]
frozen food dondurulmuş
yiyecekler [dondoorool-m**oo**sh
yee-yejekl**er**]
fruit meyva [mayv**a**]
fruit juice meyva suy**u**
fry kızartmak [kuhzartm**a**k]

frying pan tav**a**
full dol**u**
it's full of ... ... ile dolu [eel**eh**]
I'm full doyd**um**
full board tam pansiy**on**
fun: it was fun eğlendik
[eh-lendee**k**]
funeral cenaze [jenaz**eh**]
funny (strange) gar**ip**
(amusing) kom**ik**
furniture mobily**a**
further ileride [ilereed**eh**]
it's further down the road
yolun ilerisinde [eeleree-
se**e**ndeh]

•••••• DIALOGUE ••••••

how much further is it to Troy?
Truva'ya daha ne kadar var?
[neh]
about 5 kilometres yaklaşık beş
kilometre [yaklash**uh**k –
keelometr**eh**]

fuse sigorta
the lights have fused sigorta
attı [att**uh**]
fuse box sigorta kutus**u**
fuse wire sigorta tel**i**
future gelecek [gelej**ek**]
in future gelecekte
[gelejekt**eh**]

G

Gallipoli Gelibolu
gallon* galon
game (cards etc) oy**un**
(match) maç [mach]
(meat) av et**i**

garage (for fuel) benzin
istasyonu
(for repairs) tamirhane
[tameerhaneh]
(for parking) garaj [garaJ]

Filling stations are amazingly
numerous throughout most of
the country, and open long
hours. On the main roads they
are often advertized a few miles
in advance and are open 24
hours. Some also have adjoining
service facilities which are also
open 24 hours. Self service is
unusual and a tip is
appreciated.
Diesel is mazot, while petrol
is benzin, available in normal
(3-star/regular) or süper
(4-star/premium) grades.
Kurşunsuz (lead-free) is
becoming increasingly common,
but is still almost impossible to
come by in the remote east.
Avoid Petrol Ofisi and its
affiliate Türkpetrol in favour of
private filling stations run by
BP, Shell or Mobil.

garden bahçe [baʜcheh]
garlic sarmısak [sarmuhsak]
gas gaz
(US: petrol) benzin
see garage
gas cylinder (camping gas) gaz
tüpü [tewpew]
gasoline benzin
see garage

gas permeable lenses gaz
geçirgen lensler [gecheergen]
gas station benzin istasyonu
gate kapı [kapuh]
(at airport) çıkış kapısı
[chuhkuhsh kapuhsuh]
gay homoseksüel
[homoseksewel]
gay bar eşcinsellerin barı
[eshjensellereen baruh]
gearbox vites kutusu
gear lever vites kolu
gears vitesler
general (adj) genel
gents (toilet) erkekler
(tuvaleti)
genuine (antique etc) gerçek
[gerchek]
Georgia Gürcistan [gewrjeestan]
Georgian (adj) Gürcü [gewrjew]
German (adj) Alman
(language) Almanca [almanja]
German measles kızamıkçık
[kuhzamuhk-chuhk]
Germany Almanya
get (fetch) getirmek
(obtain, buy) almak, bulmak
will you get me another one,
please? bana bir tane daha
getirir misiniz, lütfen?
[taneh – lewtfen]
how do I get to ...? ...-'e nasıl
gidebilirim? [-eh nasuhl]
do you know where I can get
them? onlardan nerede
bulabilirim acaba, biliyor
musunuz? [neredeh – ajaba]

•••••• DIALOGUE ••••••

can I get you a drink? bir şey
içmek ister misiniz? [shay
eechmek]
no, I'll get this one, what would
you like? olmaz, bu sefer ben
alacağım, ne istersiniz? [alaja-
uhm neh]
a glass of red wine bir bardak
kırmızı şarap

get back (return) dönmek
[durnmek]
get in (arrive) gelmek
get off inmek
where do I get off? nerede
inmem lazım? [neredeh –
lazuhm]
get on (to train etc) binmek
get out (of car etc) inmek
get up (in the morning) kalkmak
gift hediye [hedee-yeh]
gift shop hediyelik eşya
dükkanı [esh-ya dewkkanuh]
gin cin [jeen]
a gin and tonic, please bir
cintonik, lütfen [lewtfen]
girl kız [kuhz]
girlfriend kız arkadaş [arkadash]
give vermek
can you give me some bread/
milk? bana biraz ekmek/süt
verebilir misiniz?
I gave it to him/her ona
verdim
will you give this to ...?
bunu ...-e verir misiniz? [-eh]
give back iade etmek [ee-adeh]
glad memnun

glass (material) cam [jam]
(tumbler) bardak
(wine glass) kadeh
a glass of wine bir kadeh
şarap
a glass of tea bir bardak çay
glasses gözlük [gurzlewk]
gloves eldiven
glue (noun) zamk
go gitmek
we'd like to go to the Topkapı
Palace Topkapı Sarayı'na
gitmek istiyoruz [topkapuh
sarī-uh-na]
where are you going? nereye
gidiyorsunuz? [nerayeh]
where does this bus go? bu
otobüs nereye gidiyor?
let's go! haydi gidelim!
[hīdee]
he/she's gone (left) gitti
where has he gone? nereye
gitti?
I went there last week oraya
geçen hafta gittim [orī-a
gechen]
hamburger to go paket
hamburger
go away çekilip gitmek
[chekeeleep]
go away! çekil git! [chekeel
geet]
go back (return) dönmek
[durnmek]
go down (the stairs etc) inmek
go in girmek
go out çıkmak [chuhkmak]
do you want to go out tonight?
bu akşam çıkmak ister

misiniz? [aksham chuhkmak]
go through geçmek [gechmek]
go up (the stairs etc) çıkmak
 [chuhkmak]
goat keçi [kechee]
goat's cheese keçi peyniri
 [payneeree]
God Allah
god tanrı [tanruh]
goddess tanrıça [tanruhcha]
goggles koruyucu gözlük
 [koroo-yoojoo gurzlewk]
gold altın [altuhn]
golf golf
golf course golf sahası
 [sahasuh]
good iyi
 good! iyi!
 it's no good boşuna, yararsız
 [boshoona yararsuhz]
goodbye (general use) hoşça
 kalın [hosh-cha kaluhn]
 (said by person leaving)
 Allahaısmarladık [alaha-
 uhsmarladuhk]
 (said to person leaving) güle güle
 [gewleh]
good evening iyi akşamlar
 [akshamlar]
good morning günaydın
 [gewnīduhn]
good night iyi geceler [gejeler]
goose kaz
got: we've got to leave
 gitmemiz gerek
 have you got any ...?
 hiç ...-nız var mı?
 [heech ...-nuhz var muh]
government hükümet

[hewkewmet]
gradually giderek
grammar gramer
gram(me)* gram
granddaughter torun
grandfather büyükbaba
 [bewyewk-baba]
grandmother büyükanne
 [bewyewk-anneh]
grandson torun
grapefruit greyfrut [grayfroot]
grapefruit juice greyfrut suyu
grapes üzüm [ewzewm]
grass ot
grateful minnettar
gravy sos
great (excellent) fevkalade
 [fevkaladeh]
 that's great! mükemmel!
 [mewkemmel]
 a great success büyük bir
 başarı [bewyewk beer
 basharuh]
Great Britain Büyük Britanya
Greece Yunanistan
greedy açgözlü [achgurzlew]
Greek (adj) Yunan
 (language) Rumca [roomja]
 (person) Yunanlı [yoonanluh]
 (adj, person: living in Turkey) Rum
 [room]
Greek Cypriot (adj) Kıbrıs Rum
 [kuhbruhs]
 (person) Kıbrıslı Rum
 [kuhbruhsluh]
Greek Orthodox Rum Ortodoks
green yeşil [yesheel]
green card (car insurance) yeşil
 kart

greengrocer's man**av**

greeting people

On meeting or leaving a person of the same gender, men and women kiss on the cheeks, at least once each side – but when greeting a person of the opposite sex you should just shake hands, unless you know them very well. You will please many old people if you kiss their hand when introduced. For this you do not really kiss but put the hand first towards your lips then to your forehead. If you are a woman, some older men may not give their hand at all.

grey gri [gree]
grill (noun) ızgara [uhzg**a**ra]
grilled ızgara [uhzg**a**ra]
grocer's bakk**a**l
ground yer
  on the ground yerde [yerd**eh**]
ground floor zem**i**n kat
group grup
guarantee (noun) garant**i**
  is it guaranteed? garantisi var mı? [muh]
guest mis**a**fir
guesthouse pansiy**o**n

Often the most pleasant places to stay are **pansiyons**, small guesthouses which increasingly have en suite facilities. If there are vacancies in season, touts →

in the coastal resorts and other tourist targets descend on every incoming bus, dolmuş or boat; at other places or times, look for the sign **boş oda var** (literally: empty rooms free).
The Turkish pansiyon breakfast is often served in the common gardens or terraces that are this kind of accommodation's strong point. Rooms tend to be sparse but clean. Laundry facilities – even if just a drying line and a plastic bucket – are almost always present. Hot showers are rarely charged for separately; if they are, count on an extra dollar a go, as in modest hotels.

guide (person, book) rehber [r**e**Hb**e**r]
guidebook rehber
guided tour rehberli tur
guitar gitar
gum (in mouth) dişeti [deeshet**ee**]
gun (rifle) tüfek [tewf**e**k]
  (pistol) tabanca [tab**a**nja]
gym spor salon**u**
gypsy çingene [cheegen**eh**]

H

hair saç [sach]
hairbrush saç fırçası [fuhrchas**uh**]
haircut (man's) saç tıraşı [tuhr**a**shuh]
  (woman's) saç kesme [kesm**eh**]

hairdresser's (men's) berber
(women's) kuaför [kwafur]

In Turkey most hairdressers
are open long hours every day
of the week except Sundays.
However, some hairdressers
and barbers at resorts may open
on Sundays if they think they
may get customers.

hairdryer saç kurutma
makinesi [sach]
hair gel jel [Jel]
hairgrips saç tokaları [sach
tokalaruh]
hair spray saç spreyi [sprayee]
half yarım [yaruhm]
half an hour yarım saat [sa-at]
half a litre yarım litre [leetreh]
about half that onun yarısı
kadar [yaruhsuh]
half board yarım pansiyon
half-bottle yarım şişe
[sheesheh]
half fare yarım tarife [tareefeh]
half price yarı fiyat [yaruh]
ham jambon [Jambon]
hamburger hamburger
[hamboorger]
hammer (noun) çekiç [chekeech]
hand el
handbag el çantası [chantasuh]
handbrake el freni
handkerchief mendil
handle (on door) kol
(on suitcase etc) sap
hand luggage el bagajı
[bagaJuh]

hang-gliding hang-gliding
hangover içkiden gelen baş
ağrısı [eechkeeden – bash
a-ruhsuh]
I've got a hangover çok
içtiğim için başım ağrıyor
[chok eechtee-eem eecheen
bashuhm]
happen olmak
what's happening? ne oluyor?
[neh]
what has happened? ne oldu?
happy mutlu
I'm not happy about this bu
hiç hoşuma gitmiyor [heech
hoshooma]
harbour liman
hard sert
(difficult) zor
hard-boiled egg lop yumurta
hard lenses sert lensler
hardly ancak [anjak]
hardly ever hemen hemen hiç
[heech]
hardware shop nalbur
hat şapka [shapka]
hate (verb) nefret etmek
have* sahip olmak
can I have a ...? bir ... rica
edebilir miyim? [reeja]
can we have some ...?
biraz ... rica edebilir miyiz?
do you have ...? sizde ...
bulunur mu? [seezdeh – muh]
what'll you have? ne alırsınız?
[neh aluhrsuhnuhz]
I have to leave now şimdi
gitmek zorundayım
[sheemdee – zoroondï-uhm]

do I have to ...? ...-m lazım
mı? [lazuhm muh]
hayfever saman nezlesi
hazelnuts fındık [fuhnduhk]
he* o
head baş [bash]
headache baş ağrısı [a-ruhsuh]
headlights farlar
headphones kulaklıklar
[koolakluhklar]
healthy sağlıklı [sa-luhkluh]
hear duymak [doo-imak]

•••••• DIALOGUE ••••••

can you hear me? beni
duyabiliyor musunuz?
I can't hear you, could you repeat
that? sizi duyamıyorum, tekrar
söyler misiniz? [doo-yamuh-yoroom
– suh-iler]

hearing aid işitme cihazı
[eesheetmeh jeehazuh]
heart kalp
heart attack kalp krizi
heat sıcaklık [suhjakluhk]
heater (in room) ısıtıcı
[uhsuhtuhjuh]
(in car) radyatör [radyatur]
heating ısıtma [uhsuhtma]
heavy ağır [a-uhr]
heel (of foot, shoe) topuk
could you heel these?
bunların topuklarını yapar
mısınız? [boonlaruhn
topooklaruhnuh – muhsuhnuhz]
heelbar kundura tamircisi
[tameerjeesee]
height (of person) boy
(of mountain) yükseklik

[yewksekleek]
helicopter helikopter
hello merhaba
(answer on phone) alo
helmet (for motorcycle) kask
help (noun) yardım [yarduhm]
(verb) yardım etmek
help! imdat!
can you help me? bana
yardım edebilir misiniz?
thank you very much for your
help yardımınız için çok
teşekkür ederim
[yarduhmuhnuhz eecheen chok
teshekkewr]
helpful yardımcı [yarduhmjuh]
hepatitis hepatit
her*: her ... ...-i, ...-si
(emphatic) onun ...
it's her towel onun havlusu
I haven't seen her onu
görmedim [gurmedeem]
to her ona
with her onunla
for her onun için [eecheen]
that's her işte o [eeshteh]
herbal tea bitkisel çay [chī]
herbs çeşni veren otlar
[cheshnee]
here burada
here is/are ... işte ... [eeshteh]
here you are (offering) buyrun
[boo-iroon]
hers* onunki
that's hers şu onunki [shoo]
hey! hey!
hi! (hello) merhaba!
hide (verb) saklamak
high yüksek [yewksek]

highchair bebek iskemlesi
highway otoyol
  see road
hill tepe [tep**eh**]
him*: I haven't seen him on**u**
  görmedim [g**u**rmedeem]
  to him on**a**
  with him onunl**a**
  for him onun için [eech**ee**n]
  that's him over there şuradaki
  o işte [shoorad**a**kee o eesht**eh**]
hip kalça [kalch**a**]
Hippodrome At Meydanı
  [maydan**uh**]
hire kiralamak
  for hire kiralık [keeral**uh**k]
  where can I hire a bike?
  nereden bir bisiklet
  kiralayabilirim? [keeralī-
  ab**ee**leereem]
  see bargaining and rent
his*: his ... ...-i, ...-si
  (emphatic) onun ...
  it's his car onun otomobili
  that's his şu onunki [shoo]
hit (verb) vurmak
hitch-hike otostop yapmak
hobby merak
hold (verb) tutmak
hole delik
holiday tatil
  on holiday tatilde [tateeld**eh**]
Holland Hollanda
home ev
  at home (in my house etc) evde
  [evd**eh**]
  (in my country) bizde [b**ee**zdeh]
  we go home tomorrow yarın
  evimize gidiyoruz [yar**uh**n

  eveemeez**eh**]
honest dürüst [dewr**ew**st]
honey bal
honeymoon balayı [balī-uh]
hood (US) motor kapağı
  [kapa-**uh**], kap**u**t
hookah nargile [nargeel**eh**]
hope umut
  I hope so umarım öyledir
  [oomar**uh**m uh-iled**ee**r]
  I hope not umarım öyle
  değildir [uh-il**eh** deh-**ee**ldeer]
hopefully inşallah [eenshall**ah**]
horn (of car) klakson, korna
horrible korkunç [kork**oo**nch]
horse at
horse riding binicilik
  [beeneejeel**ee**k]
hospital hastane [hast**a**neh]
hospitality konukseverlik
  thank you for your hospitality
  konukseverliğiniz için
  teşekkürler [kon**oo**kseverlee-
  een**ee**z ich**ee**n teshekkewler]
hot sıcak [s**uh**jak]
  (spicy) acı [aj**uh**]
  I'm hot sıcak bastı [bast**uh**]
  it's hot today bugün hava
  sıcak [boog**ew**n – suhj**a**k]
hotel otel

Turkish hotels are graded on a
scale of one to five stars by the
Ministry of Tourism; there is
also a lower tier of unstarred
establishments rated by
municipalities. At the four- and
five-star level you're talking →

Sheraton-type mod cons and prices. Two- or three-star outfits are less expensive and may have slightly more character; one-star establishments are basic but usually clean. Their exact price depends on the location and the presence or absence of a bath, and to some extent on the season; out of season you can often bargain prices down considerably in lower category hotels. Breakfast is often included in the rates, but it's almost invariably unexciting. The unrated hotels licensed by municipalities can be virtually as good as the lower end of the one-star class. On average, though, expect spartan rooms with possibly a washbasin and certainly a shower (never a tub), with a squat toilet down the hall. Washbasins may not have plugs.

In remote areas, especially in the east, hoteliers may refuse to take unmarried couples. Wedding rings might convince some people, but documentary proof might be demanded. If the proprietor is adamant, there is nothing you can do except look for somewhere else.

It is customary to remove your shoes when entering a house, even in households with a European lifestyle. Your host will usually offer you a pair of slippers; some hosts may tell you not to bother taking your shoes off but you should still remove them.

In rural areas single men should never enter a dwelling where only women and/or children are present, even if invited – you would be deemed to have violated the honour and good reputation of the family should the head of the household return, and you would be treated accordingly.

hovercraft hoverkraft
how nasıl [nasuhl]
   how many? kaç tane? [kach taneh]
   how do you do? memnun oldum!

•••••• DIALOGUES ••••••

   how are you? nasılsınız? [nasuhl-suhnuhz]
   fine, thanks, and you? iyiyim, teşekkür ederim, ya siz? [teshekkewr]

   how much is it? kaça? [kacha]
   150,000 lira yüz elli bin lira
   I'll take it alıyorum [aluh-yoroom]

hotel room otel odası [odasuh]
hour saat [sa-at]
house ev

humid nemli
hungry: I'm hungry acıktım

[ajuhkt**uh**m]
 are you hungry? acıktınız mı?
 [ajuhktuhn**uh**z muh]
hurry (verb) acele etmek
 [aj**e**leh]
 I'm in a hurry acelem var
 [aj**e**lem]
 there's no hurry aceleye
 gerek yok [ajelay**eh**]
 hurry up! çabuk ol! [chab**oo**k]
hurt (verb) incitmek
 [eenjeetm**e**k], acımak
 [achuhm**a**k]
 it really hurts gerçekten çok
 acıyor [g**e**rchekten chok
 ajuh-y**o**r]
husband koca [koj**a**]
hydrofoil kızaklı tekne
 [kuhzakl**uh** tekn**e**h], hidrofoil
 [h**ee**drofoyl]

I

I ben
ice buz [booz]
 with ice buzl**u**
 no ice, thanks buz istem**e**z,
 teşekkür eder**i**m
 [teshekk**e**wr]
ice cream dondurma
ice-cream cone dondurma
 külahı [kewl-**a**huh]
iced coffee buzl**u** kahve
 [ka**H**v**e**h]
ice lolly eskim**o**®
idea fik**i**r
idiot apt**a**l
if eğer [eh-**e**r]
ignition kont**a**k

ill hast**a**
 I feel ill kendim**i** hasta
 hissediy**o**rum
illness hastalık [hastal**uh**k]
imitation (leather etc) takl**i**t
immediately hemen
important önemli [urneml**ee**]
 it's very important çok
 önemlid**i**r [chok]
 it's not important önemli değil
 [deh-**ee**l]
impossible imkansız
 [eemkans**uh**z]
impressive etkileyici [etkeelay-
 eej**ee**]
improve iyileştirmek
 [eey**ee**lesh–], geliştirmek
 [gel**ee**shteerm**e**k]
 I want to improve my Turkish
 Türkçemi geliştirmek
 istiy**o**rum [t**e**wrkchemee
 gel**ee**sht**ee**rmek]
in: it's in the centre merkezde
 [merkezd**eh**]
 in my car arabamda
 in İstanbul İstanbul'da
 in two days from now iki
 güne kad**a**r [gewn**e**h]
 in five minutes beş dakik**a**
 içinde [**ee**cheendeh]
 in May mayısta
 in English İngilizce
 [eengeel**ee**zjeh]
 in Turkish Türkçe [t**e**wrkcheh]
 is he in? orda mı? [muh]
inch* inç [eench]
include dahil etmek [da**H**ee**l]
 does that include meals? buna
 yemekler dahil mi?

is that included? bu dahil mi?
inconvenient elverişsiz
[elvereesh-seez]
incredible inanılmaz
[eenanuhlmaz]
Indian (adj) Hint
indicator sinyal
indigestion hazımsızlık
[hazuhm-suhzluhk]
indoor pool kapalı havuz
[kapaluh]
indoors içerde [eecherdeh]
inexpensive ucuz [oojooz]
infection enfeksiyon
infectious bulaşıcı
[boolashuhjuh]
inflammation iltihap
informal fazla resmi olmayan
[olmī-an]
information bilgi
do you have any information
about ...? sizde ... hakkında
bilgi var mı? [hakkuhnda –
muh]
information desk danışma
masası [danuhshma masasuh]
injection enjeksiyon
[enJeksee-yon]
injured yaralı [yaraluh]
she's been injured yaralandı
[yaralanduh]
inner tube (for tyre) iç lastik
[eech]
innocent masum
insect böcek [burjek]
insect bite böcek sokması
[sokmasuh]
do you have anything for
insect bites? sizde böcek

sokmasına karşı bir şey
bulunur mu? [seezdeh –
karshuh beer shay]
insect repellent böcek ilacı
[eelachuh]
inside: inside the hotel otelin
içinde [eecheendeh]
let's sit inside içerde oturalım
[eecherdeh otooraluhm]
insist: I insist ısrar ediyorum
insomnia uykusuzluk
[oo-ikoosoozlook]
instant coffee neskafe
[neskafeh]
instead yerine [yereeneh]
give me that one instead
yerine şunu verin [shoonoo]
instead of ... ...-in yerine
insulin insülin [eensewleen]
insurance sigorta
intelligent zeki
interested: I'm interested in ...
...-e ilgi duyuyorum [-eh]
interesting ilginç [eelgeench]
that's very interesting çok
ilginç [chok]
international uluslararası
[oolooslararasuh]
interpret tercüme etmek
[terjewmeh]
interpreter tercüman
[terjewman]
intersection kavşak [kavshak]
interval (at theatre) ara
into: into the ... ...-in içine
[eecheeneh]
I'm not into ... ... ilgimi
çekmiyor [chekmee-yor]
introduce tanıştırmak

[tanuhshtuhrmak]
may I introduce ...? size ...-i
tanıştırabilir miyim?
[seezeh ...-ee
tanuhsh-tuhrabeeleer]
invitation davet
invite davet etmek
Iran İran [eeran]
Iraq Irak [uhrak]
Ireland İrlanda [eerlanda]
Irish İrlanda
I'm Irish İrlandalıyım
[eerlandaluh-yuhm]
iron (for ironing) ütü [ewtew]
can you iron these for me?
bunları benim için ütüler
misiniz? [boonlaruh – eecheen
ewtewler]
is* -dir
Islam İslam [eeslam]
Islamic İslami
island ada
İstanbul İstanbul [eestanbool]
it o
it is ... o ...-dir
is it ...? ... mu?
where is it? nerede? [neredeh]
it's him/her odur
it was ... ... idi
Italian (adj, person) İtalyan
[eetalyan]
(language) İtalyanca
[eetalyanja]
Italy İtalya
itch: it itches kaşınıyor
[kashuhnuh-yor]

J

jack (for car) kriko
jacket ceket [jeket]
jam reçel [rechel]
jammed: it's jammed takıldı
[takuhlduh]
January ocak [ojak]
jar (noun) kavanoz
jaw çene [cheneh]
jazz caz [jaz]
jealous kıskanç [kuhskanch]
jeans blucin [bloojeen]
jellyfish denizanası [–suh]
jersey kazak
jetty iskele [eeskeleh]
jeweller's kuyumcu [koo-
yoomjoo]
jewellery mücevherat
[mew-jevherat]
Jewish Yahudi
job iş [eesh]
jogging koşu [koshoo]
to go jogging koşu yapmak
joke şaka [shaka]
journey yolculuk [yoljoolook]
have a good journey! iyi
yolculuklar!
jug sürahi [sewrahee]
a jug of water bir sürahi su
juice: ... juice ... suyu
July temmuz
jump (verb) atlamak
jumper kazak
jump leads buji telleri [booJee]
junction kavşak [kavshak]
June haziran
just (only) sadece [sa-dejeh]
just two sadece iki tane

[taneh]
just for me yalnız benim için
[yaln**uh**z – eech**ee**n]
just here tam burada
not just now şimdi değil
[sh**ee**mdee deh-**ee**l]
we've just arrived henüz
geldik [hen**ew**z]

K

kebab kebap
  (mild) Bursa kebabı
  [kebab**uh**]
  (very spicy) Urfa kebabı
keep tutmak
  keep the change üstü kalsın
  [ewst**ew** kals**uh**n]
  can I keep it? bende kalabilir
  mi? [bend**eh**]
  please keep it sizde kalsın
  [seezd**eh**]
ketchup keçap [kech**a**p]
kettle çaydanlık [ch**ī**danl**uh**k]
key anahtar [ana**H**t**a**r]
  the key for room 201, please
  iki yüz bir numaralı odanın
  anahtarı, lütfen [yewz beer
  noomaral**uh** odan**uh**n
  ana**H**tar**uh** lew**t**fen]
keyring anahtarlık [ana**H**tarl**uh**k]
kidneys (in body) böbrekler
  [burbrek**l**er]
  (food) böbrek
kill (verb) öldürmek
  [urldewrm**e**k]
kilo* kilo
kilometre* kilometre
  [keelometr**eh**]

how many kilometres is it
to …? … buradan kaç
kilometre? [kach]
kind (generous) nazik, iyi
that's very kind çok naziksiniz
[chok]

DIALOGUE ••••••

which kind do you want?
hangisinden istiyorsunuz?
I want this/that kind bu/şu türden
istiyorum [shoo tewrden]

king kral
kiosk büfe [bewf**eh**]
kiss (noun) öpücük [urpewj**ew**k]
  (verb) öpmek [urpm**e**k]

---

kissing
Couples should not indulge in
visible displays of affection
beyond holding hands – and in
rural areas even that might be
thought improper. Kissing on a
park bench, for example, might
get you pelted with a half-full
soft-drink can, or worse.

---

kitchen mutfak
Kleenex® kâğıt mendil [k**a**-uht]
knee diz
knickers külot [kewl**o**t]
knife bıçak [buhch**a**k]
knitwear örgü [urg**ew**]
knock (verb) vurmak
knock down çarpmak
  [charpm**a**k]
  he's been knocked down
  araba çarpmış [charpm**uh**sh]
knock over (object) devirmek

(pedestrian) çarpmak
[charpmak], çiğnemek [chee-
nemek]
know (somebody) tanımak
[tanuhmak]
(something) bilmek
I don't know bilmiyorum
I didn't know that onu
bilmiyordum
do you know where I can
find ...? ...-i nerede
bulabilirim, biliyor
musunuz? [neredeh]

L

label etiket
ladies' (toilets) bayanlar
[bī-anlar]
ladies' wear kadın giyim eşyası
[kaduhn – esh-yasuh]
lady bayan [bī-an]
lager bira
see beer
lake göl [gurl]
lamb (meat) kuzu
lamp lamba
lane (motorway) şerit [shereet]
(small road) dar yol
language dil
language course dil kursu
large büyük [bewyewk]
last (final) son
last week geçen hafta
[gechen]
last Friday geçen Cuma
last night dün gece [dewn
gejeh]
what time is the last train to

Ankara? Ankara'ya son tren
kaçta? [kachta]
late geç [gech]
sorry I'm late geciktiğim için
özür dilerim [gejeektee-eem
eecheen urzewr]
the train was late tren gecikti
[gejeektee]
we must go – we'll be late
gitmemiz gerek – geç
kalacağız [kalaja-uhz]
it's getting late geç oluyor
[gech]
later daha sonra
I'll come back later sonra
tekrar gelirim
see you later görüşmek üzere
[gurewshmek ewzereh]
later on daha sonra
latest en son
by Wednesday at the latest en
geç Çarşambaya kadar
[gech]
laugh (verb) gülmek [gewlmek]
launderette, laundromat
otomatlı çamaşırhane
[otomatluh chamashuhr-haneh]
laundry (clothes) çamaşır
[chamashuhr]
(place) çamaşırhane
[chamashuhr-haneh]
lavatory tuvalet
law kanun
lawn çimen [cheemen]
lawyer avukat
laxative müshil [mews-heel],
laksatif
lazy tembel
lead (electrical) kablo

where does this lead to? bu
nereye çıkıyor? [nerayeh
chuhkuh-yor]
leaf yaprak
leaflet broşür [broshewr]
leak (noun) sızıntı [suhzuhntuh]
(verb) sızmak [suhzmak]
the roof leaks dam akıyor
[akuh-yor]
learn öğrenmek [ur-renmek]
least: not in the least hiç de
değil [heech deh deh-eel]
at least en azından [en
azuhndan]
leather deri
leave (verb) bırakmak
[buhrakmak]
(go away) ayrılmak [īruhlmak]
I am leaving tomorrow yarın
hareket ediyorum [yaruhn]
he left yesterday dün gitti
[dewn]
may I leave this here? bunu
burada bırakabilir miyim?
[buhraka-beeleer]
I left my coat in the bar
paltomu barda bıraktım
[buhraktuhm]
when does the bus for Bursa
leave? Bursa otobüsü ne
zaman kalkıyor? [neh –
kalkuh-yor]
Lebanon Lübnan [lewbnan]
leeks pırasa [puhrasa]
left sol
on the left solda
to the left sola
turn left sola dönün
[durnewn]

there's none left hiç kalmadı
[heech kalmaduh]
left-handed solak
left luggage (office) emanet
leg bacak [bajak]
lemon limon
lemonade limonata
lemon tea limonlu çay
[leemonloo chī]
lend ödünç vermek [urdewnch]
will you lend me your ... ?
...-inizi ödünç verir misiniz?
[urdewnch]
lens (of camera) objektif
[objekteef]
lesbian sevici [seveejee]
less daha az
less than ... ...-den daha az
less expensive daha az pahalı
lesson ders
let (allow) -a izin vermek
will you let me know? bana
haber verir misiniz?
I'll let you know ben size
haber veririm [seezeh]
let's go for something to eat
hadi gidip bir şeyler yiyelim
[shayler]
let off bırakmak [buhrakmak]
will you let me off at ...?
beni ...-da bırakır mısınız?
[buhrakuhr muhsuhnuhz]
letter mektup
do you have any letters for
me? bana mektup var mı?
[muh]
letterbox mektup kutusu

Letterboxes are yellow and are
clearly labelled with categories
of destination: **yurtdışı** for
overseas, **yurtiçi** for inland,
şehiriçi for local. Street-corner
letterboxes are rare so you will
need to go to a post office.

lettuce yeşil salata [yesh**eel**]
lever (noun) manivela
library kütüphane
   [kewtewp-h**a**neh]
licence izin belges**i**
   (driving) ehli**y**et
lid kapak
lie (verb: tell untruth) yala**n**
   söylemek [suh-ilem**ek**]
lie down uzanmak
life hayat [h**ī**-a**t**]
lifebelt can kemer**i** [jan]
lifeguard cankurtaran
   [jankoortara**n**]
life jacket can yeleğ**i** [jan
   yeleh-**ee**]
lift (in building) asansör [asans**ur**]
   could you give me a lift? beni
   de arabanıza alır mısınız?
   [deh arabanuhza al**uhr**]
   would you like a lift? sizi de
   götürebilir miyim?
   [gurtewrebeel**eer**]
light (noun) ışık [uhsh**uhk**]
   (not heavy) ha**f**if
   do you have a light? (for
   cigarette) ateşiniz var mı?
   [atesheen**eez** var muh]
   light green açık yeşil [ach**uhk**
   yesh**eel**]

light bulb amp**ul**
   I need a new light bulb ban**a**
   yeni bir amp**ul** lazım
   [laz**uhm**]
lighter çakmak [chakm**ak**]
lightning şimşek [sheemsh**ek**]
like (verb) hoşlanmak
   [hoshlanm**ak**], sevm**ek**
   I like it beğendim [beh-
   end**eem**]
   I like going for walks yürüyüşe
   çıkmayı severim [yewrew-
   yewsh**eh** chuhkmī-**uh**]
   I like you sizden
   hoşlanıyorum
   [hoshlan**uh**-yoroom]
   I don't like it hoşuma
   gitmiyor [hoshoom**a**]
   do you like ...? ... sever
   misin**iz**?
   I'd like a beer bir bira
   istiyorum
   I'd like to go swimming
   yüzmeye gitmek istiyorum
   [yewzmay**eh**]
   would you like a drink? bir şey
   içmek ister misiniz? [shay
   eechm**ek**]
   **would you like to go for a
   walk?** yürüyüşe çıkmak ister
   misiniz? [yewrew-yewsh**eh**
   chuhm**ak**]
   what's it like? nasıl bir şey?
   [nas**uhl**]
   I want one like this bunun
   gibi bir şey istiyorum
lime misket limon**u**
lime cordial konsantre limon
   suy**u** [konsantr**eh**]

line (on paper) çizgi [cheezgee]
(phone) hat
could you give me an outside
line? bana bir dış hat verir
misiniz? [duhsh]
lips dudaklar
lip salve dudak merhemi
lipstick ruj [rooJ]
liqueur likör [leekur]
listen dinlemek
listen! dinle! [deenleh]
litre* litre [leetreh]
a litre of white wine bir litre
beyaz şarap [bayaz sharap]
little küçük [kewchewk]
just a little, thanks yalnız çok
az bir şey, teşekkür ederim
[yalnuhz chok – shay
teshekkewr]
a little milk biraz süt [sewt]
a little bit more biraz daha
live (verb) yaşamak [yashamak]
we live together birlikte
yaşıyoruz [beerleekteh yashuh-
yorooz]

•••••• DIALOGUE ••••••

where do you live? nerede
oturuyorsunuz? [neredeh]
I live in London Londra'da
oturuyorum

lively (person) canlı [janluh]
(town) hareketli
liver (in body) karaciğer
[karajee-er]
(food) ciğer
loaf somun
lobby (in hotel) lobi
lobster istakoz

local yerel
can you recommend a local
restaurant? yörede bir
lokanta tavsiye edebilir
misiniz? [yuredeh – tavsee-
yeh]
lock (noun) kilit
(verb) kilitlemek
it's locked kilitli
lock in içeri kilitlemek
[eecheree]
lock out dışarıda bırakmak
[duhsharuhda buhrakmak]
I've locked myself out dışarıda
kaldım [duhsharuhda
kalduhm]
locker (for luggage etc) emanet
kasası [kasasuh]
lollipop lolipop
London Londra
long uzun
how long will it take to fix it?
tamir etmesi ne kadar
sürer? [neh – sewrer]
how long does it take? ne
kadar sürer?
a long time uzun süre
[sewreh]
one day/two days longer bir
gün/iki gün daha
long-distance call şehirlerarası
konuşma [sheheerler-arasuh
konooshma]
look: I'm just looking, thanks
şöyle bir bakıyorum,
teşekkür ederim [shuh-ileh
beer bakuh-yoroom teshekkewr]
you don't look well iyi
görünmüyorsunuz

[gurewnmew–]
look out! dikkat!
can I have a look? bir
bakabilir miyim?
look after -a bakmak
look at -a bakmak
look for aramak
  I'm looking for ... ...-i
  arıyorum [aruh-yoroom]
look forward to iple çekmek
  [eepleh chekmek]
  I'm looking forward to it onu
  iple çekiyorum [eepleh
  chekee-yoroom]
loose (handle etc) gevşek
  [gevshek]
lorry kamyon
lose kaybetmek [kī-betmek]
  I'm lost, I want to get to ...
  yolumu kaybettim, ...-'e
  gitmek istiyordum
  [kībetteem ...-eh]
  I've lost my bag çantamı
  kaybettim [chantamuh]
lost property (office) kayıp eşya
  [kī-uhp esh-ya]
lot: a lot, lots çok [chok]
  not a lot çok değil [deh-eel]
  a lot of people bir çok insan
  a lot bigger çok daha büyük
  I like it a lot çok beğendim
  [beh-endeem]
lotion losyon
loud (noise) gürültülü
  [gewrewl-tewlew]
  (voice) yüksek sesle [yewksek
  sesleh]
lounge (in house, hotel) salon
  (airport) yolcu salonu [yoljoo]

love (noun) sevgi
  (verb) sevmek
  I love Turkey Türkiye'ye
  aşığım [tewrkee-yeh-yeh
  ashuh-uhm]
lovely çok güzel [chok gewzel]
low alçak [alchak]
luck şans [shans]
  good luck! bol şanslar!
luggage bagaj [bagaɹ]
luggage trolley eşya arabası
  [esh-ya arabasuh]
lump (on body) yumru
lunch öğle yemeği [urleh
  yemeh-ee]
lungs akciğerler [akjee-erler]
luxurious (hotel, furnishings) lüks
  [lewks]
luxury lüks

M

macaroon acıbadem
  kurabiyesi [ajuhbadem]
machine makina
mad (insane) deli
  (angry) kızgın [kuhzguhn]
magazine dergi
maid (in hotel) oda hizmetçisi
  [–cheesee]
maiden name kızlık adı
  [kuhzluhk aduh]
mail (noun) posta
  (verb) postalamak
  is there any mail for me? bana
  mektup var mı? [muh]
  see post and post office
mailbox mektup kutusu

main esas
main course ana yemek
main post office merkez
  postanesi
main road (in town) ana cadde
  [jaddeh]
  (in country) anayol
mains switch şalter [shalter]
make (brand name) marka
  (verb) yapmak
  I make it 500,000 lira benim
  hesabıma göre beş yüz bin
  lira ediyor [hesabuhma gureh]
  what is it made of? neden
  yapılmış? [yapuhlmuhsh]
make-up makyaj [makyaɪ]
man adam
manager yönetici [yurneteejee]
  can I see the manager?
  yöneticiyi görebilir miyim?
  [yurneteejee-yee gurebeeleer]
manageress yönetici bayan

manners
Invitations to drink tea are
almost impossible to turn down
without risking offence; offers of
meals are rarer but can also
create delicate situations. If the
offer is perfunctory it will not be
repeated after a polite refusal,
but if it's repeated three times
or more your benefactor is in
earnest. Declining an invitation
can be done with a polite excuse
like 'hiç vaktim yok, kusura
bakmayın' [heech – bakmī-
uhn] (I haven't got any time,
please forgive me).
→

Other points to remember are:
do not scrape your plates
clean in a restaurant; it's
considered polite to leave a
small quantity of food. Do not
smoke, chew gum or eat
in public during Ramadan;
foreigners are supposedly
exempt from these restrictions,
but there have been numerous
attacks on unwitting offenders
by fundamentalists.

manual düz [dewz]
  (car) düz vitesli
many çok [chok]
  not many az
map (city plan) şehir planı
  [sheh-heer planuh]
  (road map, geographical) harita

Stock up on touring maps
before you leave, as Turkish
ones are not very detailed or
accurate. The tourist offices in
İstanbul, Ankara, Antalya and
İzmir stock reasonable city
street plans.

March mart
margarine margarin
market pazar, çarşı [charshuh]
marmalade portakal reçeli
  [rehchelee]
married: I'm married evliyim
  are you married? evli misiniz?
mascara rimel
match (football etc) maç [mach]

matches kibrit
material (fabric) kumaş
  [koom**a**sh]
matter: it doesn't matter önemli
  değil [urneml**ee** deh-**ee**l]
  what's the matter? ne ol**u**yor?
  [neh]
mattress şilte [sheelt**eh**]
May mayıs [mī-**uh**s]
may: may I have another one?
  bir tane daha alabilir
  miyim? [tan**eh**]
  may I come in? girebilir
  miy**i**m?
  may I see it? on**u** görebilir
  miy**i**m? [gurebeel**ee**r]
  may I sit here? buraya
  oturabilir miy**i**m? [boorī-**a**]
maybe belki
mayonnaise mayonez [mī-on**e**z]
me* beni, ban**a**
  that's for me o ben**i**m için
  [eech**ee**n]
  send it to me on**u** ban**a**
  gönder**i**n
  me too ben de [deh]
meal yemek

did you enjoy your meal? yemek
hoşunuz**a** gitti mi? [hoshoonooz**a**]
it was excellent, thank you
mükemmeldi, teşekkür ederim
[m**e**wkemmeldee teshekk**e**wr]

mean: what do you mean? ne
demek istiy**o**rsunuz? [neh]

what does this word mean? bu
kelimenin anlamı ne? [anlam**uh**
neh]
it means ... in English
İngilizcede ... demekt**i**r
[eengeeleezjed**eh**]

measles kızamık [kuhzam**uh**k]
meat et
meat restaurant kebapçı
  [kebapch**uh**]
mechanic tamirci [tameerj**ee**]
medicine ilaç [eel**a**ch]
Mediterranean Akdeniz
medium (adj: size) ort**a**
medium-dry dömi sek [durm**ee**]
medium-rare orta pişmiş
  [peeshm**ee**sh]
medium-sized orta büyüklükte
  [bewyew-klewkt**eh**]
meet buluşmak [boolooshm**a**k]
  (at airport) karşılamak
  [karshuhlam**a**k]
  nice to meet you memn**u**n
  old**u**m
  where shall I meet you?
  nerede buluşalım? [n**e**redeh
  boolooshal**uh**m]
meeting toplantı [toplant**uh**]
meeting place buluşma yeri
  [boolooshm**a**]
melon kavun
men adaml**a**r
mend on**a**rmak
  could you mend this for me?
  bunu ben**i**m için onarabilir
  misin**i**z? [eech**ee**n]
menswear erkek giyim eşyası

[esh-yasuh]

mention (verb) bahsetmek
[baHsetmek]
don't mention it bir şey değil
[shay deh-eel]
menu yemek listesi
may I see the menu, please?
yemek listesini görebilir
miyim, lütfen? [gurebeeleer –
lewtfen]
see menu reader page 227
message mesaj [mesaj]
are there any messages for
me? bana mesaj var mı?
[muh]
I want to leave a message
for ... ... için bir mesaj
bırakmak istiyorum [eecheen
– buhrakmak]
metal metal
metre* metre [metreh]
microwave (oven) mikro dalga
midday öğle üzeri [ur-leh
ewzeree]
at midday öğleyin [ur-layeen]
middle: in the middle ortada
in the middle of the night gece
yarısı [gejeh yaruhsuh]
the middle one ortadaki
midnight gece yarısı
at midnight gece yarısı
might: I might come belki
gelirim
I might not go gitmeyebilirim
I might want to stay another
day bir gün daha kalmak
isteyebilirim
migraine migren
mild (taste) hafif

(weather) ılıman [uhluhman]
mile* mil
milk süt [sewt]
milkshake milkşeyk
[meelkshayk]
millimetre* milimetre
[meeleemetreh]
minaret minare [meenareh]
minced meat kıyma [kuh-ima]
mind: never mind zarar yok
I've changed my mind fikrimi
değiştirdim
[deh-eeshteerdeem]

•••••• DIALOGUE ••••••

do you mind if I open the window?
pencereyi açmamın bir mahzuru
var mı? [penjerayee achmamuhn
beer maHzooroo]
no, I don't mind hayır, benim için
farketmez [hī-uhr eecheen]

mine*: it's mine o benim,
benimki
mineral water maden suyu
mints nane şekeri [naneh
shekeree]
minute dakika
in a minute birazdan
just a minute bir dakika
mirror ayna [īna]
Miss Bayan [bī-an]
miss: I missed the bus otobüsü
kaçırdım [kachuhrduhm]
missing eksik [ekseek]
one of my ... is
missing ... lerimden biri
eksik
there's a suitcase missing bir
bavul eksik

mist sis
mistake (noun) hata
  I think there's a mistake
  sanırım bir yanlışlık var
  [sanuh**ruhm** – yanluhshl**uhk**]
  sorry, I've made a mistake
  özür dilerim, hata yaptım
  [urz**ewr** – yapt**uhm**]
misunderstanding yanlış
  anlama [–l**uh**sh]
mix-up: sorry, there's been a
  mix-up özür dilerim, bir
  karışıklık olmuş [urz**ewr** –
  karuhshuhkl**uhk** olm**oo**sh]
modern modern [mod**ai**rn]
modern art gallery çağdaş sanat
  galerisi [cha-d**a**sh]
moisturizer nemlendirici krem
  [–ree**jee**]
moment: I'll be back in a
  moment hemen geliyorum
monastery manastır
  [manast**uh**r]
Monday pazartesi
money para
month ay [ī]
monument anıt [an**uh**t]
moon ay [ī]
moped moped
more* daha
  can I have some more water,
  please? bir**a**z daha su
  alabil**i**r miy**i**m, lütfen?
  [l**ew**tfen]
  more expensive/interesting
  daha pahalı/ilginç
  more than 50 elliden fazla
  more than that ond**a**n daha
  fazla

a lot more çok daha fazla
  [chok]

•••••• DIALOGUE ••••••

would you like some more? biraz
daha ister misiniz?
no, no more for me, thanks hayır,
teşekkür ederim, bu kad**a**r yet**e**r
ban**a** [hī-**uh**r – teshekke**wr**]
how about you? ya siz?
I don't want any more, thanks ben
daha fazla istemiy**o**rum,
teşekkür ederim

morning sabah [sab**a**H]
  this morning bu sabah [boo]
  in the morning sabahleyin
  [sab**a**Hlayeen]
mosaic mozaik [moza-**eek**]
mosque cami [jam**ee**]

There's no admission fee for
entry to mosques but you
may be asked by the caretaker
or **imam** to make a small
donation. If so, put it into the
collection box rather than
someone's hand. Larger
mosques are frequented by
tourists and are open all the
time; others only for **namaz**,
or Muslim prayer, five times a
day. Whether or not you're
required to, it's a courtesy for
women to cover their heads
before entering a mosque, and
for both men and women
to cover their legs (shorts
are considered particularly
→

offensive) and upper arms – in some mosques pieces of material are distributed at the door. Shoes should always be removed.

mosquito sivrisinek
mosquito repellent sivrisinek ilacı [eelaj**uh**]
most: I like this one most of all en çok bundan hoşlanıyorum [chok – hoshlan**uh**-yoroom]
most of the time çoğu zaman [choh-**oo**]
most tourists çoğu turist
mostly çoğunlukla [choh-oonl**oo**kla]
mother anne [ann**eh**]
mother-in-law kayınvalide [kī-uhnvaleed**eh**]
motorbike motosiklet
motorboat deniz motoru
motorway otoyol
  see road
mountain dağ [da]
in the mountains dağlarda [da-l**a**rda]
mountaineering dağcılık [da-juhl**uh**k]
mouse fare [far**eh**]
moustache bıyık [buhy**uh**k]
mouth ağız [a-**uh**z]
mouth ulcer aft, pamukçuk [pamookch**oo**k]
move (verb: oneself) hareket etmek
  (something) oynatmak

(house) taşınmak [tashuhnm**a**k]
he's moved to another room başka bir odaya taşındı [b**a**shka beer od**ī**-a tashuhnd**uh**]
could you move your car? arabanızı çeker misiniz? [arabanuhz**uh** chek**e**r]
could you move up a little? biraz yukarı gider misiniz? [y**oo**karuh]
where has it moved to? nereye taşındı? [neray**eh** tashuhnd**uh**]
where has it been moved to? (painting etc) nereye kaldırıldı? [kalduhruhld**uh**]
movie film
movie theater sinema
  see cinema
Mr Bay [bī]
Mrs Bayan [bī-an]
Ms Bayan
much çok [chok]
much better/worse çok daha iyi/daha kötü
much hotter çok daha sıcak
not much pek değil [deh-**ee**l]
not very much çok fazla değil
I don't want very much çok fazla istemiyorum
mud çamur [cham**oo**r]
mug (for drinking) kupa
I've been mugged saldırıya uğradım [salduhr**uh**-ya oo-rad**uh**m]
mum anne [ann**eh**]
mumps kabakulak
museum müze [mewz**eh**]

Museums are generally open from 8.30 or 9 a.m. until 5 or 6 p.m., and closed on Monday, though in the case of some smaller museums you may have to find the **bekçi** (caretaker) yourself and ask him to open up. All sites and museums are closed on the mornings of public holidays.

Major archeological sites have variable opening hours, but are generally open daily from just after sunrise until just before sunset. Some smaller archeological sites are only guarded during the day, and left unfenced, permitting a free wander around in the evening. Permission is required for photographing and filming in museums and ancient ruins and a fee is charged in addition to the entrance fee.

mushrooms mant**a**r
music müzik [mewz**ee**k]
musician müzisy**e**n
Muslim (adj, person) Müslüman
  [mewslewm**a**n]
mussels midye [meed-y**eh**]
must: I must … …-meliyim
  I mustn't drink alcohol
  alkol alm**a**mam lazım
  [laz**uh**m]
mustard hard**a**l
my* -im, -ım [-**uh**m], -um, -üm
  [-ewm], -m

myself*: **I'll do it myself** kend**i**m
  yaparım [yapar**uh**m]
  by myself yalnız baş**ı**ma
  [yaln**uh**z bash**uh**ma]

N

nail (finger) tırnak [tuhrn**a**k]
  (metal) çivi [cheev**ee**]
nailbrush tırnak fırçası [tuhrn**a**k
  fuhrchas**uh**]
nail varnish tırnak cilası
  [jeel**a**suh]
name ad
  my name's John adım John
  [ad**uh**m]
  what's your name? adınız
  n**e**dir? [aduhn**uh**z]
  **what is the name of this
  street?** bu caddenin adı ne?
  [jadden**ee**n ad**uh** n**eh**]

In formal situations the first name followed by **beyefendi** equates to the English Mr. The feminine version, **hanımefendi**, is used in the same way and equates to Mrs, Ms and Miss. **Sayın** followed by the surname is also used as a very formal way of addressing a man or a woman. Beyefendi and hanımefendi are also used on their own when inquiring very formally about absent partners etc; for example, 'hanımefendi nasıllar?' is literally 'how is your (lady) wife?'

→

A less formal way of address is the first name followed by **Bey** (Mr) or **Hanım** (Mrs/Ms/Miss). First names are only used between friends and relatives. It is not usual to use first names for much older people no matter what the relationship is unless you attach an **amca** (uncle), **teyze** (aunty), **abla** (older sister) or **ağabey/abi** (older brother) to the first names, even if they are not relatives.

napkin peçete [pech**eteh**]
nappy çocuk bezi [choj**ook**]
narrow (street) dar
nasty (person, weather, taste) iğrenç [**ee**grench]
   (cut, accident) kötü [kurt**ew**]
national ulusal
nationality vatandaşlık [vatandashl**uhk**]
natural doğal [doh-**al**]
nausea mide bulantısı [m**ee**deh boolantuhs**uh**]
navy (blue) lacivert [lajeev**e**rt]
near: near the ... ...-in yakınında [yakuhn**uh**nda]
   is it near the city centre? şehir merkezine yakın mı? [m**uh**]
   do you go near Aya Sophia? Ayasofya'nın yakınından geçecek misiniz? [ī-asof**ya**-nuhn yakuhnuhnd**an** gechej**ek**]
   where is the nearest ...? en yakın ... nerede? [n**e**redeh]
nearby yakında [yak**uh**nda]

nearly neredeyse [n**e**redayseh]
necessary gerekli
neck boyun
necklace kolye [kol-yeh]
necktie kravat
need: I need ... ...-e ihtiyacım var [-eh ee**H**tee-yaj**uh**m]
   do I need to pay? para ödemem gerekiyor mu? [urdem**e**m]
needle iğne [ee-n**eh**]
negative (film) negat**if**
neither: neither (one) of them hiç biri [h**ee**ch]
   neither ... nor ... ne ... ne ... [n**eh**]
nephew yeğen [yeh-**e**n]
net (in sport) ağ [a]
Netherlands Hollanda
network map şebeke planı [shebek**eh** plan**uh**]
never hiçbir zaman [h**ee**chbeer]

•••••• DIALOGUE ••••••

have you ever been to Bursa?
Bursa'ya hiç gittiniz mi?
no, never, I've never been there
hayır, oraya hiç gitmedim [hī-**uh**r orī-a]

new yeni
news (radio, TV etc) haber
newsagent's gazete bayii [gazet**eh** bī-ee-**ee**]
newspaper gazete
newspaper kiosk gazete satış büfesi [satuhsh bewfes**ee**]
New Year Yeni Yıl [yuhl]

New Year's Eve is widely celebrated. This might be at home with family and friends perhaps with a special meal, playing games, and watching special programmes on the TV. Alternatively Turks might go to a **gazino** (a restaurant cum nightclub) or to a dance. It is also quite common to exchange presents on New Year's Eve.

•••••• DIALOGUE ••••••

do you have a single room for one night? bir gece için tek kişilik bir odanız var mı? [gej**eh** eech**een** tek keeshee**leek** beer odan**uh**z var m**uh**]
yes, madam evet, ef**e**ndim
how much is it per night? gecesi ne kadar? [gejes**ee** neh]
it's 600,000 lira for one night bir gece için altı yüz bin lira
thank you, I'll take it tut**u**yorum, teşekkür ederim [teshekk**ewr**]

Happy New Year! Yeni Yılınız Kut**lu** Olsun! [yuhluhn**uhz**]
New Year's Eve Yılbaşı Gecesi [yuhlbash**uh** gejes**ee**]
New Zealand Yeni Zel**a**nda
New Zealander: I'm a New Zealander Yeni Zelandalıyım [zelandal**uh**yuhm]
next bir s**o**nraki
the next turning/street on the left s**o**lda, bir s**o**nraki sap**a**k/ cadde
at the next stop bir s**o**nraki durakt**a**
next week gelecek haft**a** [gelej**e**k]
next to ... ...-in bitişiğinde [beeteeshee-eend**eh**]
nice (food, day) güzel [gewz**e**l]
(person, looks, view) hoş [hosh]
Nicosia Lefk**o**şe [lefk**o**sha]
niece yeğen [yeh-**e**n]
night gece [gej**eh**]
at night geceleyin [gej**e**lay-een]
good night iyi geceler [gej**e**ler]

nightclub gece kulübü [koolewb**ew**]
nightdress gecelik [gejel**ee**k]
night porter gece bekçisi [bekchees**ee**]
no hayır [h**ī**-**uh**r]
I've no change hiç bozuğum yok [heech bozoo-**oo**m]
there's no ... left hiç ... kalmadı [kalmad**uh**]
no way! katiyen olm**a**z!
oh no! (upset) hay aksi! [h**ī**]

The body language for 'no' is either raised eyebrows, an abrupt tilting back of the head, or a clicking of the tongue against the teeth — or sometimes all three at once.

nobody hiç kimse [heech keems**eh**]
there's nobody there hiç kimse yok **o**rda
noise gürültü [gewrewlt**ew**]
noisy: it's too noisy fazla

gürültülü

non-alcoholic alkolsüz [–se**w**z]

none hiç [heech]

nonsmoking compartment
sigara içmeyenlere mahsus
kompartıman
[eechmayenler**eh** maH**soo**s
kompartuhm**an**]

noon öğle [**ur**-leh]

no-one hiç kimse [heech
keems**eh**]

nor: nor do I ne de ben [neh
deh]

normal normal [nor-m**al**]

north kuzey [koo**zay**]
in the north kuzeyde
[koozayd**eh**]
to the north kuzeye [koo**zay**eh]
north of Ankara Ankara'nın
kuzeyi [ankara-n**uhn**]

northeast kuzeydoğu
[koozaydoh-**oo**]

northern kuzey

Northern Ireland Kuzey İrlanda
[**ee**rlanda]

northwest kuzey batı [bat**uh**]

Norway Norveç [**n**orvech]

Norwegian (adj) Norveç
(language) Norveççe [norvech-
ch**eh**]

nose bur**u**n

nosebleed burun kanaması
[kanamas**uh**]

not* değil [deh-**ee**l]
no, I'm not hungry hayır, aç
değilim [h**ī**-**uhr** ach
deh-eel**ee**m]
I don't want any, thank you hiç
istemiyorum, teşekkür

ederim [heech – teshekk**ewr**]
it's not necessary gerekli
değil [deh-**ee**l]
I didn't know that onu
bilmiyordum
not that one – this one o değil
– bu

note (banknote) kâğıt para
[ka-**uh**t]

notebook not defteri

notepaper (for letters) mektup
kağıdı [ka-uhd**uh**]

nothing hiç bir şey [heech beer
shay]
nothing for me, thanks ben bir
şey istemem, teşekkür
ederim [teshekk**ewr**]
nothing else hepsi o kadar

novel roman

November kasım [kas**uh**m]

now şimdi [sh**ee**mdee]

number* (amount) sayı [s**ī**-**uh**]
(telephone) numar**a**
I've got the wrong number
yanlış numara [yanl**uh**sh]
what is your phone number?
telefon numaranız nedir?
[noomaran**uh**z]

number plate plaka

nurse hasta bakıcı [bakuhj**uh**]

nursery slope acemi pisti
[ajem**ee**]

nut (for bolt) som**u**n

nuts fıstık [fuhst**uh**k]

O

occupied (US) meşgul
[meshg**oo**l]

o'clock*: ... o'clock saat ...
[sa-**a**t]

October ekim

odd (strange) tuhaf

of* -in

off (lights) kapalı [kapal**uh**]
it's just off İstiklal Caddesi/
Taksim Meydanı hemen daha
İstiklal Caddesi'ne/Taksim
Meydanı'na çıkmadan
[eesteekl**al** jaddesee-n**eh**/
taks**ee**m maydanuh-n**a**
chuhkmad**an**]
we're off tomorrow yarın
ayrılıyoruz [yar**uh**n īruhl**uh**-
yorooz]

offensive çirkin [cheerk**ee**n]

office büro [b**ew**ro]

officer (said to policeman) memur
bey [bay]

often sık sık [suhk]
not often ara sıra [suhr**a**]
how often are the buses?
otobüsler ne kadar sık? [neh]

oil (for car, for salad) yağ [ya]

ointment merhem

OK tamam
are you OK? iyi misin?
is that OK with you? siz ne
dersiniz? [neh]
is it OK to ...? ...-nin bir
mahzuru var mı? [muh]
that's OK, thanks tamam,
teşekkür ederim
[teshekk**ew**r]

I'm OK (nothing for me) ben
böyle iyiyim [buh-il**eh**]
(I feel OK) ben iyiyim
is this train OK for ...? için
bu tren doğru mu? [eech**ee**n
– doh-r**oo**]
I said I'm sorry, OK özür
diledim ya [urz**ew**r]

old (person) yaşlı [yashl**uh**]
(thing) eski

•••••• DIALOGUE ••••••

how old are you? kaç
yaşındasınız? [kach
yashuhnd**a**-suhnuhz]
I'm 25 yirmi beş yaşındayım
[yashuhnd**ī**-uhm]
and you? ya siz?

old-fashioned eski moda

old town (old part of town) eski
şehir [sheh-h**ee**r]

olive oil zeytinyağı
[zayt**ee**nya-uh]

olives zeytin
black/green olives siyah/yeşil
zeytin [yesh**ee**l]

omelette omlet

on*: on the ... ...-in üstünde
[ewstewnd**eh**]
(light) açık [ach**uh**k]
on the street/beach caddede/
plajda [jadded**eh**/plaJd**a**]
is it on this road? bu yol
üzerinde mi? [ewzereend**eh**]
on the plane uçakta
[oochakt**a**]
on Saturday Cumartesi günü
[gewn**ew**]
on television televizyonda

I haven't got it on me yanımda
değil [yanuhmda deh-**eel**]
this one's on me (drink) bu
benden
the light wasn't on ışık
yanmıyordu [uhsh**uh**k
y**a**nmuh-yordoo]
what's on tonight? bu akş**a**m
ne var? [neh]
once (one time) bir kere [ker**eh**]
at once (immediately) h**e**men
one* bir
the white one bey**a**z ol**a**n
one-way ticket gidiş bilet**i**
[geed**ee**sh]
onion soğan [soh-**a**n]
only yalnız [y**a**lnuhz]
only one yalnız bir tane
[tan**eh**]
it's only 6 o'clock saat henüz
altı [sa-**a**t hen**e**wz]
I've only just got here ancak
şimdi geldim [anj**a**k
sheemd**ee**]
on/off switch açıp/kapama
düğmesi [ach**uh**p – dew-
mes**ee**]
open (adj) açık [ach**uh**k]
(verb) açmak [achm**a**k]
when do you open? saat
kaçta açıyorsunuz? [sa-**a**t
k**a**chta ach**uh**–]
I can't get it open
açamıyorum [ach**a**muh–]
in the open air açık hav**a**da
opening times açılış ve kapanış
saatleri [ach**u**hl**uh**sh veh
kapan**uh**sh sa-**a**tleree]
open ticket açık bilet [ach**uh**k]

operation (medical) ameliy**a**t
operator (telephone) santr**a**l
memur**u**
see directory enquiries
opposite: the opposite direction
aksi yön [yurn]
the bar opposite karş**ı**daki
bar [karshuhdak**ee**]
opposite my hotel otelimin
karşısında [karshuhs**uh**nda]
optician gözlükçü
[gurzlewkch**ew**]
or veya [v**a**y-**a**]
orange (fruit) portak**a**l
(colour) turuncu [tooroonj**oo**]
orange juice portak**a**l suy**u**
orchestra orkestr**a**
order: can we order now? (in
restaurant) yemekleri şimdi
söyleyebilir miyiz?
[sh**ee**mdee suh-ilayebeel**ee**r]
I've already ordered, thanks
ben ısmarladım, teşekkür
ederim [uhsmarlad**uh**m
teshekk**ew**r]
I didn't order this ben bun**u**
ısmarlamadım
out of order bozuk
ordinary olağan [ola-**a**n]
other diğer [dee-**e**r]
the other one öbürü
[urbewr**ew**]
the other day geçen gün
[gech**e**n gewn]
I'm waiting for the others
diğerlerini bekliyorum
do you have any others?
başka var mı? [bashk**a** var
muh]

otherwise yoksa

our* -miz, -mız
[-muhz], -muz, -müz [-mewz]

ours* bizimki

out: he's out yok, dışarda
[duhsharda]
three kilometres out of town
şehrin üç kilometre dışında
[shehreen ewch keelometreh
duhsuhnda]

outdoors açık havada
[achuhk]

outside: outside the ... ...-in
dışında [duhshuhnda]
can we sit outside? dışarda
oturabilir miyiz? [duhsharda]

oven fırın [fuhruhn]

over: over here burada
over there orada
over 500 beş yüzden fazla
[besh]
it's over bitti

overcharge: you've overcharged
me benden fazla para
aldınız [alduhnuhz]

overcoat palto

overlooking: I'd like a room
overlooking the courtyard
avluya bakan bir oda
istiyorum

overnight (travel) gece [gejeh]

overtake geçmek [gechmek]

owe: how much do I owe you?
size borcum ne kadar?
[seezeh borjoom neh]

own: my own ... benim
kendi ...-m
are you on your own? tek
başına mısınız? [bashuhna

muhsuhnuhz]
I'm on my own tek
başımayım [bashuhmı-uhm]

owner sahibi

P

pack (verb) paketlemek
a pack of ... bir paket ...

package (parcel) paket, koli

package holiday paket tur

packed lunch piknik paketi

packet: a packet of cigarettes bir
paket sigara

padlock asma kilit

page (of book) sayfa [sīfa]
could you page Mr ...?
Sayın ...-i çağırtabilir
misiniz? [sī-uhn ...-ee cha-
uhrtabeeleer]

pain ağrı [a-ruh]
I have a pain here şuramda
bir ağrı var [shooramda beer
a-ruh var]

painful ızdıraplı [uhzduhrapluh]

painkillers ağrı kesiciler [a-ruh
keseejeeler]

paint (noun) boya

painting resim

pair: a pair of ... bir çift ...
[cheeft]

Pakistani (adj, person) Pakistanlı
[-luh]

palace saray [sarī]

pale solgun
pale blue uçuk mavi
[oochook]

pan tencere [tenjereh]

panties külot [kewlot]

pants (underwear: men's) **don**
(women's) **külot** [kewl**o**t]
(US) **pantolon**
pantyhose **külotlu çorap**
[kewlotl**oo** chor**a**p]
paper **kâğıt** [ka-**uh**t]
(newspaper) **gazete** [gaz**e**teh]
a piece of paper **bir parça
kağıt** [parch**a**]
paper handkerchiefs **kağıt
mendil**
parcel **koli**
pardon (me)? (didn't understand/
hear) **efendim?**
parents **anne baba** [ann**eh**]
park (noun) **park**
(verb) **park etmek**
can I park here? **buraya park
edebilir miyim?** [boor**ī-a**]
parking lot **otopark**
part (noun) **parça** [parch**a**]
partner (boyfriend, girlfriend etc)
arkadaş [arkad**a**sh]
party (group) **grup**
(celebration) **parti**
pass (in mountains) **geçit**
[gech**ee**t]
passenger **yolcu** [yolj**oo**]
passport **pasaport**

It is advisable to carry your
passport with you at all times.
Hotels ask for it when checking
in. You probably won't need to
produce it whilst on the beach
at major resorts, but the police
and military sometimes have
road checks, where both Turks
→

and foreigners are obliged to
produce their ID cards or
passports.

past: in the past **geçmişte**
[gechmeesht**eh**]
just past the information office
**danışma bürosunu geçer
geçmez** [danuhshm**a**
bewrosoon**oo** gech**e**r gechm**e**z]
path **patika, yol**
pattern **desen**
pavement **kaldırım**
[kalduhr**uh**m]
on the pavement **kaldırımda**
pay (verb) **ödemek** [urdem**e**k]
can I pay, please? **ödeyebilir
miyim, lütfen?**
[urdayebeel**ee**r]
it's already paid for **ödendi
bile** [urdend**ee** beel**eh**]

•••••• DIALOGUE ••••••

who's paying? **kim ödüyor?**
[urdew-y**o**r]
I'll pay **ben ödeyeceğim** [urdayejeh-
eem]
no, you paid last time, I'll pay
**olmaz, siz geçen sefer ödediniz,
ben ödeyeceğim** [gechen –
urdedeen**e**ez ben urdayejeh-**ee**m]

pay phone **umumi telefon**
peaceful **sakin**
peach **şeftali** [sheftal**ee**]
peanuts **yerfıstığı**
[yerfuhstuh-**uh**]
pear **armut**
peas **bezelye** [bezelyeh]

peculiar (strange) tuhaf

pedestrian crossing yaya geçidi
[yī-**a** gecheed**ee**]

> Be careful when crossing city
> roads: drivers, if they can get
> away with it, prefer not to stop
> at pedestrian crossings.

pedestrian precinct yayalara
mahsus bölge [ma**H**s**oo**s
burlg**eh**]

peg (for washing) mand**al**
(for tent) kaz**ı**k [kaz**uh**k]

pen mürekkepli kalem
[mewrek-kepl**ee**]

pencil kurşun kalem
[koorsh**oo**n]

penfriend mektup arkadaşı
[arkadash**uh**]

penicillin penisilin

penknife çakı [chak**uh**]

pensioner emekli

people insanl**ar**
  the other people in the hotel
  oteldeki diğer kişiler [dee-er
  keesheel**er**]
  too many people fazla sayıda
  insan [sī-**uh**da]

pepper biber
  green pepper yeşil biber
  [yesh**ee**l]
  red pepper kırmızı biber
  [kuhrmuhrz**uh**]

peppermint (sweet) nane şekeri
[nan**eh** shekeree]

per: per night bir gecesi
[gejes**ee**]
  how much per day? gündeliği

kaça? [gewndelee-**ee** kach**a**]

per cent yüzde [yewzd**eh**]

perfect mükemmel
[mewkemm**el**]

perfume parfüm [parf**ew**m]

perhaps belki
  perhaps not belki de değil
  [deh deh-**ee**l]

period (of time) süre [sewr**eh**]
  (menstruation) **a**det dönem**i**

perm perm**a**

permit (noun) iz**in**

person kişi [keesh**ee**]

personal stereo walkman®

petrol benzin
  see garage

petrol can benzin bidon**u**

petrol station
  benzin istasyon**u**

pharmacy eczane [ejz**a**neh]

> For minor complaints head for
> the nearest **eczane** (pharmacy)
> – even the smallest town will
> have at least one. Pharmacists
> in Turkey are able to dispense
> medicines that would ordinarily
> require a prescription abroad.
> In larger towns, **eczane** staff
> may know some English or
> German. Foreign visitors have
> to pay for prescriptions.
> Medication prices are low, but
> you may find it difficult to
> find exact equivalents to your
> home prescription, so take
> anything you need with you.
> Night-duty pharmacies are →

known as **nöbetçi**; a list of the current rota is posted in every pharmacist's front window.

phone (noun) telef**o**n
(verb) telefon etm**e**k

The best place to make phone calls is the **PTT** (post and telephone office) or mobile PTT services in holiday resorts. Inside or just adjacent there is usually a range of alternatives: a **jeton** (token) phone, a cardphone and/or a **konturlu** (metered, clerk-attended) phone, sometimes in a closed booth. Phones elsewhere are relatively rare, though you will find them in public parks and at filling stations. Jetons theoretically come in small (**küçük**), medium (**orta**) and large (**büyük**) sizes, for local, trunk and international use respectively, though the medium-sized ones are often in short supply. Partly used tokens are not returned, so don't use bigger sizes for local calls. While you're in Turkey it's a good idea to carry a few on you – they're not always on sale when you need them. Drop at least one token in the slot before dialling; when the red light comes on and a warning tone sounds, you have about ten seconds to feed in →

more. Never attempt to call from a jeton-operated phone box where the square, red 'out of service' light is illuminated. For trunk or overseas calls, phonecards (available in 30, 60 and 100 units) or metered booths inside PTTs are better value. Overseas rates are not cheap, but there is a 25 per cent discount on normal rates after 10 p.m. and on Sunday. Try not to make anything other than local calls from a hotel room – there is usually a one-hundred per cent surcharge on the already hefty rates.

phone book telef**o**n rehberi [reнberee]
phone box telefon kulübesi [koolewbesee]
phonecard telefon kartı [kart**uh**]
phone number telefon numarası [noomaras**uh**]
photo fot**o**ğraf [foto-r**a**f]
  excuse me, could you take a photo of us? **a**ffedersiniz, bir fotoğrafımızı çekebilir misin**iz**? [foto-rafuhmuhz**uh** chekebeel**ee**r]
phrasebook konuşma kılavuzu [konooshm**a** kuhlavooz**oo**]
piano piy**a**no
pickpocket yankesici [yankeseej**ee**]
pick up: will you be there to pick

me up? beni almaya gelecek
misiniz? [almī-**a** gelej**ek**]
picnic piknik
picture resim
pie (meat) etli börek [bur-r**ek**]
(fruit) turt**a**
piece parça [parch**a**]
a piece of ... bir parça ...
pill doğum kontrol hapı [doh-
oom – hahp**uh**]
I'm on the pill doğum kontrol
hapı alıyorum [hap**uh** aluh-
y**oo**room]
pillow yastık [yast**uh**k]
pillow case yastık kılıfı
[kuhluhf**uh**]
pin (noun) toplu iğne [ee-n**eh**]
pineapple ananas
pineapple juice ananas suyu
pink pembe [pemb**eh**]
pipe (for smoking) pipo
(for water) boru
pistachio antep fıstığı
[fuhst**uh**-uh]
pity: it's a pity yazık [yaz**uh**k]
pizza pizza
place (noun) yer
is this place taken? bu yerin
sahibi var mı? [muh]
at your place sende [send**eh**],
sizin evde [evd**eh**]
at his place onda, onun
evinde [eveend**eh**]
plain (not patterned) düz [dewz]
plane uçak [ooch**ak**]
by plane uçakla
plant bitki
plaster cast alçı [alch**uh**]
plasters flaster, yara bandı

[band**uh**]
plastic plastik
(credit cards) kredi kartları
[kartlar**uh**]
plastic bag naylon torba [nīlon]
plate tabak
platform peron
which platform is it for Bursa?
Bursa treni hangi perondan
kalkıyor? [kalkuh-y**or**]
play (verb) oynamak
(noun: in theatre) oy**u**n
playground çocuk bahçesi
[choj**oo**k ba**H**chese**e**]
pleasant hoş [hosh]
please lütfen [l**e**wtfen]
yes please lütfen
could you please ...?
lütfen ...-ebilir miydiniz?
[mee-ideen**ee**z]
please don't do that lütfen
yapmayın
pleased to meet you!
tanıştığımıza memnun
oldum! [tanuhshtuh-uhmuhz**a**]
pleasure: my pleasure rica
ederim [r**ee**ja]
plenty: plenty of ... bol bol ...
there's plenty of time bol bol
vakit var
that's plenty, thanks teşekkür
ederim, yeter [teshekk**ewr**]
pliers kerpeten
plug (electrical) fiş [feesh]
(in sink) tıkaç [tuhk**ach**]
(for car) buji [b**oo**Jee]
plumber tesisatçı [teseesatch**uh**]
p.m.*: ... p.m. (afternoon)
öğleden sonra ... [ur-leden]

(evening) akşam ... [aksham]

poached egg kaynar suya kırılmış yumurta [kīnar – kuhruhlm**uh**sh]

pocket cep [jep]

point: two point five iki nokt**a** beş
there's no point anlamı yok [anlam**uh**]

points (in car) kesici platinler [keseej**ee**]

poisonous zehir**li**

police polis
call the police! polis çağırın! [cha-**uh**ruhn]

Civilian police come in a variety of subdivisions. The green-uniformed **Polis** are the everyday security force in the towns and cities. The **Trafik Polisi**, recognized by their white caps, are a branch of this service. The **Turizm Polisi** patrol tourist areas dressed in beige uniforms and maroon berets, and should have some knowledge of English, German or Arabic. In the towns you're also likely to see the **Belediye Zabıtası** or navy-clad market police, who patrol the markets and bazaars to ensure that tradesmen aren't ripping off customers.

In most rural areas, particularly as you move further east, law enforcement is in the hands of the **Jandarma**, a division of the →

regular army charged with law enforcement duties. Dial 155 for the police, 156 for the Jandarma and 154 for the traffic police. The call costs one small **jeton**, or one phonecard unit.

policeman polis

police station polis karakol**u**

policewoman kadın polis [kad**uh**n]

polish (noun) cila [jeel**a**]

polite nazik

polluted kir**li**

pony midi**lli**

pool (for swimming) hav**uz**

poor (not rich) fak**ir**
(quality) kalite**siz**

pop music pop müzik [mewz**ee**k]

pop singer pop şarkıcısı [sharkuhjuhs**uh**]

popular sevi**len**

population nüfus [newf**oos**]

pork dom**uz** eti

port (for boats) lim**an**
(drink) porto şarabı [sharab**uh**]

porter (in hotel) kapıcı [kapuhj**uh**]

portrait portre [**p**ortreh]

posh kib**ar**

possible mümkün [mewmk**ewn**]
is it possible to ...? ...-mak mümkün mü? [mew]
as ... as possible olduğunca ... [oldoo-oonj**a**]

post (noun: mail) post**a**

(verb) postalamak
could you post this for me?
bunları benim için
postalayabilir miydiniz?
[boonlar**uh** – eech**ee**n postalī-
abeel**ee**r mee-ideen**ee**z]
postbox posta kutus**u**
postcard kartpostal
postcode posta kodu
poster (for room) post**e**r
(in street) afiş [af**ee**sh]
poste restante postrestant
post office postane [postaneh]

The Turkish postal and
telephone service is run by the
PTT (**P**osta, **T**elgraf, **T**elefon),
easily identified by a black-on-
yellow logo. In larger towns and
tourist resorts, the phone
division of the main PTT
building is open 24 hours, with
mail accepted from 8 a.m. until
7 p.m. Elsewhere expect both
facilities to be available from
8 a.m. to 10 p.m. Monday to
Saturday, and from 9 a.m. to
7 p.m. on Sunday.
The outgoing service is efficient,
but make sure that the clerk has
charged you for airmail (uçakla
[ooch**a**kla]) and not the
cheaper and slower surface rate.
The best advice on sending
packages is not to send anything
over two or three kilos. Boxes
must be left open for inspection,
though at main branches folded
packing kits are sold.

potato patates
pots and pans mutfak eşyası
[esh-yas**uh**]
pottery (objects) seramik,
toprak eşya [esh-ya]
pound* (money) sterlin
(weight) libre [l**ee**breh]
power cut elektrik kesilmesi
power point priz
practise: I want to practise my
Turkish Türkçe pratik
yapmak istiyorum
[t**ew**rkcheh]
prawns karides
prayer dua
prayer mat seccade [sejj**a**deh]
prefer: I prefer ... ... tercih
ederim [terj**ee**H]
pregnant gebe [geb**e**h]
premium süper [sewp**e**r]
prescription (for medicine) reçete
[rech**e**teh]
see **pharmacy**
present (gift) hediye [hedee-y**e**h]
president (of country)
cumhurbaşkanı
[joomHoor-bashkan**uh**]
pretty güzel [gewz**e**l]
it's pretty expensive oldukça
pahalı [old**oo**kcha]
price fiyat
priest rahip
prime minister başbakan
[b**a**shbakan]
printed matter matbua
priority (in driving) öncelik
[**u**rnjeleek]
prison hapishane
[hapeesh**a**neh]

private özel [urzel]
private bathroom özel banyo
probably belki
problem problem
  no problem! hiç sorun değil!
  [heech – deh-**eel**]
program(me) (noun) program
promise: I promise söz
  veriyorum [surz]
pronounce: how is this
  pronounced? bu nasıl telaffuz
  edilir? [na**suhl**]
properly (repaired, locked etc)
  hakkıyla [hakk**uh**-yuhla], iyice
  [**ee**-yeejeh]
protection factor koruma
  faktörü [fakt**urew**]
Protestant Protestan
public convenience umumi hela
public holiday resmi tatil
pudding (dessert) sütlü tatlı
  [sewtl**ew** tatl**uh**], puding
pull çekmek [chekm**ek**]
pullover kazak
puncture (noun) lastik
  patlaması [patlamas**uh**]
purple eflatun
purse (for money) para çantası
  [chantas**uh**]
  (US) el çantası [chantas**uh**]
push itmek
pushchair puset
put koymak
  where can I put ...? ...-i nereye
  koyabilirim? [nerayeh]
  could you put us up for the
  night? bu gece bizi konuk
  edebilir misiniz? [gej**eh**]
pyjamas pijama [pee**J**ama]

Q

quality kalite [kaleet**eh**]
quarantine karantina
quarter çeyrek [chayrek]
quayside: on the quayside
  rıhtımda [ru**H**tuhmd**a**]
question soru
queue (noun) kuyruk [koo-ir**oo**k]
quick çabuk [chab**oo**k]
  that was quick ne kadar
  çabuk oldu [neh]
  what's the quickest way there?
  oraya en çabuk nasıl gidilir?
  [na**suhl**]
  fancy a quick drink? çabucak
  bir şey içelim ister misin?
  [chaboo**j**ak beer shay
  eechel**eem**]
quickly hızla [huhzl**a**]
quiet (place, hotel) sakin [sak**ee**n]
quiet! gürültü yapmayın!
  [gewrewlt**ew** yapm**ı**-uhn]
quite (fairly) oldukça
  [old**oo**kcha]
  (very) tamamen, pek, çok
  [chok]
  that's quite right çok doğru
  [chok doh-r**oo**]
  quite a lot oldukça çok
  [old**oo**kcha]

R

rabbit tavşan [tavsh**an**]
race (for runners, cars) yarış
  [yar**uh**sh]
racket (tennis, squash) raket
radiator radyatör [rad-yat**ur**]

radio radyo
 on the radio radyoda
rail: by rail trenle [trenleh]
railway demiryolu
rain (noun) yağmur [ya-moor]
 in the rain yağmurda
 it's raining yağmur yağıyor
 [ya-uh-yor]
raincoat yağmurluk
Ramadan Ramazan
rape (noun) ırza geçme [uhrza
 gechmeh]
rare (uncommon) nadide
 [nadeedeh]
 (steak) az pişmiş [peeshmeesh]
rash (on skin) isilik
raspberry ahududu
 [aHoodoodoo]
rat sıçan [suhchan]
rate (for changing money) kur
rather: it's rather good oldukça
 iyi [oldookcha]
 I'd rather ... ...-yi tercih
 ederim [terjeeH]
razor ustura
 (electric) elektrikli tıraş
 makinesi [tuhrash]
razor blades jilet [Jeelet]
read okumak
ready hazır [hazuhr]
 are you ready? hazır mısınız?
 [muhsuhnuhz]
 I'm not ready yet henüz hazır
 değilim [henewz –
 deh-eeleem]

•••••• DIALOGUE ••••••

when will it be ready? ne zaman
 hazır olur? [neh]

it should be ready in a couple of
 days bir kaç güne kadar hazır
 olur [kach gewneh]

real gerçek [gerchek]
really gerçekten [gerchekten]
 I'm really sorry gerçekten
 üzgünüm [ewzgewnewm]
 that's really great gerçekten
 çok iyi [chok]
 really? (doubt) yok canım?
 [januhm]
 (polite interest) sahi mi?
rear lights arka lambalar
rearview mirror dikiz aynası
 [īnasuh]
reasonable (prices etc) akla
 yakın [yakuhn]
receipt makbuz
recently geçenlerde
 [gechenlerdeh]
reception (in hotel) resepsiyon
 (for guests) davet
 at reception resepsiyonda
reception desk resepsiyon
 masası [masasuh]
receptionist resepsiyon
 memuru
recognize tanımak [tanuhmak]
recommend: could you
 recommend ...? ... tavsiye
 edebilir misiniz? [tavsee-yeh]
record (noun: music) plak
red kırmızı [kuhrmuhzuh]
red wine kırmızı şarap [sharap]
refund (noun) iade [ee-adeh]
 can I have a refund? paramı
 geri alabilir miyim?
 [paramuh]

region bölge [burlg**eh**]

registered: by registered mail
taahhütlü [ta-a-hewtl**ew**]

registration number kayıt
numarası [kī-**uht** noomaras**uh**]

regular gas normal [nor-m**al**]

relative (noun) akrab**a**

religion din [deen]

remember: I don't remember
hatırlamıyorum [hatuhrlamuh-
y**o**room]

I remember hatırlıyorum
[hatuhrluh-y**o**room]

do you remember? hatırlıyor
musun**uz**?

rent (noun: for apartment etc) kir**a**
(verb: car etc) kiralam**a**k

for rent kiralık [keeral**uh**k]

• • • • • • DIALOGUE • • • • • •

I'd like to rent a car bir otomobil
kiralamak istiyorum

for how long? ne kadar süre için?
[neh – sewr**eh** eech**ee**n]

two days iki gün [gewn]

this is our range elimizdekiler
bunl**a**r

I'll take the ... ...-yi alayım [alī-
uhm]

is that with unlimited mileage?
kilometre sınırı yok değil mi?
[keelometr**eh** suhnuh-ruh y**o**k deh-
eel]

it is evet

can I see your licence please?
ehliyetinizi görebilir miyim
lütfen? [e**H**lee-yeteeneez**ee**
gurebeel**eer** – l**ew**tfen]

and your passport ve
pasaportunuz**u** [veh]

is insurance included? sigorta
içinde mi? [eecheend**eh**]

yes, but you pay the first 6,000,000
lira evet, fakat ilk altı milyon
lirayı siz ödeyeceksiniz [leerī-uh
s**ee**z urdayejekseen**ee**z]

can you leave a deposit of
1,000,000 lira? bir milyon lira
depozito bırakabilir misiniz?
[buhrakabeel**eer**]

rented car kiralık otomobil
[keeral**uh**k]

repair (verb) onarm**a**k

can you repair it? on**u**
onarabilir misin**iz**?

repeat tekrarlam**a**k

could you repeat that? on**u**
tekrarlar mısınız?
[muhsuhn**uh**z]

reservation rezervasyon

I'd like to make a reservation
bir rezervasyon yapm**a**k
istiyorum

• • • • • • DIALOGUE • • • • • •

I have a reservation
rezervasyon**um** var

yes sir, what name please? evet
efendim, isim neydi lütfen?
[nayd**ee**]

reserve (verb) ayırtm**a**k
[ī-uhrtm**a**k]

• • • • • • DIALOGUE • • • • • •

can I reserve a table for tonight? bu
akşam için bir masa ayırtabilir
miyim? [aksh**a**m eech**ee**n –
ī-uhrtabeel**eer**]

yes madam, for how many people?

evet efendim, kaç kişi için? [kach
keeshee]
for two iki kişi için
and for what time? ve saat kaç
için? [veh sa-at]
for eight o'clock sekiz için
and could I have your name,
please? adınızı alabilir miyim,
lütfen? [aduhnuhzuh-abeeleer –
lewtfen]
see alphabet for spelling

rest: I need a rest dinlenmeye
ihtiyacım var [–mayeh eeнtee-
yajuhm]
the rest of the group grubun
geri kalan kısmı [kuhsmuh]
restaurant lokanta, restoran

A lokanta is a restaurant, as
is a restoran. A kebapçı or
köfteci specializes in the
preparation of kebabs and
köfte respectively, with a
limited number of side dishes.
Most budget-priced restaurants
are içkisiz or alcohol-free; any
place marked içkili (licensed) is
likely to be more expensive.
Many places don't have menus:
you'll need to ascertain the
prices of the main courses
beforehand, and review bills
carefully when finished.
In many restaurants lone
women will be ushered into the
family parlour, which is often
upstairs or behind a curtain.

restaurant car yemekli vagon

restroom tuvalet [toovalet]
see toilet
retired: I'm retired emekliyim
return: a return to ... ...-'e bir
gidiş dönüş bilet [-eh beer
geedeesh durnewsh]
return ticket gidiş dönüş bileti
see ticket
reverse charge call ödemeli
konuşma [urdemelee
konooshma]
reverse gear geri vites
revolting iğrenç [ee-rench]
Rhodes Rodos
rib kaburga
rice (uncooked) pirinç
[peereench]
(cooked) pilav
rich (person) zengin
(food) ağır [a-uhr]
ridiculous gülünç [gewlewnch]
right (correct) doğru [doh-roo]
(not left) sağ [sa]
you were right haklıymışsınız
[hakluh-ımuhsh-suhnuhz]
that's right doğru
this can't be right bu doğru
olamaz
right! tamam!
is this the right road for ...? bu
yol ...-e gider mi? [-eh]
on the right sağda [sa-da]
turn right sağa dönün
[durnewn]
right-hand drive sağdan
direksiyonlu [sa-dan]
ring (on finger) yüzük [yewzewk]
I'll ring you sizi telefonla
ararım [araruhm]

ring back geri aramak
(telefonla)
ripe (fruit) olgun
rip-off: it's a rip-off tam bir
kazık [kazuhk]
rip-off prices kazık fiyatlar
risky rizikolu
river nehir [neh-Heer]
road yol
is this the road for ...?
bu ... yolu mudur?
down the road yolun
ilerisinde [eelereeseendeh]

Ordinary main roads are usually
adequately paved, but often
dangerously narrow. Toll
highways are springing up, and
are well worth the modest tolls.
International roads have 'E'
before a number (meaning
Europe) and state roads have
'D' (meaning 'devlet' state).
The main motorway (otoyol)
connecting İstanbul to Ankara is
called the TEM (Trans
European Motorway); a toll is
charged depending on the
distance travelled.

road accident trafik kazası
[kazasuh]
road map karayolu haritası
[hareetasuh]
roadsign trafik işareti
[eesharetee]
rob: I've been robbed soyuldum
rock kaya [kı-a]
(music) rock müziği

[mewzee-ee]
on the rocks (with ice) buzlu
roll (bread) sandviç ekmeği
[sandveech ekmeh-ee]
roof dam
roof rack üst bagaj yeri [ewst
bagaɹ]
room oda
in my room odamda
•••••• DIALOGUE ••••••
do you have any rooms? boş
odanız var mı? [bosh odanuhz var
muh]
for how many people? kaç kişi
için? [kach keeshee eecheen]
for one/for two bir/iki kişi için
yes, we have rooms free evet, boş
odamız var [odamuhz]
for how many nights will it be? kaç
gece için olacak? [gejeh – olajak]
just for one night sadece bir gece
için [sa-dejeh]
how much is it? ne kadar? [neh]
... with bathroom and ... without
bathroom banyolu ... ve
banyosuz ... [veh]
can I see a room with bathroom?
banyolu odayı görebilir miyim?
[odī-uh gurebeeleer]
OK, I'll take it tamam, tutuyorum

room service oda servisi
rope halat
rosé (wine) pembe şarap
[pembeh sharap]
roughly (approximately) kabaca
[kabaja]
round: it's my round bu sefer
sıra bende [suhra bendeh]

roundabout (for traffic) göbek [gurbek]

round trip ticket gidiş dönüş bileti

route yol
what's the best route? en iyi hangi yoldan gidilir?

rubber (material) lastik (eraser) silgi

rubber band lastik bant

rubbish (waste) çöp [churp]
(poor quality goods) uyduruk şeyler [oo-idooruhk shayler]
rubbish! (nonsense) saçma! [sachma]

rucksack sırt çantası [suhrt chantasuh]

rude kaba

rug (for floor) kilim
(blanket) battaniye [battanee-yeh]

ruins harabeler

rum rom
rum and coke rom ve koka kola [veh]

run (verb: person) koşmak [koshmak]
how often do the buses run? otobüslerin arası ne kadar? [arasuh neh]
I've run out of money param bitti

rush hour kalabalık saatler [kalabaluhk sa-atler]

S

sad üzgün [ewzgewn]

saddle (for horse) eyer [ay-er]
(for bike) sele [seleh]

safe (not in danger) güvenli [gewvenlee]
(not dangerous) güvenilir

safety pin çengelli iğne [chengellee ee-neh]

sail (noun) yelken

sailboard (noun) yelkenli sörf [surf]

sailboarding sörf yapmak

salad salata

salad dressing salata sosu

sale: for sale satılık [satuhluhk]

salmon som balığı [baluh-uh]

salt tuz

same: the same aynı [inuh]
the same as this bunun aynısı [inuhsuh]
the same again, please aynısından bir tane daha, lütfen [inuhsuhndan beer taneh – lewtfen]
it's all the same to me benim için hepsi bir [eecheen]

sand kum [koom]

sandals sandal

sandwich sandviç [sandveech]

sanitary napkin kadın bağı [kaduhn ba-uh]

sanitary towel kadın bağı

sardines sardalya

Saturday cumartesi [joomartesee]

sauce sos

saucepan tencere [tenjereh]

saucer fincan tabağı [feenjan
taba-**uh**]
sauna sauna [sa-**oo**na]
sausage sosis
say (verb) demek, söylemek
[suh-ilem**ek**]
how do you say ... in Turkish?
Türkçe ... nasıl denir?
[te**w**rkcheh ... n**a**suhl]
what did he/she say? ne dedi?
[neh]
he/she said ... ... dedi
could you say that again?
tekrarlar mısınız?
[muhsuhn**uh**z]
scarf (for neck) atkı [atk**uh**]
(for head) eşarp [esh**a**rp]
scenery manzara
schedule (US) tarife [taree**feh**]
scheduled flight tarifeli sefer
school okul
scissors: a pair of scissors
makas
scooter küçük motosiklet
[kewch**ew**k]
scotch viski
Scotch tape® seloteyp
[sel**o**tayp]
Scotland İskoçya [eesk**och**-ya]
Scottish İskoç
I'm Scottish İskoçyalıyım
[eeskoch-yaluh-y**uh**m]
scrambled eggs karılmış
sahanda yumurta
[karuhlm**uh**sh]
scratch (noun) çizik [cheez**eek**]
screw (noun) vida
screwdriver tornavida
sea deniz

by the sea deniz kıyısında
[kuh-yuhsuhnd**a**]
seafood deniz ürünleri
[ewrewnler**ee**]
seafood restaurant balık
lokantası [bal**uh**k lokantas**uh**]
seafront sahil [saH**eel**]
on the seafront sahilde
[saHeeld**eh**]
seagull martı [mart**uh**]
Sea of Marmara Marmara
Denizi
search (verb) aramak
seashell deniz kabuğu [deneez
kab**oo**-oo]
seasick: I feel seasick beni
deniz tutt**u**
I get seasick beni deniz tutar
seaside: by the seaside deniz
kenarında [kenaruhnd**a**]
seat oturacak yer [otoorajak]
is this anyone's seat? bu yerin
sahibi var mı? [muh]
seat belt emniyet kemeri
sea urchin deniz kestanesi
seaweed yosun
secluded kuytu [koo-it**oo**]
second (adj) ikinci [eek**een**jee]
(of time) saniye [sanee-y**eh**]
just a second! bir saniye!
[beer]
second class (travel) ikinci sınıf
[eek**een**jee suhn**uh**f]
second floor ikinci kat
[eek**een**jee]
(US) birinci kat [beer**een**jee]
second-hand elden düşme
[dewshm**eh**]
see görmek [gurmek]

can I see? görebilir miyim?
[gurebeel**ee**r]
have you seen ...? ...-i
gördünüz mü? [-ee
gurdewn**ew**z mew]
I saw him/her this morning
onu bu sabah gördüm
[gurd**ew**m]
see you! görüşürüz!
[g**u**rewshewrewz]
I see (I understand) anlıyorum
[anl**uh**-yoroom]
self-catering apartment
pansiyon (yemek pişirme
olanaklı) [peesheerm**eh**
olanakl**uh**]
self-service self servis
sell satmak
do you sell ...? ... satıyor
musun**uz**? [satuh-y**or**]
Sellotape® seloteyp [sel**o**tayp]
send göndermek [gurndermek]
I want to send this to England
bunu İngiltere'ye
göndermek istiyorum
[**ee**ngeeltereh-yeh]
senior citizen yaşlı vatandaş
[yashl**uh** vatand**a**sh]
separate ayrı [**î**r**uh**]
separated: I'm separated
eşimden ayrı yaşıyorum
[esheemd**e**n – yashuh-yor**oo**m]
separately (pay, travel) ayrı ayrı
[**î**r**uh**]
September eylül [ayl**ew**l]
septic mikroplu
serious ciddi [jeedd**ee**]
service charge (in restaurant)
servis ücreti [ewjret**ee**]

service station servis istasyonu
serviette peçete [pech**e**teh]
set menu tabldot [tabld**o**t]
several birkaç [beerk**a**ch]
sew dikmek
could you sew this back on?
bunu yerine dikebilir
misiniz? [yereen**eh**]
sex seks
(gender) cinsiyet [jeensee-y**et**]
sexy cazibeli [jazeebel**ee**]
shade: in the shade gölgede
[gurlged**eh**]
shake: let's shake hands
tokalaşalım [tokalashal**uh**m]
shallow (water) sığ [s**uh**]
shame: what a shame! ne yazık!
[neh yaz**uh**k]
shampoo (noun) şampuan
[shampoo-**a**n]
shampoo and set yıkama ve
mizanpli [y**uh**kama veh]
share (verb: room, table etc)
paylaşmak [pîlashm**a**k]
sharp (taste, knife) keskin
(pain) şiddetli [sheeddetl**ee**]
shattered (very tired)
yorgunluktan bitmiş
[beetm**ee**sh]
shaver tıraş makinesi [tuhr**a**sh]
shaving foam tıraş köpüğü
[kurpew-**ew**]
shaving point tıraş makinesi
prizi
she* o
is she here? o burada mı?
[muh]
sheep's cheese beyaz peynir
[bay**a**z payn**ee**r]

sheet (for bed) çarşaf [charshaf]

shelf raf

shellfish kabuklu deniz
ürünleri [ewrewnleree]

sherry şeri [sheree]

ship gemi

by ship gemiyle [gemee-ileh]

shirt gömlek [gurmlek]

shit! şimdi hapı yuttuk!
[sheemdee hapuh]

shock (noun) şok [shok]

I got an electric shock from
the ... ...-den elektrik çarptı
[charptuh]

shock-absorber amortisör
[amorteesur]

shocking korkunç [korkoonch]

shoe ayakkabı [ī-akkabuh]

a pair of shoes bir çift
ayakkabı [cheeft]

shoelaces ayakkabı bağı
[ba-uh]

shoe polish ayakkabı cilası
[jeelasuh]

shoe repairer kundura
tamircisi [–jeesee]

shop dükkân [dewkkan]

Ordinary shops are open
continuously from 8.30 or 9 a.m.
until 7 or 8 p.m., depending on
the owner. Craftsmen and
bazaar stallholders keep long
hours, often working from 9
a.m. to 8 or 9 p.m., Monday to
Saturday, with only the hastiest
of breaks for meals, tea or
prayers. Even on Sunday the
→

tradesmen's area may not be
completely shut down – though
don't count on this.

shopping: I'm going shopping
ben alış-verişe çıkıyorum
[aluhsh-vereesheh chuhkuh-
yoroom]

shopping centre alış-veriş
merkezi

shop window vitrin

shore sahil [saнeel]

short kısa [kuhsa]

shortcut kestirme [kesteermeh]

shorts şort [short]

should: what should I do? ne
yapmam lazım? [neh –
lazuhm]

you should ... ...-malıydınız
[-maluh-iduhnuhz]

you shouldn't ...
...-mamalıydınız

he should be back soon
birazdan gelmesi lazım

shoulder omuz [omooz]

shout (verb) bağırmak
[ba-uhrmak]

show (in theatre) gösteri
[gursteree]

could you show me? bana
gösterebilir misiniz?
[gursterebeeleer]

shower (in bathroom) duş [doosh]
(rain) sağanak [sa-anak]

with shower duşlu [dooshloo]

shower gel duş jeli [doosh]

shut (verb) kapatmak

when do you shut? saat kaçta

kapatıyorsunuz? [sa-**at** kacht**a**
kapat**uh**-yorsoonooz]
when does it shut? ne zaman
kapanıyor? [neh kapanuh-**yor**]
they're shut kapalılar
[kapal**uh**-lar]
I've shut myself out anahtarı
içerde unutt**um** [ana**н**tar**uh**
eech**er**deh]
shut up! kapa çeneni!
[chenen**ee**]
shutter (on camera) örtücü
[urtewj**ew**], obtüratör
[obdewrat**ur**]
(on window) kep**e**nk
shy çekingen [chekeeng**e**n]
sick (ill) hast**a**
I'm going to be sick (vomit)
kusacağım g**a**liba [koosaja-
uhm]
side yan
the other side of the street
cadd**e**nin öbür tarafı
[urb**ew**r taraf**uh**]
side lights park lambaları
[lambalar**uh**]
side salad garnitür sal**a**ta
[garneet**ew**r]
side street yan sok**a**k
sidewalk kaldırım [kalduhr**uh**m]
on the sidewalk kaldırımd**a**
sight: the sights of ... ...-nin
görmeye değer yerler**i**
[gurmay**eh** deh-**er**]
**sightseeing: we're going
sightseeing** geziye çıkıyoruz
[gezee-y**eh** chuhkuh-y**orooz**]
sightseeing tour gezi, tur
sign (roadsign etc) işaret

[eeshar**et**]
**signal: he/she didn't give a
signal** (driver, cyclist) işaret
vermedi
signature imza
signpost işaret levhası [ishar**et**
levhas**uh**]
silence sessizlik
silk ipek
silly (person) sersem
(thing to do) saçma [sachm**a**]
silver (noun) gümüş [gewm**ew**sh]
silver foil aluminy**um** foly**o**
similar benzer
simple (easy) kolay [kol**ī**]
since: since last week geçen
haftadan beri [gech**e**n]
since I got here buraya
geldiğimden beri [boorī-**a**
geldee-eemd**e**n]
sing şarkı söylemek [shark**uh**
suh-ilem**e**k]
singer şarkıcı [sharkuhj**uh**]
single: a single to ... ...-e bir
gidiş bileti [-**eh** beer
geed**ee**sh]
I'm single bek**a**rım [bek**a**ruhm]
see ticket
single bed tek kişilik yat**a**k
[keesheel**ee**k]
single room tek kişilik bir od**a**
sink (in kitchen) evye [ev-yeh],
bulaşık lavabosu
[boolash**uh**k]
sister kız kardeş [kuhz kard**e**sh]
sister-in-law (wife's sister) baldız
[bald**uh**z]
(husband's sister) görümce
[gurrewmj**eh**]

(brother's wife) yenge [yeng**eh**]

sit: can I sit here? buraya
oturabilir miyim? [b**oo**rī-a]
is anyone sitting here? burada
oturan var mı? [muh]

sit down oturmak
sit down otur**un**

size boy

ski (noun) kayak [kī-**ak**]
(verb) kayak yap**mak**
a pair of skis bir çift kayak
[ch**eeft**]

skiing kayakçılık [kī-ak-
chuhl**uhk**]

ski-lift telesiyej [telesee-ye**J**]

skin cilt [jeelt]

skin-diving balık adamlık
[bal**uh**k adaml**uh**k]

skinny sıska [suhsk**a**]

skirt et**ek**

sky gök [gurk]

sleep (verb) uyumak
[oo-yoom**ak**]
did you sleep well? iyi
uyudunuz mu?
[oo-yoodoon**ooz**]

sleeper (on train) yataklı vagon
[yatakl**uh**]

sleeping bag uyku tulumu
[oo-ik**oo**]

sleeping car yataklı vagon
[yatakl**uh**]

sleeping pill uyku hapı [oo-ik**oo**
hap**uh**]

sleepy: I'm feeling sleepy
uyk**u**m geldi

sleeve kol

slide (photographic) diya

slip (garment) kombinez**on**

slippers terlik

slippery kaygan [kīg**a**n]

slow yavaş [yav**a**sh]
slow down! (driving, speaking)
yavaşla!

slowly yavaşça [yav**a**sh-cha]
very slowly çok yavaş [chok]

small küçük [kewch**ew**k]

smell: it smells (smells bad) kötü
kokuyor [kurt**ew**]

smile (verb) gülümsemek
[gewlewm-sem**e**k]

smoke (noun) duman
do you mind if I smoke?
izninizle sigara içebilir
miyim? [–l**eh** – eechebeel**eer**]
I don't smoke ben sigara
kullanmıyorum
[kooll**a**nmuh–]
do you smoke? sigara içiyor
musun**uz**? [eechee-y**or**]

snack hafif yemek, meze
[mez**eh**]
just a snack yalnız hafif bir
şeyler [yaln**uh**z – shayl**er**]

Many workers start the morning
with a **börek**, a rich, flaky,
layered pastry containing bits of
mince or cheese; these are sold
either at a tiny **büfe** (stall-café)
or from street carts. Others
content themselves with a
simple **simit** (bread rings
speckled with sesame seeds) or
a bowl of **çorba** (soup) with
lemon.
Later in the day, vendors hawk
lahmacun, small, round Arab-
→

style pizzas with a thin meat-based topping. Also available are sandwiches (**sandviç**) with various fillings (spicy sausage, cheese, **kokoreç** offal, or fish). In coastal cities **midye tava** (deep-fried mussels) are often available, as are **midye dolması** (mussels stuffed with rice, pine nuts and allspice). At lunchtime you can buy **pide**, Turkish pizza – flat bread with various toppings, served in a **pideci** or **pide salonu**.

sneeze (noun) hapşırık [hapshuh**ruh**k]
snorkel şnorkel [shn**o**rkel]
snow (noun) kar
  it's snowing kar yağıyor [ya-uh-y**o**r]
so: it's so good! öyle iyi ki! [uh-il**eh**]
  it's so expensive! öyle pahalı ki!
  not so much o kad**a**r çok değil [chok deh-**ee**l]
  not so bad pek kötü değil [kurt**ew**]
  so am I ben de öyle [deh]
  so do I ben de
  so-so şöyle böyle [sh**uh**-**i**leh b**uh**-**i**leh]
soaking solution (for contact lenses) koruyucu sıvı [koroo-yooj**oo** suhv**uh**]
soap sabun
soap powder sabun tozu

sober ayık [ī-**uh**k]
sock çorap [ch**o**rap]
socket (electrical) priz
soda (water) maden sodası [sodas**uh**]
sofa divan
soft (material etc) yumuşak [yoomoosh**a**k]
soft-boiled egg rafadan yumurta
soft drink alkolsüz içecek [alkols**ew**z eechej**e**k], meşrubat [meshroob**a**t]
soft lenses yumuşak kontak lensleri [yoomoosh**a**k]
sole (of shoe, of foot) taban
  could you put new soles on these? bunlara pençe yapar mısınız? [pench**eh** – muhsuhn**uh**z]
some: can I have some water? biraz su alabilir miyim?
  can I have some biscuits? birkaç bisküvi alabilir miyim? [beerk**a**ch]
  can I have some? biraz alabilir miyim?
somebody, someone birisi
something bir şey [shay]
something to eat yiyecek bir şey [yee-yej**e**k]
sometimes bazen
somewhere bir yerde [beer yerd**eh**]
son oğul [o-**oo**l]
song şarkı [shark**uh**]
son-in-law damat
soon yakında [yakuhnd**a**]
  I'll be back soon birazdan

dönerim
  as soon as possible en kısa
  zamanda [kuhsa]
sore: it's sore acıyor [ajuh-yor]
sore throat boğaz ağrısı [bo-az
  a-ruhsuh]
sorry: (I'm) sorry özür dilerim
  [urzewr]
  sorry? (didn't hear etc) efendim?
sort: what sort of ...? ne tür ...?
  [neh tewr]
soup çorba [chorba]
sour (taste) ekşi [ekshee]
south güney [gewnay]
  in the south güneyde
  [gewnaydeh]
South Africa Güney Afrika
South African (adj) Güney
  Afrika
  I'm South African Güney
  Afrikalıyım [–luh-yuhm]
southeast güney doğu [doh-oo]
southwest güney batı [batuh]
souvenir hatıra [hahtuhra]
Spain İspanya [eespanya]
Spanish (adj, person) İspanyol
  (language) İspanyolca
  [eespanyolja]
spanner somun anahtarı
  [anaHtaruh]
spare part yedek parça [parcha]
spare tyre yedek lastik
spark plug buji [boojee]
speak: do you speak English?
  İngilizce biliyor musunuz?
  [eengeeleezjeh]
  I don't speak ...
  ... bilmiyorum
  can I speak to ...? ... ile

görüşebilir miyim? [eeleh
  gurew-shebeeleer]

•••••• DIALOGUE ••••••

can I speak to Sinan? Sinan'la
  görüşebilir miyim?
  [gurewshebeeleer]
who's calling? kim arıyor? [aruh-
  yor]
it's Patricia Patricia
I'm sorry, he's not in, can I take a
  message? üzgünüm evde değil,
  mesaj alabilir miyim?
  [ewzgewnewm evdeh deh-eel
  mesaj]
no thanks, I'll call back later hayır
  teşekkür ederim, ben sonra
  tekrar ararım [hī-uhr teshekkewr
  – araruhm]
please tell him I called lütfen
  aradığımı söyleyin [lewtfen
  araduh-uhmuh suh-ilayeen]

spectacles gözlük [gurzlewk]
speed (noun) hız [huhz]
speed limit azami hız
speedometer hızölçer
  [huhzurlcher]
spell: how do you spell it? nasıl
  yazılıyor? [nasuhl yazuhluh-
  yor]
  see alphabet
spend harcamak [harjamak]
spider örümcek [urewmjek]
spin-dryer santrifüjlü kurutma
  makinesi [santreefewJlew]
splinter kıymık [kuh-imuhk]
spoke (in wheel) jant [Jant]
spoon kaşık [kashuhk]
sport spor

sprain: I've sprained my ... ...-m
burkuldu
spring (season) ilkbahar
(of car, seat) yay [yī]
square (in town) meydan
[maydan]
stairs merdiven
stale bayat [bī-at]
stall: the engine keeps stalling
motor sık sık duruyor [suhk]
stamp (noun) pul

•••••• DIALOGUE ••••••

a stamp for England, please
İngiltere'ye bir pul, lütfen
[eengeeltereh-yeh – lewtfen]
what are you sending? ne
gönderiyorsunuz? [gurnderee-
yorsoonooz]
this postcard bu kartpostalı
[–postaluh]

Stamps are only available from
the PTT (post and telephone
office).

standby yedek, standby
star yıldız [yuhlduhz]
(in film) film yıldızı
start (noun) başlangıç
[bashlanguhch]
(verb) başlamak [bashlamak]
when does it start? ne zaman
başlayacak? [neh – bashlī-
ajak]
the car won't start araba
çalışmıyor [chaluhshmuh-yor]
starter (of car) marş [marsh]
(food) ordövr [ordurvr], meze

[mezeh]
starving: I'm starving çok
acıktım [chok ajuhktuhm]
state (country) devlet
the States (USA) Birleşik
Amerika [beerlesheek]
station istasyon
statue heykel [haykel]
stay: where are you staying?
nerede kalıyorsunuz?
[neredeh kaluh-yorsoonooz]
I'm staying at ... ...-de
kalıyorum [-deh kaluh-
yoroom]
I'd like to stay another two
nights iki gece daha kalmak
istiyorum [gejeh]
steak biftek
steal çalmak [chalmak]
my bag has been stolen
çantam çalındı [chantam
chaluhnduh]
steep (hill) dik
steering direksiyon sistemi
step: on the steps merdivende
[merdeevendeh]
stereo stereo
sterling sterlin
steward (on plane) kabin
memuru
stewardess hostes
sticky tape seloteyp [selotayp]
sticking plaster flaster, yara
bandı [banduh]
still: I'm still here hâlâ
buradayım [hala booradī-uhm]
is he/she still there? hâlâ
orada mı? [muh]
keep still! kımıldamayın!

[kuhmuhl-damī-uhn]
sting: I've been stung beni
böcek soktu [burjek]
stockings çoraplar [choraplar]
stomach mide [meedeh]
stomach ache mide ağrısı
[a-ruhsuh]
stone (rock) taş [tash]
stop (verb) durmak
  please, stop here (to taxi driver
  etc) lütfen, burada durun
  [lewtfen]
  do you stop
  near ...? ... yakınında
  duruyor musunuz?
  [yakuhnuhnda]
  stop it! kes (artık)! [artuhk]
stopover ara durak
storm fırtına [fuhrtuhna]
straight (whisky etc) sek
  it's straight ahead dümdüz
  ilerde [dewmdewz eelerdeh]
straightaway hemen şimdi
  [sheemdee]
strange (odd) acayip [ajī-eep]
stranger yabancı [yabanjuh]
  I'm a stranger here buranın
  yabancısıyım [booranuhn
  –suh-uhm]
strap (on watch, suitcase) kayış
  [kī-uhsh]
  (on dress) askı [askuh]
strawberry çilek [cheelek]
stream dere [dereh]
street sokak
  on the street sokakta
streetmap şehir planı [sheheer
  planuh]
string ip

strong (person) güçlü [gewchlew]
  (drink) sert
stuck: it's stuck sıkıştı
  [suhkuhshtuh]
student öğrenci [ur-renjee]
stupid aptal
subway (US) metro
suburb banliyö [banlee-yur]
suddenly aniden
suede süet [sewet]
sugar şeker [sheker]
sugared almonds badem şekeri
suit (man's) takım elbise
  [takuhm elbeeseh]
  (woman's) tayyör [tī-ur]
  it doesn't suit me (jacket etc)
  bana yakışmıyor
  [yakuhshmuh-yor]
  it suits you size yakışıyor
  [seezeh yakuhshuh-yor]
suitcase bavul
summer yaz
  in the summer yazın [yazuhn]
sun güneş [gewnesh]
  in the sun güneşte
  [gewneshteh]
  out of the sun gölgede
  [gurlgedeh]
sunbathe güneş banyosu
  yapmak
sunblock (cream) güneş
  merhemi [gewnesh]
sunburn güneş yanığı
  [yanuh-uh]
sunburnt güneşte yanmış
  [gewneshteh yanmuhsh]
Sunday pazar
sunglasses güneş gözlüğü
  [gewnesh gurzlew-ew]

sun lounger şezlong [shezlong]

sunny: it's sunny hava güneşli [gewneshlee]

sunroof (in car) güneşlik [gewneshleek], sunroof

sunset günbatımı [gewnbatuhmuh]

sunshade gölgelik [gurlgeleek], güneş şemsiyesi [gewnesh shemsee-yesee]

sunshine güneş ışığı [uhshuh-uh]

sunstroke güneş çarpması [charpmasuh]

suntan bronz ten

suntan lotion güneş losyonu [gewnesh los-yonoo]

suntanned bronzlaşmış [bronzlashmuhsh]

suntan oil güneş yağı [gewnesh ya-uh]

super fevkalade [fevkaladeh]

supermarket süpermarket [sewpermarket]

supper akşam yemeği [aksham yemeh-ee]

supplement (extra charge) ek ücret [ewjret]

sure: are you sure? emin misiniz?

sure! tabii! [tabee-ee]

surfboard sörf tahtası [surf tahtasuh]

surname soyadı

swearword küfür [kewfewr]

sweater kazak

sweatshirt svetşört [svetshurt]

Sweden İsveç [eesvech]

Swedish (adj) İsveç

(language) İsveççe [eesvech-cheh]

sweet (dessert) tatlı [tatluh]

it's too sweet fazla tatlı

sweets şeker [sheker]

swelling şişlik [sheeshleek]

swim (verb) yüzmek [yewzmek]

I'm going for a swim yüzmeye gidiyorum [yewzmayeh]

let's go for a swim hadi yüzmeye gidelim

swimming costume mayo [mī-o]

swimming pool yüzme havuzu [yewzmeh]

swimming trunks mayo [mī-o]

switch (noun) elektrik düğmesi [dewmesee]

switch off kapamak

switch on açmak [achmak]

swollen şişmiş [sheeshmeesh]

Syria Suriye [sooree-yeh]

T

table masa

a table for two iki kişilik bir masa [keesheeleek]

tablecloth masa örtüsü [urtewsew]

table tennis masatopu

table wine sofra şarabı [sharabuh]

tailback (of traffic) taşıt kuyruğu [tashuht koo-iroo-00]

tailor terzi

take (verb: lead) götürmek [gurtewmek]

(accept) almak

(room etc) tutmak

can you take me to the ...?
beni ...-'e götürür müsünüz?
[-eh gurtew-**rewr**
mewsewn**ewz**]

do you take credit cards? kredi
kartı kabul ediyor
musun**uz**? [kart**uh**]

fine, I'll take it tam**am**,
alıyorum [al**uh**-y**o**room]

(room) tam**am**, tut**u**yorum

can I take this? (leaflet etc)
bun**u** alabil**ir** miy**im**?

how long does it take? ne
kadar sürer? [neh – sewr**er**]

it takes three hours üç saat
sürer [ewch sa-**at**]

is this seat taken? bu yerin
sahi**b**i var mı? [muh]

hamburger to take away pak**et**
hamburger

can you take a little off here?
(to hairdresser) burad**an** bir**az**
alır mısınız? [al**uhr**
muhsuhn**uhz**]

talcum powder talk pudrası
[tahlk poodras**uh**]

talk (verb) konuşmak
[konooshm**ak**]

tall (person) uzun boyl**u**
(building) yüksek [yewks**e**k]

tampons tamp**on**

tan (noun) bronz ten
to get a tan güneşte yanmak
[gewnesht**eh**], bronzlaşmak
[bronzlashm**ak**]

tank (of car) depo

tap musluk

tape (for cassette) teyp [tayp]

tape measure şerit metre
[sh**e**ret metr**eh**], mezür
[mez**ewr**]

tape recorder teyp [tayp]

taste (noun) tat
can I taste it? tadına bakabil**ir**
miy**im**? [tad**uh**n**a**]

taxi taksi
will you get me a taxi? bana
bir taksi bul**ur** musunuz?
where can I find a taxi?
nerede bir taksi bulabilirim?
[n**e**redeh]

•••••• DIALOGUE ••••••

to the airport/to the ... Hotel, please
havaalanına/Hotel ...-'e, lütfen
[hava-alan**uh**na – ...-eh l**e**wtfen]

how much will it be? ne kadar
tut**ar**? [neh]

250,000 lira iki yüz elli bin lira

that's fine right here, thanks tam**am**
burası iyi, teşekkürler [booras**uh**
– teshekkewrl**er**]

Yellow city taxis are everywhere,
and ranks crop up at
appropriate places, though in
rush hour finding a free cab can
be difficult. Hailing one in the
street is the best way to find a
cab, but in suburban areas
there are useful street corner
telephones from which you can
call cabs if you can make
yourself understood. Urban
vehicles all have working,
digital-display meters, and fares
are among the lowest in the
→

Mediterranean. Out in the country, you'll have to bargain. A Turkish institution is the **dolmuş** or shared transport. This is a car or minibus which runs along set routes, picking passengers up and dropping them off along the way. To stop a dolmuş, give a hand signal as for a normal taxi, and if there's any room at all, they'll stop and let you on. Generally dolmuşes run between 7 or 8 a.m. and 7 p.m. in summer, stopping earlier to match the hour of sunset in winter or extending until 10 or 11 p.m. near popular resorts. Dolmuşes do not operate to a timetable but leave when they are full or when there is hope of picking up passengers en-route.

tea is decanted into tiny tulip-shaped glasses, then diluted with more water to taste: **açık** [ach**uh**k] is weak, **demli** or **koyu** strong. Sugar comes as cubes on the side; milk is never added. If you're frustrated by the usual tiny glass at breakfast, ask for a **düble çay** [**dew**bleh] (a 'double', served in a juice glass).
Herbal teas are also popular in Turkey, particularly **ıhlamur** [uhHlam**oor**] (linden flower) and **ada çayı** [ch**ī**-uh] ('island' tea), an infusion of a type of sage. The much-touted **elma çayı** (apple tea) in fact contains only chemicals and not a trace of apple essence.

taxi-driver taksi şoförü [shofur**ew**]
taxi rank taksi durağı [door**a**-uh]
tea (drink) çay [ch**ī**]
  tea for one/two, please bir/iki çay, lütfen [l**ew**tfen]

Tea is the national drink and is properly prepared in a double-boiler apparatus, with a larger water chamber underneath the smaller receptacle (**demlik**) containing dry leaves, to which a small quantity of hot water is added. After a suitable wait the →

teabags torb**a** çay
teach: could you teach me? ban**a** öğretir misini**z**? [ur-ret**ee**r]
teacher öğretmen [ur-retm**e**n]
team ekip
  (sporting) takım [tak**uh**m]
teaspoon çay kaşığı [ch**ī** kashuh-**uh**]
tea towel kurul**a**ma bez**i**
teenager (male/female) delikanlı [deleekanl**uh**], genç kız [gench kuhz]
telegram telgr**af**
telephone tel**efo**n
  see **phone**
television televizy**o**n

tell: could you tell him/her ...?
ona ...-i söyler misiniz? [suh-
iler]
temperature (weather) sıcaklık
[suhjakl**uhk**]
(fever) ateş [at**e**sh]
temple tapınak [tapuhn**a**k]
tennis tenis
tennis ball tenis top**u**
tennis court tenis kort**u**
tennis racket tenis raket**i**
tent çadır [chad**uhr**]
term (at university, school) dönem
[durn**e**m]
terminus (rail) son istasy**o**n
terrible berb**a**t
terrific müthiş [mewt-h**ee**sh]
than* -den
smaller than -den küçük
[kewch**e**wk]
thank: thank you teşekkür
ederim [teshekk**e**wr]
thanks teşekkürler
[teshekkewrl**e**r]
thank you very much çok
teşekkür ederim [chok]
thanks for the lift arabanıza
aldığınız için teşekkür
ederim [–nuhz**a** alduh-uhn**uh**z]
no thanks hayır, teşekkür
ederim [h**ı**-uhr]

•••••• DIALOGUE ••••••

thanks teşekkürler
don't mention it bir şey değil [shay
deh-**ee**l]

that*: that rug (nearby) şu kilim
[shoo]
(further away) o kilim

that one (nearby) şu
(further away) o
I hope that ... umarım ki ...
[oomar**uh**m]
that's nice o iy**i**
is that ...? şu ... mı? [muh]
that's it (that's right) tam**a**m
işte [eesht**e**h]
the*
theatre tiyatro
their* onların -leri [onlar**uh**n]
theirs* onlar**ı**nk**i**
them* onları [onlar**uh**]
for them onlar için [eech**ee**n]
with them onlarla
to them onlar**a**
who? – them kim? – onl**a**r
then (at that time) o zam**a**n
(after that) s**o**nra
there or**a**da
over there şurada [sh**oo**rada],
or**a**da
up there yukarıda
[yook**a**ruhda]
is there/are there ...? ... var
mı? [muh]
there is/there are ... ... var
there you are (giving something)
buyrun [b**oo**-iroon]
thermal spring kaplıca
[kapluhj**a**]
thermometer termometre
[termom**e**treh]
thermos flask term**o**s
these*: these men/women bu
adaml**a**r/kadınl**a**r
I'd like these bunları
isti**y**orum [boonlar**uh**]
they* onl**a**r

thick kalın [kaluhn]
(stupid) kalın kafalı [kafaluh]
thief hırsız [huhrsuhz]
thigh but [boot]
thin ince [eenjeh]
thing şey [shay]
my things benim eşyam [esh-yam]
think düşünmek [dewshewnmek]
I think so bence öyle [benjeh uh-ileh]
I don't think so bence öyle değil [deh-eel]
I'll think about it düşüneceğim [dewshewnejeh-eem]
third party insurance mecburi trafik sigortası [mejbooree – seegortasuh]
thirsty: I'm thirsty susadım [soosaduhm]
this: this rug bu kilim
this one bu
this is my wife bu eşim [esheem]
is this ...? bu ... mi?
those*: those men (nearby) şu adamlar [shoo]
(further away) o adamlar
which ones? – those hangileri? – şunlar [shoonlar]
thread (noun) iplik
throat boğaz [bo-az]
throat pastilles boğaz pastilleri
through içinden [eecheenden]
does it go through ...? (train, bus) ...-den geçiyor mu? [gechee-yor]
throw (verb) atmak, fırlatmak [fuhrlatmak]

throw away (verb) atmak
thumb başparmak [bashparmak]
thunderstorm gök gürültülü fırtına [gurk gewrewltewlew fuhrtuhna]
Thursday perşembe [pershembeh]
ticket bilet

•••••• DIALOGUE ••••••

a return to İzmir İzmir'e bir gidiş-dönüş [eezmeer-eh beer geedeesh-durnewsh]
coming back when? dönüş ne zaman?
today/next Tuesday bugün/gelecek salı
that will be 200,000 lira iki yüz bin lira ediyor

ticket office (bus, rail) bilet gişesi [geeshesee]
tide gel-git olayı [olī-uh]
tie (necktie) kravat
tight (clothes etc) dar
it's too tight fazla dar
tights külotlu çorap [kewlotloo chorap]
till (cash desk) kasa
time* zaman
what's the time? saat kaç? [sa-at kach]
this time bu sefer
last time geçen sefer [gechen]
next time gelecek sefer [gelejek]
three times üç kez
timetable tarife [tareefeh]
tin (can) konserve kutusu [konserveh]

tinfoil alüminyum folyo
[alewmeen-yoom]

tin-opener konserve açacağı
[konserveh achaja-uh]

tiny minik

tip (to waiter etc) bahşiş
[baH-sheesh]

Restaurants usually add a
service charge to the bill, but if
it is not included in the price it
is customary to leave a tip of
10-15%. Taxi drivers do not
expect tips but you can round
off the fare to a suitable
amount. It is customary to put
something in the pockets of
barbers and hairdressers (10-
15%).

---

tired yorgun [yorgoon]
I'm tired yorgunum
[yorgoonoom]

tissues kâğıt mendil [ka-uht]

to: ⓦ Bursa/London Bursa'ya/
Londra'ya [londrī-a]
to Turkey/England Türkiye'ye/
İngiltere'ye [tewrkee-yeh-yeh/
eengheeltereh-yeh]
to the post office postaneye
[postanayeh]

toast (bread) kızarmış ekmek
[kuhzarmuhsh]

today bugün [boogewn]

toe ayak parmağı [ī-ak
parma-uh]

together beraber
we're together (in shop etc)
beraberiz

toilet tuvalet [toovalet]
where is the toilet? tuvalet
nerede? [neredeh]
I have to go to the toilet
tuvalete gitmem lazım
[toovaleteh – lahzuhm]

Except in the fancier resort
hotels and restaurants, most
public toilets are of the
squathole variety, found either
in public parks or (more
infallibly) next to any mosque.
Keep small coins handy for the
custodian. Keep a supply of
toilet paper with you (available
in Turkey) – Turks wash
themselves off either with the
bidet-spout or the special vessel
filled from the handy floor-level
tap.

---

toilet paper tuvalet kâğıdı
[ka-uhduh]

tomato domates

tomato juice domates suyu

tomato ketchup ketçap
[ketchap]

tomorrow yarın [yaruhn]
tomorrow morning yarın
sabah [sabaH]
the day after tomorrow öbür
gün [urbewr gewn]

toner (cosmetic) toner

tongue dil

tonic (water) tonik

tonight bu gece [gejeh]

tonsillitis bademcik iltihabı
[bademjeek eelteehabuh]

too (excessively) fazla
(also) de [deh]
  too hot fazla sıcak
  too much çok fazla [chok]
  me too ben de [deh]
tooth diş [deesh]
toothache diş ağrısı [a-ruhs**uh**]
toothbrush diş fırçası
[fuhrchas**uh**]
toothpaste diş macunu
[majoon**oo**]
top: on top of ... ...-in üstünde
[ewstewnd**eh**]
  at the top en üstte [ewstt**eh**]
  at the top of ... ...-in en
  üstünde
top floor üst kat [ewst]
topless göğüsleri açık [gur-
ewsler**ee** ach**uh**k], üstsüz
[ewsts**ewz**]
torch el feneri
total (noun) toplam
tour (noun) tur
  is there a tour of ...? ... tur**u**
  var mı? [muh]
tour guide rehber
tourist turist
tourist information office turizm
danışma bürosu [danuhshm**a**
bewros**oo**]
tour operator tur operatörü
[operatur**ew**]
towards -e doğru [-eh doh-
r**oo**]
towel havlu
tower kule [kool**eh**]
town kasaba
  in town şehirde [sheheerd**eh**]
  just out of town şehrin

hemen dışında [sheh**ree**n –
duhshuhnd**a**]
town centre şehir merkezi
town hall belediye binası
[beledee-y**eh**]
toy oyuncak [o-yoonj**ak**]
track (US) per**o**n
tracksuit eşofman [eshofm**an**]
traditional geleneksel
traffic trafik
traffic jam trafik tıkanıklığı
[tuhkanuhkl**uh**-uh]
traffic lights trafik ışıkları
[uhshuhk-lar**uh**]
trailer (for carrying tent etc) römork
[rurm**ork**], trayler [tr**ī**ler]
(US) karav**a**n
trailer park kamp**i**ng
train tren
  by train trenle [tr**e**nleh]

> Turkey's train network is far
> from exhaustive and it's best
> used to span the distances
> between the three main ci.es
> and the provincial centres.
> Trains often follow tortuous
> routes and may take up to
> twice as long as buses. They
> do, however, have the advantage
> of additional comfort at
> comparable or lower prices.
> The better services, west of
> Ankara, called mavi tren or
> ekspres, almost match long-
> distance buses in speed and
> frequency. Avoid any departure
> labelled posta (mail train) or
> →

yolcu (local) as they're very slow. On major train routes it's a good idea to make a reservation. You can do this for any journey in the country in İstanbul, İzmir and Ankara. On long-haul journeys you have a choice between a first- and second-class seat. There are fare reductions for students, return tickets and groups.

•••••• DIALOGUE ••••••

is this the train for Ankara? bu Ankara treni mi?

sure tabi

no, you want that platform there hayır, sizin şu öbür perona gitmeniz lazım [hı-**uh**r – shoo ewb**ew**r – laz**uh**m]

trainers (shoes) spor ayakkabısı [ı-akkabuh**suh**]
train station tren istasyonu
tram tramvay [tramv**ı**]
translate tercüme etmek [terjewm**eh**]
could you translate that? bun**u** tercüme edebilir misiniz?
translation tercüme
translator tercüm**a**n
trash çöp [churp]
trashcan çöp tenekes**i**
travel seyahat [sayah**a**t]
we're travelling around geziy**o**ruz
travel agent's seyahat acentası [sayah**a**t ajentas**uh**]
traveller's cheque seyahat çek**i**

[chek**ee**]
see **cheque**
tray teps**i**
tree ağaç [a-**a**ch]
tremendous muazzam [moo-azz**a**m]
trendy (restaurant, club) şık [shuhk], mod**a**
(clothes) modaya uygun [mod**ı**-a oo-ig**oo**n]
(person) şık [shuhk]
trim: just a trim please (to hairdresser) lütfen yalnız uçlarından biraz alın [l**ew**tfen yaln**uh**z oochlaruhnd**a**n – al**uh**n]
trip (excursion) yolculuk [yoljool**oo**k]
I'd like to go on a trip to ... bir ... gezisi yapmak istiy**o**rum
trolley el arabası [arabas**uh**]
trolleybus troleybüs [trolaybe**ws**]
trouble (noun) dert
I'm having trouble with ... ... ile başım dertte [eel**eh** bash**uh**m dertt**eh**]
trousers pantol**o**n
Troy Truv**a**
true gerçek [gerch**e**k]
that's not true o doğru değil [doh-r**oo** deh-**ee**l]
trunk (US) bagaj [baga**ᴊ**]
trunks (swimming) mayo [m**ı**-o]
try (verb) denemek
can I have a try? (at doing something) bir deneyebilir miyim? [denayebeel**eer**]

try on prova etmek
  can I try it on? üstümde
  deneyebilir miyim?
  [ewstewmd**eh** denayebeel**eer**]
T-shirt tişört [tee-sh**urt**]
Tuesday salı [sal**uh**]
tuna ton balığı [bal**uh**-uh]
tunnel tünel [tewn**el**]
Turk Türk [tewrk]
Turkey Türkiye [t**e**wrkee-yeh]
Turkish (adj) Türk
  (language) Türkçe [tewrkch**eh**]
Turkish bath hamam

Virtually all Turkish towns of
any size have at least one
hamam per neighbourhood.
Baths are usually signposted,
but if in doubt look for the
distinctive external profile of
the roof domes, visible from the
street. Baths are either
permanently designated for
men or women, or sexually
segregated on a schedule – look
for the words erkekler (men)
and kadınlar (women), followed
by a time range written on a
placard by the door.
On entering, you will usually
leave your valuables in a small
drawer, the key of which (often
on a wrist/ankle thong) you
keep with you for the duration
of your wash. Bring soap,
shampoo and a shaving mirror
– these are either not supplied
or are expensive; the basic →

admission charge varies
depending on the level of
luxury.
Men will be supplied with a
peştamal, a thin, wraparound
sarong; both sexes get takunya,
wooden clogs, and later a havlu
or proper drying towel.

Turkish coffee Türk kahvesi
  [tewrk kaHv**e**see]
Turkish Cypriot (adj) Kıbrıs Türk
  [k**uh**bruhs]
  (person) Kıbrıslı Türk
  [kuhbr**uh**sluh]
Turkish delight lokum
Turkish wrestling yağlı güreş
  [ya-l**uh** gewr**e**sh]
turn: turn left/right sola/sağa
  dönün [durn**ew**n]
turn off: where do I turn off?
  nereden sapmalıyım? [–luh-
  yuhm]
  can you turn the heating off?
  kaloriferi kapatabilir
  misiniz?
turn on: can you turn the heating
  on? kaloriferi yakabilir
  misiniz?
turning (in road) sapak
TV TV [tee vee]
tweezers cımbız [juhmb**uh**z]
twice iki kez
  twice as much iki misli
  [meesl**ee**]
twin beds çift yatak [cheeft]
twin room çift yataklı oda
  [yatakl**uh**]

twist: I've twisted my ankle ayak
   bileğimi burktum [ī-ak
   beeleh-eemee]
type (noun) tip [teep]
   another type of ... başka tip
   bir ... [bashka]
typical tipik
tyre lastik

U

ugly çirkin [cheerkeen]
UK Birleşik Krallık [beerlesheek
   kralluhk]
ulcer ülser [ewlser]
umbrella şemsiye [shemsee-yeh]
uncle amca [amja]
unconscious baygın [bīguhn]
under: under
   the ... (position) ...-in altında
   [altuhnda]
   (less than) ...-den az
underdone (meat) az pişmiş
   [peeshmeesh]
underground (railway) metro
underpants külot [kewlot]
understand: I understand
   anlıyorum [anluh-yoroom]
   I don't understand
   anlamıyorum [anlamuh-
   yuhoroom]
   do you understand? anlıyor
   musunuz? [anluh-yor]
unemployed işsiz [eesh-seez]
United States Birleşik Amerika
   [beerlesheek]
university üniversite [ewnee-
   verseeteh]
unleaded petrol kurşunsuz

benzin [koorshoonsooz]
unlimited mileage kilometre
   kısıtlamasız [keelometreh
   kuhsuhtlamasuhz]
unlock kilidi açmak [achmak]
unpack eşyaları bavuldan
   çıkarmak [esh-yalaruh –
   chuhkarmak]
until -e kadar [-eh]
unusual alışılmamış
   [aluhshuhl-mamuhsh]
up yukarı [yookaruh]
   up there yukarıda
   [yookaruhda]
   he's not up yet (not out of bed)
   daha kalkmadı [kalkmaduh]
   what's up? (what's wrong?) ne
   oldu? [neh oldoo]
upmarket sükseli [sewkselee]
upset stomach mide bozukluğu
   [meedeh bozookloo-oo]
upside down baş aşağı [bash
   asha-uh]
upstairs üst katta [ewst]
urgent acil [ajeel]
us* bizi
   with us bizimle [beezeemleh]
   for us bizim için [eecheen]
USA ABD [a beh deh]
use (verb) kullanmak
   may I use ...? ...-i kullanabilir
   miyim?
useful yararlı [yararluh]
usual olağan [ola-an]
   the usual (drink etc) her
   zamanki

V

vacancy: do you have any
  vacancies? (hotel) boş odanız
  var mı? [bosh odan**uh**z var
  muh]
  see room
vacation tatil
  on vacation tatilde [tateeld**eh**]
vaccination aşılama [ashuhlam**a**]
vacuum cleaner elektrik
  süpürgesi [sewpewrges**ee**]
valid (ticket etc) geçerli
  [gecherl**ee**]
  how long is it valid for? ne
  zaman**a** kad**a**r geçerli? [neh]
valley vadi
valuable (adj) değerli
  [deh-erl**ee**]
  can I leave my valuables here?
  değerli eşyalarımı bur**a**da
  bırakabilir miy**i**m? [esh-
  yalaruhm**uh** – buhraka-beel**ee**r]
value (noun) değer [deh-**er**]
van kamyonet
vanilla vanilya
  a vanilla ice cream vanily**a**lı
  dondurma [vaneel-yal**uh**]
vary: it varies değişir [deh-
  eesh**ee**r]
vase vazo
veal dana eti
vegetables sebze [sebz**eh**]
vegetarian (noun) etyem**e**z
vending machine otom**a**t
very çok [chok]
  very big çok b**ü**yük
  very little for me ban**a** azıcık
  [azuhj**uh**k]

I like it very much çok
  beğeniyorum [beh-enee-
  y**o**room]
vest (under shirt) fanil**a**
via üzerinden [ewzereend**en**]
video video
view manzara
villa villa
village köy [kuh-i]
vinegar sirke [seerk**eh**]
vineyard bağ [ba]
visa vize [v**ee**zeh]
visit (verb) ziyaret etmek
  I'd like to visit ... ...-i ziyaret
  etmek ister**i**m
vital: it's vital that ... ...-si şart
  [shart]
vodka votka
voice ses
voltage voltaj [volt**a**ʝ]

> The supply is 220V. British
> appliances need a 3-to-2-pin
> plug adaptor; North American
> ones both an adaptor and a
> transformer (except for dual
> voltage shavers, which need only
> the former).

vomit kusmak

W

waist bel
waistcoat yelek
wait (verb) beklemek
  wait for me beni bekleyin
  [beklay**ee**n]
  don't wait for me beni

beklemeyin [bekl**e**mayeen]
can I wait until my partner gets
here? eşim gelinceye kadar
bekleyebilir miyim? [esh**ee**m
geleenjay**eh** – beklayebeel**ee**r]
can you do it while I wait?
beklerken yapabilir misiniz?
could you wait here for me?
beni burada bekler misiniz?
waiter garson
  waiter! bakar mısınız!
  [muhsuhn**uh**z]
waitress garson kız [kuhz]
  waitress! bakar mısınız!
  [muhsuhn**uh**z]
wake: can you wake me up at
  5.30? beni beş buçukt**a**
  uyandırır mısınız?
  [oo-yanduhr**uh**r muhsuhn**uh**z]
wake-up call telefonl**a**
  uyandırma [oo-yanduhrm**a**]
Wales Galler
walk: is it a long walk?
  yürüyerek uzak mıdır?
  [yewrew-yer**e**k – m**uh**duhr]
  it's only a short walk
  yürüyerek çok yakın [chok
  yak**uh**n]
  I'll walk yürüyeceğim [yewrew-
  yejeh-**ee**m]
  I'm going for a walk ben
  yürüyüşe çıkıyorum [yewrew-
  yewsh**eh** chuhkuh-y**o**room]
Walkman® walkman®
wall duvar
wallet cüzdan [jewzd**a**n]
wander: I like just wandering
  around amaçsızca dolaşmayı
  severim [amachsuhzj**a**

dolashmī-**uh**]
want: I want
  a ... bir ... istiyorum
  I don't want any ...
  ... istemiyorum
  I want to go home eve gitmek
  istiyorum [ev**eh**]
  I don't want to ...
  ...-mek istemiyorum
  he wants to ... ...-mek istiyor
  what do you want? ne
  istiyorsunuz? [neh]
ward (in hospital) koğuş
  [ko-**oo**sh]
warm sıcak [suhj**a**k]
  I'm so warm sıcak bastı
  [bast**uh**]
was*: he/she/it was -di
wash (verb) yıkamak
  [yuhkam**a**k]
  can you wash these? bunları
  yıkayabilir misiniz?
  [boonlar**uh** yuhkī-abeel**ee**r]
washer (for bolt etc) rondela
washhand basin lav**a**bo
washing (clothes) çamaşır
  [chamash**uh**r]
washing machine çamaşır
  makinesi
washing powder çamaşır tozu
washing-up liquid deterjan
  [deterj**a**n]
wasp eşek arısı [esh**e**k aruhs**uh**]
watch (wristwatch) saat [sa-**a**t]
  will you watch my things for
  me? eşyalarıma göz kulak
  olur musunuz? [esh-
  yalaruhm**a** gurz]
watch out! dikkat!

---

watch strap saat kayışı [sa-at kī-uhsh**uh**]

water su
  may I have some water? bir**az** su ver**ir** misin**iz**?

water pipe nargile [nargeel**eh**]

waterproof (adj) su geçirmez [gecheerm**ez**]

waterskiing su kayağı [kī-**a**-uh]

wave (in sea) dal**ga**

way: it's this way bu taraftan
  it's that way şu taraftan [shoo]
  is it a long way to ...? ... buraya uzak mı? [b**oo**rī-a – muh]
  no way! katiyen olm**az**! [katee-y**en**]

•••••• DIALOGUE ••••••

could you tell me the way to ...? ...-e nereden gidilir söyleyebilir misiniz? [-eh – suh-ilayebeel**eer**]

go straight on until you reach the traffic lights trafik ışıklarına kadar dümdüz gidin [uhsh**uh**klaruhn**a** – dewmd**ewz**]

turn left sola dönün [durn**ewn**]

take the first on the right sağdan ilk yola sapın [sa-d**an** – sap**uh**n]

see where

we* biz

weak (person) zayıf [zī-**uh**f], güçsüz [g**ew**chsewz]
  (drink) hafif
  (tea) açık [ach**uh**k]

weather hav**a**

•••••• DIALOGUE ••••••

what's the weather forecast? hava raporu nasıl? [n**a**suhl]

it's going to be fine hava güzel olacak [gewz**el** olaj**ak**]

it's going to rain yağmur yağacak [ya-m**oor** ya-aj**ak**]

it'll brighten up later sonra hava açacak [achaj**ak**]

wedding düğün [dew-**ewn**]

wedding ring alyans

Wednesday çarşamba [charsh**a**mba]

week haft**a**
  a week (from) today haftaya bugün [haftī-**a** boog**ewn**]
  a week (from) tomorrow yarından itibaren bir hafta sonra [yaruhnd**an**]

weekend hafta son**u**
  at the weekend hafta sonun**da**

weight ağırlık [a-uhrl**uh**k]

weird tuhaf [tooh**af**]

weirdo kaçık [kach**uh**k]

welcome: welcome to ... ...-e hoş geldiniz [-**eh** hosh]
  you're welcome (don't mention it) bir şey değil [shay deh-**eel**]

well: I don't feel well kendimi iyi hissetmiyorum
  he/she's not well iyi değil [deh-**eel**]
  you speak English very well çok iyi İngilizce konuşuyorsunuz [chok – eengeel**ee**zjeh konooshoo-yorsoon**ooz**]

ENGLISH ✦ TURKISH | We

139

well done! aferin!

this one as well bu da

well well! (surprise) hayret!
[hīret]

•••••• DIALOGUE ••••••

how are you? nasılsınız?
[nasuhlsuhnuhz]

very well, thanks, and you? çok
iyiyim, teşekkür ederim, ya siz?
[chok – teshekkewr]

well-done (meat) iyi pişmiş
[peeshmeesh]

Welsh (adj) Galler

I'm Welsh Galliyim

were*: we were -dik

you were -diniz

they were -diler

west batı [batuh]

in the west batıda

West Indian (adj) Batı Hint
[batuh]

wet ıslak [uhslak]

what? ne? [neh]

what's that? o nedir?

what should I do? ne
yapsaydım? [yapsiduhm]

what a view! ne manzara!

what bus do I take? hangi
otobüse binmem lazım?
[lazuhm]

wheel tekerlek

wheelchair tekerlekli iskemle
[eeskemleh]

when? ne zaman?

when we get back biz
dönünce [dewnewnjeh]

when's the train/ferry? tren/
feribot kaçta? [kachta]

where? nerede? [neredeh]

I don't know where it is
nerede olduğunu
bilmiyorum [oldoo-oonoo]

•••••• DIALOGUE ••••••

where is the Topkapı museum?
Topkapı müzesi nerede?
[topkapuh mewzesee]

it's over there şurada [shoorada]

could you show me where it is on
the map? haritada yerini gösterir
misiniz? [gurstereer]

it's just here tam burada

see way

which: which bus? hangi
otobüs?

•••••• DIALOGUE ••••••

which one? hangisi?

that one şu [shoo]

this one? bu mu?

no, that one hayır, şu [hī-uhr]

while: while I'm here ben
buradayken [booradīken]

whisky viski

white beyaz [bayaz]

white wine beyaz şarap
[sharap]

who? kim?

who is it? kim o?

the man who … …-an adam

whole: the whole week bütün
hafta [bewtewn]

the whole lot hepsi

whose: whose is this? bu
kimin?

why? niçin? [neecheen]

why not? neden olmasın?

[olmas**uhn**]
wide geniş [gen**ee**sh]
wife hanım [han**uh**m]
will: will you do it for me? bun**u**
benim için yapar mısınız?
[eech**ee**n – muhsuhn**uh**z]
wind (noun) rüzgâr [r**ew**z**g**ar]
window (of house, car) pencere
[**pe**njereh]
(of shop) vit**r**in
near the window pencere**n**in
yakı**n**ında [yakuhnuhnd**a**]
in the window (of shop)
vitrinde [veetreend**eh**]
window seat pencere yanı
[yan**uh**]
windscreen araba ön camı [urn
jam**uh**]
windscreen wiper silecekler
[seelejekl**er**]
windsurfing yelkenli sörf
[yelkenl**ee** surf]
windy rüzgârlı [r**ew**zgarl**uh**]
wine şarap [shar**ap**]
can we have some more wine?
bize bir**az** daha şarap ver**ir**
misiniz? [beez**eh**]

Wine from vineyards scattered
across western Anatolia
between Cappadocia, the
Euphrates Valley, Thrace and
the Aegean, is often better than
average; names to watch for
include **Kavaklıdere**, **Doluca**,
Turasan, **Narbağ** and
Kavalleros. The best white
wines come from around İzmir.
→

Red is kırmızı [kuhrmuhz**uh**],
white beyaz [b**a**yaz] and
rosé pembe [pemb**eh**]/roze
[roz**eh**].

wine list şarap listes**i** [shar**ap**]
winter kış [kuhsh]
in the winter kışın [kuhsh**uh**n]
winter holiday kış tatil**i** [kuhsh]
wire tel
(electric) k**a**blo
wish: best wishes en iy**i**
dileklerimle [deeleklereeml**eh**]
with ile [eel**eh**]
I'm staying with ... ...-de
kalıyorum [-deh kaluh-y**o**room]
without -siz
witness tanık [tan**uh**k]
will you be a witness for me?
benim için tanıklık ed**er**
misiniz? [eech**ee**n tanuhkl**uh**k]
woman kadın [kad**uh**n]

women
Turkish society is deliberately
gender-segregated, and if you
want to avoid men completely,
even if you're travelling alone,
it's not too difficult. Simply seek
the company of Turkish women
at every opportunity, and you
will generally be protected by
them. Turkish women suffer
from harassment themselves,
and their methods of dealing
with it can be very successfully
imitated. Avoid eye contact with
men, and try to look as
→

142

confident and purposeful as
possible. When all else fails, the
best way of neutralizing
harassment is to make a public
scene.
see bus

wonderful harikulade [–ladeh]
won't*: it won't start çalışmıyor
[chaluhshmuh-yor]
wood (material) tahta [taHta]
woods (forest) orman
wool yün [yewn]
word kelime [keleemeh]
work (noun) iş [eesh]
it's not working çalışmıyor
[chaluhshmuh-yor]
I work in … …-'da
çalışıyorum [chaluhshuh-
yoroom]
world dünya [dewnya]
worry: I'm worried
kaygılanıyorum [kīguhlanuh-
yoroom]
worry beads tesbih [tesbeeH]
worse: it's worse daha kötü
[kurtew]
worst en kötü
worth: is it worth a visit? ziyaret
etmeye değer mi? [etmayeh
deh-er]
would: would you give this
to …? bunu …-e verir
misiniz? [-eh]
wrap: could you wrap it up?
paket yapar mısınız?
[muhsuhnuhz]
wrapping paper ambalaj kağıdı

[ambalaJ ka-uhduh]
wrist bilek
write yazmak
could you write it down? yazar
mısınız? [muhsuhnuhz]
how do you write it? nasıl
yazılır? [nasuhl yazuhluhr]
writing paper yazı kâğıdı [yazuh
ka-uhduh]
wrong: it's the wrong key o
yanlış anahtar [yanluhsh]
this is the wrong train bu
yanlış tren
the bill's wrong hesap yanlış
sorry, wrong number
affedersiniz, yanlış numara
sorry, wrong room
affedersiniz, yanlış oda
there's something wrong
with … …-de bir sorun var
[-deh]
what's wrong? sorun nedir?

X

X-ray röntgen [rurntgen]

Y

yacht yat
yard* yarda
year yıl [yuhl]
yellow sarı [saruh]
yes evet
yesterday dün [dewn]
yesterday morning dün sabah
[sabaH]
the day before yesterday
evvelsi gün [gewn]

ENGLISH ✦ TURKISH | Wo

yet henüz [hen**ew**z]

•••••• DIALOGUE ••••••

is it here yet? dah**a** gelmed**i** mi?
no, not yet hayır, henüz değil
[hī-uhr – deh-**eel**]
you'll have to wait a little longer yet
bir**az** dah**a** beklemeniz lazım
[laz**uh**m]

yoghurt yoğurt [yo-**oort**]
you* (pl or pol) siz, sizler
(sing, fam) sen
this is for you bu siz**in** için
[eech**ee**n]
with you sizinle [seez**ee**nleh]

Siz is the formal word for 'you'
used when speaking to one
person and is also the form to
use when speaking to more than
one person in formal or
informal situations. Sizler is an
even more formal way of
addressing more than one
person. Sen is the word for 'you'
used for family members,
friends and children though in
some families parents and
grandparents may prefer to be
addressed in the formal way.

---

young genç [gench]
your* (pl or pol) -iniz, -niz
(emphatic) siz**in**
(sing, fam) -in, -n
(emphatic) sen**in**
your camera fotoğraf
makın**a**nız
yours (pl or pol) sizinki

(sing, fam) seninki
youth hostel gençlik yurd**u**
[gench**lee**k]

Z

zero sıfır [suhf**uh**r]
zip fermuar [fermoo-**ar**]
could you put a new zip on?
fermuarı değiştirir misin**iz**?
[fermoo-ar**uh** deh-eeshteer**ee**r]
zip code post**a** kod**u**
zoo hayvanat bahçesi [hīvanat
ba**H**ches**ee**]
zucchini kabak

Turkish-English

COLLOQUIAL TURKISH

The following are words you might well hear. You shouldn't be tempted to use any of the stronger ones unless you are sure of your audience.

Allah aşkına [ashkuhna] for God's sake
Allah kahretsin! damn!
Allah razı olsun! [razuh] bless you!
aslan sütü [sewtew] slang word for rakı
baksana be! [beh] hey you!
bombok shitty
çek arabanı! [chek arabanuh] get lost!
dangalak wally
defol! get out!; go away!
eline sağlık! [eeleneh sa-luhk] well done!
eşşoğlu eşşek [esh-sholoo esh-shek] ass; lout
eyvah! [ayvaн] alas!
hay Allah! [hī] damn!
hayret! [hīret] well well!
herif bloke, guy
inşallah [eenshallah] I hope so; hopefully; God willing
kapa çeneni! [chenenee] shut up!
katiyen olmaz! no way!
kuş beyinli [koosh bayeenlee] stupid, bird-brained
maşallah! [mashallah] wonderful! (used to express admiration and wonder and to avert the evil eye)
saçma! [sachma] rubbish!, nonsense!
sakın! [sakuhn] beware!; don't!
serseri tramp, vagabond
sudan ucuz [oojooz] dirt cheap
vay canına! [vī januhna] I'll be damned!
yapma be! [beh] really!

A

a! oh!
-a to
AB [a beh] EU
abartmak to exaggerate
ABD [a beh deh] USA
abi older brother
abide [abeedeh] monument
abla elder sister
abone kartı [aboneh kartuh] season ticket
abonman book of bus tickets
acaba [ajaba] I wonder
acayip [ajī-eep] odd, strange
acele [ajeleh] hurry; urgent
acele edin! hurry up!
  acele et! hurry up!
acele etmek to hurry
acemi [ajemee] beginner
acemi pisti nursery slope
acenta [ajenta] agency
acı [ajuh] bitter; hot, spicy; pain
acıkmak [ajuhkmak] to be hungry
  acıktım [ajuhktuhm] I'm hungry
acılı [ajuhluh] hot
acımak [ajuhmak] to feel pain; to ache; to hurt
acıyor [ajuh-yor] it hurts, it's sore
acil [ajeel] urgent
acildir: bu acildir! [ajeeldeer] this is an emergency!
acil durum emergency
acil servis casualty department
acil vaka emergency

aç [ach] hungry; greedy
açgözlü [achgurzlew] greedy
açık [achuhk] open; clear, obvious; (switched) on; light
açık bilet open ticket
açık havada outdoors
açık hava tiyatrosu open air theatre
açıklamak [achuhk-lamak] to explain
açık yüzme havuzu [yewzmeh] open-air swimming pool
açılır tavan [achuhluhr] sun roof
açılış saatleri [achuhluhsh sa-atleree] opening times; collection times
açılış ve kapanış saatleri [veh kapanuhsh] opening times
açıp/kapama düğmesi [achuhp – dew-mesee] on/off switch
açmak [achmak] to open; to switch on
ad name; first name
ada island
adam man
adamlar men
adaptör [adaptur] adapter
adası [adasuh] island
adet number; sum; total
âdet custom; menstruation
adı [aduh] name
adım ... [aduhm] my name is ..., I am called ...
adınız nedir? [aduhnuhz] what's your name?
adil fair
adres address

adres defteri address book

aferin! well done!

affedersiniz sorry; excuse me

afiş [afeesh] poster

afiyet olsun! enjoy your meal!

aft mouth ulcer

ağ [a] net

ağa [a-a] formerly a rank of nobility, now used as a term of respect

ağabey [a-abay] elder brother

ağaç [a-ach] tree

ağır [a-uhr] heavy; rich

ağırlık [a-uhrluhk] weight

ağız [a-uhz] mouth; dialect

ağlamak [a-lamak] to cry

ağrı [a-ruh] ache, pain

ağrı giderici ilaçlar [geedereejee eelachlar] painkillers

ağustos [a-oostos] August

ahali people

ahçı [ahchuh] cook; owner of restaurant

ahize [aheezeh] receiver, handset

Aids [aydz] AIDS

aile [a-eeleh] family

aile gazinosu [a-eeleh] family nightclub

ailesiz girilmez entry only for families

aileye mahsus only for family groups

ait: -e ait [-eh īt] belonging to; relating to

ait olmak to belong

ajanda [aЈanda] diary (business etc)

akciğerler [akjee-erler] lungs

Akdeniz Mediterranean

akıl [akuhl] intelligence

akıllı [akuhlluh] clever

akım [akuhm] current (electrical)

akıntı [akuhntuh] current (in water)

akraba relative

akrabalar relatives

akrep scorpion

aks axle

aksan accent

akşam [aksham] evening; in the evening; p.m.

akşam on 10 p.m.

bu akşam this evening

akşamleyin [akshamlayeen] in the evening

akşam yemeği [yemeh-ee] dinner, evening meal; supper

akşam yemeği yemek [yemeh-ee] to have dinner

aktarma connection

aktarmalı sefer [aktarmaluh] connecting flight

aktarma yapmak to change (trains etc)

aktör [aktur] actor

aktris actress

akü [akew] battery

alan area; field; square

alaturka Turkish-style

al bakalım [bakaluhm] here you are

alçak [alchak] low

alçı [alchuh] plaster cast

alerjik [alerЈeek] allergic

alet device; tool

alıcı [aluhj**uh**] addressee

alımlı [aluhml**uh**] attractive

alın [al**uh**n] forehead

alınan mal değiştirilmez no
refund or exchange

alınan para [aluhn**a**n] charge

alıp götürmek [al**uh**p
gurtewrm**e**k] to take away

alışılmamış [aluhsh**uh**l-mamuhsh]
unusual

alışkanlık [aluhshkanl**uh**k] habit

alış kuru [al**uh**sh] buying rate

alışmak: -e alışmak [-eh
aluhshm**a**k] to get used to

alışveriş [aluhshver**ee**sh]
shopping

alışverişe çıkmak
[aluhshvereesh**eh** chuhkm**a**k] to
go shopping

alışveriş merkezi shopping
centre

Allah God

Allahaısmarladık [all**a**ha-
uhsmarlad**uh**k] goodbye (said by
person leaving)

Allah aşkına [ashkuhn**a**] for
God's sake

Allah belanı versin! [belan**uh**]
damn you!

Allah kahretsin! damn!

Allah razı olsun [raz**uh**] bless
you

allık [all**uh**k] blusher

almak to take, to accept; to
receive; to buy; to obtain

Alman German (adj, person)

Almanca [alm**a**nja] German
(language)

Almanya Germany

alo hello

alt bottom (of road etc)

altı [alt**uh**] six

altın [alt**uh**n] gold

altıncı [alt**uh**njuh] sixth

altında [altuhnd**a**] below,
under; at the bottom of

altmış [altm**uh**sh] sixty

altta underneath

alüminyum folyo [alewmeen-
y**oo**m] tinfoil

alyans wedding ring

ama but

...-amadım [-**a**maduhm] I
couldn't ...

aman! goodness!; heavens!;
careful!

ambalaj kağıdı [ambal**a**ɹ
ka-uhd**uh**] wrapping paper

amca [amj**a**] (paternal) uncle

ameliyat operation

Amerikalı [amereekal**uh**]
American

amfiteatr amphitheatre

amortisör [amortees**u**r] shock-
absorber

amper(lik) amp

ampul light bulb

an moment

ana mother

Anadolu Anatolia, Asia Minor

anahtar [ana**H**t**a**r] key

anahtarlık [ana**H**tarl**uh**k] keyring

anavatan home, homeland

anayol main road

anayol ilerde main road ahead

anayurt home, homeland

ancak [anj**a**k] only; hardly; but

anıt [anuht] monument

ani sudden

aniden suddenly

anlam meaning

anlamadım [–maduhm] I don't understand

anlamak to understand

anlamı yok [anlamuh] there's no point

anlamıyorum [anlamuh–] I don't understand

anlatmak to explain

anlıyorum [anluh–] I understand

anne [anneh] mother

anne baba parents

Anonim Şirket [sheerket] joint stock company, corporation

antifriz antifreeze

antik ancient

antika antique(s)

antikacı [anteekajuh] antique dealer

antiseptik antiseptic

antrenman training

antrenman ayakkabısı [ī-akkabuhsuh] trainers

apaçık [apachuhk] obvious

apandisit appendicitis

apartman block of flats, apartment block

apartman dairesi [da-eeresee] flat, apartment

aptal idiot; stupid

apteshane [aptes-haneh] toilet

ara interval; gap; space

araba car; cart

arabamda in my car

araba ön camı [urn jamuh] windscreen

araba vapuru car ferry

arabesk Turkish 'art' music

araç giremez no entry

araç kurtarma [arach] breakdown service

ara durak stopover

aralık [araluhk] December

aramak to search for, to look for

Arap Arab

Arapça [arapcha] Arabic

arasında: ...-lerin arasında [arasuhnda] among the ..., between the ...

arasıra [arasuhra] now and then

ara sokak sidestreet

ardında [arduhnda] beyond

arı [aruh] bee

arı su [soo] distilled water

arıza [aruhza] breakdown

arızalı [aruhzaluh] faulty; out of order

arıza servisi faults service

arıza yapmak to break down

arka back (part)

arkada at the back; behind ...-in arkada behind the ...

arkadan binilir entry at the back

arkadan göndermek [gurndermek] to forward

arkadan inilir exit at the back

arkadaş [arkadash] friend; partner, boyfriend, girlfriend

arka lambalar rear lights

arkamdaki behind me

arka sinyal lambaları
[lambalar**uh**] rear lights
Arnavut Albanian
arnavut kaldırımı cobblestone
pavement, cobblestone
sidewalk
Arnavutluk Albania
artık [art**uh**k] no longer;
residue; remnant
artık ... yok no more ...
arzu etmek to wish for
asansör [asans**ur**] lift, elevator
aseton nail polish remover
asıl [as**uh**l] original; base;
basis; origin
asker soldier
askeri bölge military zone
askı [ask**uh**] coathanger
asla never
aslan sütü [sewt**ew**] slang word
for rakı
aslen basically; originally
asma kilit padlock
astım [ast**uh**m] asthma
Asya Asia
AŞ [a sheh] joint stock
company, corp.
aşağı [asha-**uh**] down
aşağıda [asha-uhda] down; at
the bottom; downstairs;
down there
aşçı [ash-ch**uh**] cook
aşı [ash**uh**] vaccination
aşılama [ashuhlama]
vaccination
aşmak [ashm**a**k] to cross
AT [a teh] EC
at horse
ata ancestor

ateş [at**e**sh] fire; temperature,
fever
ateşli [atesh**lee**] feverish
atınız insert (coin)
Atina Athens
atkı [atk**uh**] scarf (for neck)
atlamak to jump
atletizm athletics
atmak to throw (away)
At Meydanı [maydan**uh**]
Hippodrome
avanak idiot
avcılık [avjuhl**uh**k] hunting
avlu courtyard
Avrupa [avr**oo**pa] Europe;
European (adj)
Avrupalı [avroopal**uh**] European
(person)
avukat lawyer
Avustralya [avoostr**a**lya]
Australia; Australian
Avusturya [avoost**oo**rya] Austria;
Austrian
ay [**ī**] month; moon
ayak [**ī**-a**k**] foot
ayak bileği [beeleh-**ee**] ankle
ayakkabı [**ī**-akkab**uh**] shoe(s)
ayakkabı bağı [b**a**-uh]
shoelaces
ayakkabıcı [**ī**-akkabuhj**uh**]
shoeshop
ayakkabı cilası [jeelas**uh**] shoe
polish
ayak parmağı [**ī**-a**k** parma-**uh**]
toe
ayakta durmak [**ī**-akt**a**] to stand
aybaşı [**ī**bash**uh**] period
(menstruation); beginning of
the month; pay day

aydın [īd**uh**n] intellectual; well-lit

aydınlık [īduhnl**uh**k] well-lit

ay hali period (menstruation)

ayı [ī-**uh**] bear; jerk; blockhead

ayık [ī-**uh**k] sober; conscious

ayılmak [ī-uhlm**a**k] to come round

ayırma [ī-**uh**rma] parting

ayırmak [ī-uhrm**a**k] to separate

ayırtmak [ī-uhrtm**a**k] to reserve

ayin [ī-**ee**n] mass; religious ceremony, rite

aylık bilet [īl**uh**k] monthly season ticket

aylık taksitler monthly instalments

ayna [īna] mirror

aynı [īn**uh**] (the) same

ayrı [ī**ruh**] separate

ayrı ayrı separately

ayrıldım [īruhld**uh**m] separated

ayrılmak [īruhlm**a**k] to leave; to go away

ayrılmış [īruhlm**uh**sh] reserved

az not many; little

azami ağırlık weight limit

azami genişlik maximum width

azami hız maximum speed

azami park 1 saat parking limited to 1 hour

azami sürat speed limit

azami yükseklik maximum height

B

baba father; dad

bacak [baj**a**k] leg

bacanak [bajan**a**k] brother-in-law

bademcik iltihabı [bademj**ee**k eelteehab**uh**] tonsillitis

badem şekeri [sheker**ee**] sugared almonds

bagaj [baga**ı**] luggage, baggage; boot, (US) trunk

bagaj alma yeri baggage claim

bagaj fişi [feesh**ee**] baggage receipt

bagaj kaydı [kīd**uh**] check-in

bagaj kayıt [kī-**uh**t] check-in

bagaj kayıt masası [masas**uh**] check-in desk

bagaj kontrolü [kontrol**ew**] baggage check

bağ [ba] cord; string; bond; link; vineyard

bağımsız [ba-uhms**uh**z] independent

bağırmak [ba-uhrm**a**k] to shout

bağlantı [ba-lant**uh**] connection

bağlı: ...-a bağlı [ba-l**uh**] it depends on ...

bahçe [ba**н**ch**eh**] garden

bahsetmek [ba**н**setm**e**k] to mention

bahşiş [ba**н**sh**ee**sh] tip

bakabilir miyim? can I see it?

bakar mısınız! [muhsuhn**uh**z] excuse me!

bakım [bak**uh**m] care, attention

bakımından [bakuhmuhnd**a**n] from the point of view of

bakır [bak**uh**r] copper

bakkal grocer's, food store

bakkaliye [bakkalee-y**eh**] groceries

bakmak: -a bakmak to look at; to look after

baksana be! [beh] hey you!

balayı [bal**ī**-uh] honeymoon

baldız [bald**uh**z] sister-in-law (wife's sister)

bale [bal**eh**] ballet

balık [bal**uh**k] fish

balık adamlık [adaml**uh**k] skindiving

balıkçı [bal**uh**kchuh] fishmonger's

balıkçı köyü [kur-y**ew**] fishing village

balıkçılık [baluhkchuhl**uh**k] fishing

balık lokantası [bal**uh**k lokantas**uh**] fish restaurant

balık pazarı [pazar**uh**] fish market

balık tutmak yasaktır no fishing

balkon balcony; circle balkonlu with a balcony

balsam conditioner

balta axe

bambaşka [bamb**a**shka] quite different

bana to me

banka [b**a**nka] bank

banka hesabı [hesab**uh**] bank account

banket hard shoulder

banknot note, (US) bill

bankomatik cash dispenser, ATM, automatic teller

banliyö [banlee-y**ur**] suburbs

banliyö tren şebekesi local railway system

banyo bath; bathroom banyolu (oda) with a private bathroom

banyo etmek to develop

banyo tuzları [toozlar**uh**] bath salts

banyo yapmak to take a bath

bardak glass

barmen kız [k**uh**z] barmaid

barsak intestine

basamağa dikkat mind the step

basın(ız) press

basit simple, easy

baş [bash] head

baş ağrısı [a-ruhs**uh**] headache

başarı [bashar**uh**] success

başarmak [basharm**a**k] to succeed; to achieve

baş aşağı [asha-**uh**] upside down

başbakan [b**a**shbakan] prime minister

başka [b**a**shka] different; other(s)

başka bir another

başka bir şey [shay] something else; anything else

başka bir yer somewhere else

başka bir yerde [yerd**eh**] elsewhere

başkent [bashk**e**nt] capital city

başlamak [bashlam**a**k] to start, to begin

başlangıç [bashlang**uh**ch] beginning, start

başlangıçta [bashlanguhchta] at the beginning

başlıca [bashluhja] main, principal

başparmak [bashparmak] thumb

baş üstüne [ewstewneh] with pleasure

batı [batuh] west

batıda in the west

...-in batısında west of ...

batmak to sink

battaniye [battanee-yeh] blanket

bavul suitcase

Bay [bī] Mr

bayağı [bī-a-uh] ordinary; vulgar, common

Bayan [bī-an] Mrs; Miss; Ms

bayan lady; ladies

bayan iç çamaşırı [eech chamashuhruh] ladies' underwear

bayan konfeksiyon ladies' wear

bayanlar [bī-anlar] ladies (toilets), ladies' room

bayat [bī-at] stale

baygın [bīguhn] unconscious

bayılmak [bī-uhlmak] to faint

baylar [bīlar] gents (toilet)

baypas [bīpas] by-pass

bayrak [bīrak] flag

bazen sometimes

bazı [bazuh] some

bebek baby; doll

bebek bezi nappy, diaper

bebek iskemlesi highchair

bedava free (of charge)

beden size

bedesten covered market hall for valuable goods

beğendim [beh-endeem] I like it

beğenmek [beh-enmek] to like

bej [beJ] beige

bekar batchelor; single (unmarried)

bekârım [bekaruhm] I'm single

bekçi [bekchee] guard; watchman

beklemek: -i beklemek to wait; to expect

bekleme salonu [beklemeh] waiting room

beklemeyin [beklemayeen] don't wait

bekleyin! [beklayeen] wait! beni bekleyin wait for me

bekleyiniz! [beklayeeneez] wait!

bel spade; waist

belediye binası [beledee-yeh beenasuh] town hall

belediye sarayı [sarī-uh] town hall

... belediyesi [beledee-yesee] municipality of ...; municipal town hall

belge [belgeh] document

belki maybe, perhaps belki de değil [deh deh-eel] perhaps not

belli obvious

ben I

ben de [deh] so am I; so do I; nor do I; me too

bence öyle [benjeh ur-ileh] I think so bence öyle değil [deh-eel] I don't think so

bende [bendeh] on/in me

benden from me

beni me

benim my; it's me; speaking (phone)

  benim için [eecheen] for me

  o benimdir it's mine

benim kendi ...-m my own ...

benimki mine

benzemek to look like

benzer similar

benzin petrol, (US) gas

benzin bidonu petrol can, gas can

benzin istasyonu petrol station, gas station

benzin pompası [pompasuh] petrol pump

beraber together

berbat terrible, awful, dreadful

berber men's hairdresser, barber's

bereket blessing; abundance

bereket versin fortunately

beri here

  ...-den beri since ...

beş [besh] five

beşinci [besheenjee] fifth

Bey [bay] Mr; sir; ruler; chief; master; gentleman

beyaz [bayaz] white

beyazlar whites

beyaz zehir drugs (narcotics)

beyefendi gentleman; sir

beyin sarsıntısı [bayeen sarsuhn-tuhsuh] concussion

bez cloth

bıçak [buhchak] knife

bırakmak [buhrakmak] to leave;

to abandon; to let, to allow; to let off

bıyık [buh-yuhk] moustache

biberon baby's bottle

biçim [beecheem] shape, form; kind; manner

bijuteri [beeJooteree] jewellery

bile [beeleh] even

  ...-se bile [-seh] even if ...

bile bile deliberately

bilek wrist

bilet ticket

biletçi [beeletchee] conductor

bilet gişesi [geeshesee] ticket office; box office

biletsiz girilmez no entry without a ticket

bilezik bracelet

bilgi information

bilgisayar [beelgeesī-ar] computer

bilim science

bilinmeyen numaralar [beeleenmayen] directory enquiries

... biliyor musunuz? do you speak ...?

bilmek to know

bilmiyordum I didn't know

bilmiyorum I don't know

bin thousand

bina building

binicilik [beeneejeeleek] horse-riding

binilir get on here

biniş kartı [beeneesh kartuh] boarding card

binmek to get on; to get in

bir a, an; one

bir ... daha another ..., one
more ...

biraz some; a little, a bit
biraz daha some more; a
little bit more

birazcık [beerazjuhk] a bit, a
little bit

birazdan in a minute

bir çift ... [cheeft] a couple of ...

birçok [beerchok] a lot of, many

birey [beeray] individual

bir gecesi [gejesee] per night

biricik [beereejeek] the only,
sole, unique

bir iki tane ... [taneh] a couple
of ..., a few ...

biriktirmek to collect

birinci [beereenjee] first

birinci kat first floor, (US)
second floor

birinci sınıf [suhnuhf] first class

birisi somebody, someone

birkaç [beerkach] several, a
few

birkaç tane [taneh] a few

bir kere [kereh] once

Birleşik Amerika [beerlesheek]
the United States

Birleşik Devletler the States

Birleşik Krallık [kralluhk] the
United Kingdom

birlikte [beerleekteh] together

bir parça [parcha] a little bit

bir sonraki next

bir şey [shay] something;
anything

bir şey değil [deh-eel] you're
welcome, don't mention it,

not at all
başka bir şey? [bashka]
anything else?

bir yerde [yerdeh] somewhere

bisiklet bicycle

bisikletçi [beeseekletchee]
cyclist

bisiklete binmek [beeseekleteh]
cycling

bisiklet sporu cycling

bitirmek: -i bitirmek to finish, to
end

bitişiğinde [beeteeshee-eendeh]
next to

bitişik [beeteesheek] next to

bitki plant

bitkin exhausted, tired

bitmek to end, to come to an
end; to grow

bitti over

biz we

Bizans [beezans] Byzantine

bizde [beezdeh] on/in us

bizden from us

bize [beezeh] (to) us

bizi us

bizim our

bizim için [eecheen] for us

bizimki ours

bizimle [beezeemleh] with us

bizler we

bizzat personally, in person

blucin [bloojeen] jeans

bluz blouse

bodrum basement

bodrum kat basement

boğa [bo-a] bull

boğaz [bo-az] throat; straits

boğaz ağrısı [a-ruhsuh] sore

throat
Boğaziçi [bo-**a**zeechee] the
  Bosphorus
boğaz pastil(ler)i throat
  pastille(s)
bol wide; loose; plentiful
bol bol ... plenty of ...
bol şanslar! good luck!
bomba bomb
bombok shitty
bone [bon**eh**] bathing cap
boru pipe (for water)
boş [bosh] vacant; empty
boşanmış [boshanm**uh**sh]
  divorced
boş oda vacancy
boşta (gezer) unemployed
boş yer vacancy
boy size; height
boya paint
boyamak to paint
boyar not colourfast
boyun neck
boyunca [boyoonj**a**] along;
  throughout; during
bozmak to change
bozuk damaged; broken; out
  of order
bozuk para coins; small
  change
böbrekler [burbrekl**er**] kidneys
  (in body)
böcek [burj**ek**] insect
böcek ilacı [eelaj**uh**]
  insect repellent;
  insecticide
böceklere karşı ilaç [burjekler**eh**
  karsh**uh** eel**a**ch] insect
  repellent

böcek sokması [sokmas**uh**]
  insect bite
Boğaz [boh-az] the Bosphorus
bölge [burlg**eh**] region; district;
  zone
bölüm [burl**ewm**] department
böyle [buh-il**eh**] so, this way,
  like this; such
  böyle tamam that'll do
  nicely
böyle iken anyhow; while this
  is so
Britanya Britain
bronşit [bronsh**eet**] bronchitis
bronzlaşmak [bronzlashm**ak**] to
  get a tan
bronzlaşmış [bronzlashm**uh**sh]
  suntanned
bronzluk suntan
bronz ten suntan
broş [brosh] brooch
broşür [brosh**ewr**] brochure;
  leaflet
bu this (one); these; this is
  bu ... mi? is this ...?
  bu ne? what's this?
buçuk [booch**ook**] half; and a
  half
  ... buçuk half past ...
budala idiot
bu gece [gej**eh**] tonight
bugün [boog**ewn**] today
buji [boo**J**ee] spark plug
buji telleri jump leads
bukle [bookl**eh**] curl
Bul. Boul.
bu ...-lar these ...
bulaşıcı [boolashuhj**uh**]
  infectious

bulaşık [boolashuhk] washing-up

bulaşık bezi dishcloth

bulaşık deterjanı [deterJanuh] washing-up liquid

bulaşık lavabosu sink

bulaşık yıkamak [yuhkamak] to do the washing-up

Bulgar Bulgarian

Bulgaristan Bulgaria

bulmak to find, to discover; to reach

buluşmak [boolooshmak] to meet

buluşma yeri [boolooshma] meeting place

bulut cloud

bulutlu cloudy

bulvar boulevard

... Bulvarı [boolvaruh] ... Boulevard

bunlar these

bunları [boonlaruh] these

bunun fiyatı ne kadar? [fee-yatuh neh] how much is it?, how much is this?

burada [boorada] here; over here

burada aşağıda [asha-uhda] down here

burda here; over here

burası [boorasuh] here

burun nose

but [boot] thigh

buyrun [boo-iroon], buyurun [boo-yooroon] can I help you?; yes?; this way; please; there you are; go ahead

buz [booz] ice

buzdolabı [boozdolabuh] fridge

buzluk freezer

büfe [bewfeh] kiosk selling sandwiches

büro [bewro] office

büro malzemeleri office supplies

bütün [bewtewn] whole; all

büyük [bew-yewk] large, big; great

büyükanne [bew-yewkanneh] grandmother

büyükbaba grandfather

Büyük Britanya Great Britain

büyükelçilik [bew-yewkelcheeleek] embassy

büyük jeton [Jeton] large token

büyüklük [bew-yewlewk] size

büyük mağaza [bew-yewk ma-aza] department store

büyültme [bew-yewltmeh] enlargement

C

Cad. [jad] St; Ave

cadde [jaddeh] street; avenue

... Caddesi ... Street, ... Avenue

cam [jam] glass

cami [jamee] mosque

... Camii/Camisi ... Mosque

cam sileceği [seelejeh-ee] windscreen wiper

canım sıkılıyor [jahnuhm suh-kuhluh-yor] I'm bored

-a canim sıkılıyor I'm worried, I'm concerned

cankurtaran [jankoortaran]
 ambulance; lifeguard
canlı [janl**uh**] alive; lively;
 bright
can sıkıcı [jan suhkuhj**uh**]
 annoying
can simidi lifebelt
can yeleği [yeleh-**ee**] life jacket
can yelekleri life jackets
can yelekleri tavandadır life
 jackets up above
caz [jaz] jazz
cazibeli [jazeebel**ee**] sexy
ceket [jeket] jacket
cemiyet [jemee-yet] society
cenaze [jenaz**eh**] funeral
cep [jep] pocket
cereyanlı [jerayanl**uh**] draughty
cesur [jes**oo**r] brave
cevap [jev**a**p] answer
cevap vermek to answer
ceza [jez**a**] fine (punishment)
check-in yaptırmak
 [yaptuhrm**a**k] to check in
cımbız [juhmb**uh**z] tweezers
ciddi [jeedd**ee**] serious
cila [jeel**a**] polish
cilt [jeelt] skin
cilt temizleyici [temeezlayeej**ee**]
 skin cleanser
cins(i) [jeens(**ee**)] type; kind
cinsiyet(i) [jeensee-yet(ee)] sex,
 gender
civarında [jeevaruhnd**a**] about
coğrafya [joh-rafy**a**] geography
cuma [joom**a**] Friday
cumartesi [joom**a**rtesee]
 Saturday
cumhurbaşkanı [joomHoor-

bashkan**uh**] president
cumhuriyet [joomHooree-y**e**t]
 republic
cüzdan [jewzd**a**n] wallet

Ç

çabuk [chab**oo**k] quick
 çabuk ol! hurry up!
çadır [chad**uh**r] tent
çadır bezi tarpaulin
çadır direği [deereh-**ee**] tent
 pole
çadır kazığı [kazuh-**uh**] tent
 peg
çağ [cha] time; date; age, era
çağdaş sanat [cha-d**a**sh] modern
 art
çağdaş sanat galerisi modern
 art gallery
çağırmak [cha-uhrm**a**k] to call;
 to invite
çağlayan [cha-lī-an] waterfall
çakı [chak**uh**] penknife
çakmak [chakm**a**k] cigarette
 lighter
çalar saat [chal**a**r sa-**a**t] alarm
 clock
çalınız ring
çalışkan [chaluhshk**a**n]
 hardworking
çalışmak [chaluhshm**a**k] to try;
 to work
çalışma saatleri [chaluhshm**a** saatler**ee**] working hours
çalışmıyor [chaluhshmuh-yor] it's
 not working
çalıştırmak [chaluhshtuhrm**a**k] to
 switch on

çalkalamak [chalkalamak] to shake; to stir; to wash out; to rinse

çalmak [chalmak] to steal; to play; to ring

çamaşır [chamashuhr] laundry, washing

çamaşırhane [–haneh] laundry (place)

çamaşır ipi clothes line

çamaşır makinesi washing machine

çamaşır mandalı [mandaluh] clothes peg

çamaşır suyu bleach

çamaşır tozu washing powder

çamaşır yıkamak [yuhkamak] to do the washing

çamur [chamoor] mud

çan [chan] bell

çanak çömlek [chanak churmlek] pottery

Çanakkale Boğazı [chanakkaleh bo-azuh] the Dardanelles

çanta [chanta] bag

çapa [chapa] anchor

çarpışma [charpuhshma] crash

çarşaf [charshaf] sheet; long, baggy dress with a hood worn by religious Turkish women

çarşamba [charshamba] Wednesday

çarşı [charshuh] market, bazaar ... Çarşısı [charshuhsuh] ... Market

çartır (seferi) [chartuhr] charter flight

çatal [chatal] fork

çatal bıçak [buhchak] cutlery

çay [chī] tea; stream

çay bahçesi [baHchesee] tea garden

çaydanlık [chīdanluhk] kettle

çayevi [chī-evee] tea shop, tea house

çayhane [chī-Haneh] café (for families)

çay kaşığı [chī kashuh-uh] teaspoon

çek [chek] cheque, (US) check

çek arabanı! [arabanuh] get lost!

çek defteri cheque book

çeker [cheker] will shrink

çekici [chekeejee] attractive

çekiç [chekeech] hammer

çekil! [chekeel] go away!

çekilip gitmek [chekeeleep] to go away

çek-in [chek] check-in

çekin pull

çekingen [chekeengen] shy

çekiniz pull

çek kabul edilir cheques accepted

çek kartı [kartuh] cheque card, (US) check card

çekmece [chekmejeh] drawer

çekmek [chekmek] to pull, to draw; to suffer

çekmez unshrinkable

çene [cheneh] chin; jaw

çengelli iğne [chengellee ee-neh] safety pin

çeşit [chesheet] variety, sort, kind

çeşme [cheshmeh] fountain
... Çeşmesi [cheshmesee] ...
Fountain
çeviriniz [cheveereeneez] dial
çevirmek [cheveermek] to turn;
to translate; to dial
çevir sesi [cheveer] dialling
tone
çevir sinyali dialling tone
çevir tonu dialling tone
çevre yolu [chevreh] by-pass;
ringroad
çeyizlik [chayeezleek] trousseau
goods
çeyrek [chayrek] quarter
çığlık atmak [chuh-luhk] to
scream
çık dışarı! [chuk dusharuh] get
out!
çıkılmaz no exit
çıkış [chuhkuhsh] exit, way out
çıkış kapısı [kapuhsuh] gate
çıkmak [chuhkmak] to go out;
to go up
çıkmaz [chuhkmaz] dead-end
alley
... Çıkmazı [chuhkmazuh] ...
Cul-de-sac
çıkmaz sokak cul-de-sac; no
through road
çıkmaz yol dead end
çıplak [chuhplak] bare, naked
çiçek [cheechek] flower
çiçekçi [cheechekchee] florist
çiçekevi [cheechekevee] florist
çift [cheeft] pair; couple;
double
çiftçi [cheeftchee] farmer
çiftlik [cheeftleek] farm

çift yataklı oda [yatakluh] twin
room
çiğ [chee] raw
çiğnemek için chew
çiklet [cheeklet] chewing gum
çikolata [cheekolata] chocolate
çimen [cheemen] grass; lawn
çimenlere basmayınız keep off
the grass
çingene [cheegeneh] gypsy
çini [cheenee] tiles
çips [cheeps] crisps, (US)
potato chips
çirkin [cheerkeen] ugly;
offensive
çivi [cheevee] nail (metal)
çizgi [cheezgee] line
çizik [cheezeek] scratch
çizim [cheezeem] drawing
çizme [cheezmeh] boot (footwear)
çizmek [cheezmek] to draw
çocuk [chojook] child
çocuk arabası [arabasuh] pram
çocuk bahçesi [baHchesee]
playground
çocuk bakıcısı [bakuhjuhsuh]
baby-sitter, childminder
çocuk bezi nappy-liners,
diaper-liners
çocuk doktoru paediatrician
çocuk havuzu children's pool
çocuk konfeksiyon children's
wear
çocuklar [chojooklar] children
çocuk yatağı [yata-uh] cot
çoğu [choh-oo] many; most
(of)
çoğunlukla [choh-oonlookla]
mostly; most of the time

çok [chok] many; much; a lot,
lots; very; very much
çok daha fazla a lot more
çok daha iyi/daha kötü
[kurtew] much better/worse
çok değil [deh-eel] not much
çok fazla too much
o kadar çok değil not a lot;
not so much
çok çok very much; at the
most
çok doğru! [doh-roo] exactly!
çok yaşa! [yasha] bless you!
çorap(lar) [chorap(lar)] sock(s);
stocking(s)
çöp [churp] rubbish, garbage;
litter
çöp atmayınız no litter please
çöp kutusu bin
çöp tenekesi dustbin, trashcan
çöp torbası [torbasuh] bin
liners
çünkü [chewnkew] because
çürük [chewrewk] bruise;
rotten

D

D shared taxi stop
da too, also
-da at (the); in (the); on
(the)
İstanbul'da in Istanbul
dağ [da] mountain
dağlarda [da-larda] in the
mountains
... Dağı [da-uh] ... Mountain
... Dağları [da-laruh]
... Mountains

dağcılık [da-juhluhk] climbing;
mountaineering
dağ köyü [kur-yew] mountain
village
daha more; extra; still; yet
... daha fazla more than ...
çok daha fazla [chok] a lot
more
daha az less
daha iyi better
daha iyi olmak to improve
daha kötü [kurtew] worse
dahi also, too; even
dahil [daHeel] included
dahilen (alınır) to be taken
internally
dahil etmek to include
dahili extension
dahiliye [daHeelee-yeh] internal
dahiliyeci [daHeelee-yejee]
specialist in internal
diseases
dahiliye mütehassısı
[mewtehassuhsuh] specialist
in internal diseases
daima [da-eema] always
daire [da-eereh] circle; flat,
apartment; office;
department
dakika minute
beş dakikaya kadar [besh
dakeekī-a] in five minutes
bir dakika just a minute
dalga wave
dalmak to dive
dalma techizatı [tejheezatuh]
skin-diving equipment
dam roof
damat son-in-law

damla drop

damsız girilmez no entry without women

-dan from
İstanbul'dan Bodrum'a from Istanbul to Bodrum

-dan biraz a little bit (of)

-dan daha iyi better than

-dan beri since

dangalak wally

danışma [danuhshma] information

danışma masası [masasuh] information desk

Danimarka Danish (adj); Denmark

dans dance

dans etmek to dance

dar narrow; tight

darüşşifa [darewshsheefa] old hospital

dava trial

davet invitation; reception

davet etmek to invite

dayı [dī-uh] (maternal) uncle

de [deh] too, also; and; but

-de at (the); in (the); on (the)

debriyaj [debree-yaJ] clutch

dede [dedeh] grandfather

dedi he/she said

defa time; turn

defol! get out!; go away!

defter notebook; exercise book

değer [deh-er] value

değerli [deh-erlee] valuable

değil [deh-eel] not; he/she/it is not

değil mi? isn't it?

değiler [deh-eeler] they are not

değilim [deh-eeleem] I am not

değiliz [deh-eeleez] we are not

değilsin [deh-eelseen] you are not

değilsiniz [deh-eelseeneez] you are not

değişir [deh-eesheer] it varies

değişken [deh-eeshken] changeable

değişmek [deh-eeshmek] to change; to alter

değiştirilmez goods cannot be exchanged

değiştirmek [deh-eeshteermek] to change; to exchange

değmek [deh-mek] to be worth; to touch

deli mad, crazy

delik hole

delikanlı [deleekanluh] teenager (male)

demek to mean; to pronounce; to say

demek istemek to mean

demir iron

demiryolu railway

demiryolu geçidi [gecheedee] level crossing

demlik teapot

-den from; than; of

-den az under, less than

-den başka [bashka] apart from

den beri since (time)

-den daha az less than

denemek to try

denetçi [denetch**ee**] inspector
deniz sea
  deniz kenarında [kenar**uh**nda]
  at the seaside
  deniz kıyısı [kuh-yuhs**uh**]
  seashore; by the sea
  deniz kıyısında [kuh-yuh-
  suhnd**a**] on the seashore, by
  the sea
  denizanası [deneezanas**uh**]
  jellyfish
  deniz gezisi cruise
  deniz kabuğu [kab**oo**-oo]
  seashell
  deniz kestanesi sea urchin
  deniz motoru motorboat
  deniz yosunu seaweed
depo tank (of car)
depozito deposit
deprem earthquake
dere [der**eh**] stream
derece [derej**eh**] degree; step
dergi magazine
derhal at once, immediately
deri skin; hide; leather
deri mamulleri leather goods
derin deep
dernek society
ders lesson; class; lecture
dert pain; suffering; disease;
  illness; sorrow; trouble
deterjan [deter**J**an] washing
  powder
dev enormous, giant
devam etmek to continue
devamlı virajlar series of bends
deve [dev**eh**] camel
dev gibi enormous
devirmek to knock over, to

knock down
devlet state
devre [devr**eh**] period, term
dezenfektan disinfectant
-dir: o ...-dir it is ...
dırlar: onlar ... dırlar [duhrl**ar**]
  they are ...
dış [duhsh] exterior, outside
dışarda [duhsharda] out;
  outside; he/she's out
dışarı [duhshar**uh**] outside; out
dışarı sarkmayınız do not lean
  out
dış hatlar international flights
dışında [duhshuhnd**a**] except
-di he/she/it was
dibinde [deebeend**eh**] at the
  bottom of
Dicle [deejl**eh**] the Tigris
Didim Didyma
diğer [dee-**er**] other
dik steep
-dik we were
dikiz aynası [īnas**uh**] rearview
  mirror
dikkat! look out!; caution!
  dikkat ediniz! take care!
  dikkat et! be careful!
dikkatli careful
  dikkatli olun! be careful!
dikmek to sew; to plant
dil language; tongue
dilek: en iyi dileklerimle
  [deeleklereeml**eh**] best wishes
-diler they were
dilim slice
dil kursu language course
dil okulu language school
din [deen] religion

-diniz you were
dinle! [deenleh] listen!
dinlemek to listen (to)
dinlenme [deenlenmeh] rest
dinlenmek to rest
dip bottom
diploma degree
-dir is
direk pole; column
direksiyon steering wheel
direksiyon sistemi steering
direkt direct
dirsek elbow
disket disk, diskette
dispanser out-patients' clinic
diş [deesh] tooth
diş ağrısı [a-ruhsuh] toothache
dişçi [deesh-chee] dentist
dişeti [deeshetee] gum
diş fırçası [fuhrchasuh]
  toothbrush
diş floşu [floshoo] dental floss
diş hekimi dentist
diş ipi dental floss
diş macunu [majoonoo]
  toothpaste
diş tabibi dentist
diya [dee-ya], diyapozitif [dee-
  yapozeeteef] slide
diz knee
doğa [doh-a] nature
doğal [doh-al] natural
doğmak [doh-mak] to be born;
  to rise
doğru [doh-roo] correct, right;
  accurate; straight
  -e doğru [-eh] towards
doğrulamak [doh-roolamak] to
  confirm

doğu [doh-oo] east
  doğuda [doh-ooda] in the
  east
  ...-nın doğusu [-nuhn doh-
  oosoo] east of ...
doğum günü [doh-oom gewnew]
  birthday
  doğum gününüz kutlu olsun!
  [gewnewnewz] happy
  birthday!
doğum tarihi [tareeHee] date of
  birth
doğum yeri place of birth
doksan ninety
dokumak to weave
dokunmak to touch
dokunmayınız do not touch
dokuz nine
dokuzuncu [dokoozoonjoo] ninth
döküman [dokewman]
  document
dolap cupboard
dolayı: -den dolayı [dolī-uh]
  because of
doldurmak to fill; to fill in; to
  fill up
doldurunuz fill in; fill up
dolgu filling
dolmak to be filled; to become
  full
dolma kalem pen
dolmuş [dolmoosh] shared
  taxi
dolmuş durağı [doora-uh]
  shared taxi stand
dolmuş indirme-bindirme yeri
  [eendeermeh-beendeermeh]
  shared taxi pick-up/set-
  down point

dolu full, no vacancies; engaged; occupied; hail

doluyuz we're full

domuz pig

don underpants, panties; knickers; frost

donatım [donatuhm] equipment

dondurma külahı [kewl-ahuh] ice-cream cone

dondurulmuş yiyecekler [dondoorool-moosh yee-yejekler] frozen food

donmuş [donmoosh] frozen

donuk dull

dosdoğru [dosdoh-roo] straight ahead

dost friend

dökmek [durkmek] to pour (out); to spill

döndürmek [durndewrmek] to turn

dönel kavşak [durnel kavshak] roundabout

dönmek [durnmek] to come/go back, to return; to get back; to turn

... dönün [durnewn] turn ...

dönüş [durnewsh] return

dördüncü [durdewnjew] fourth

dört [durt] four

dört yol (ağzı) [a-zuh] crossroads, intersection

döşeme [durshemeh] furniture; upholstery; floor; floor covering

döviz [durveez] foreign currency

döviz alım belgesi [aluhm] document for purchase of foreign currency

döviz kuru exchange rate

draje [draJeh] coated pill

dudak lips

dudak merhemi lip salve

dul widow; widower

duman smoke

dur! stop!

duracak the bus is going to stop

duracak yer standing room

durak stop

durgun calm, still

durmak to stop; to stand; to lie; to remain

durmak yasaktır no stopping

duru clear

durulmaz no stopping

durum situation

duruma göre [gureh] it depends

duş [doosh] shower

duş jeli [Jelee] shower gel

duşlu with shower

duvar wall

duygu [doo-igoo] feeling

duymak [doo-imak] to hear; to feel

düğme [dewmeh] button; switch

düğün [dew-ewn] wedding

dükkân [dewkkan] shop

dümdüz devam edin [dewmdewz] go straight on

dümdüz ilerde [eelerdeh] straight ahead

dün [dewn] yesterday

dün gece [gejeh] last night

dün sabah [sabaH] yesterday morning

dünya [dewn-ya] world

dürüst [dewrewst] honest

düş kırıcı [dewsh kuhruhjuh] disappointing

düşmek [dewshmek] to fall

düşünmek [dewshewnmek] to think; to think about

düşürmek [dewshewrmek] to drop

düz [dewz] flat; plain (not patterned)

düzenlemek [dewzenlemek] to organize

düz gidin straight on

düzine [dewzeeneh] dozen yarım düzine [yaruhm] half a dozen

düz vitesli manual, with manual gears

E

-e [-eh] to; towards

...-ebilir misiniz? can you ...?, could you ...?

...-ebilir miyim? can I ...?, may I ...?

eczane [ejzaneh] chemist's, pharmacy

edebilir: ... edebilir miyim? can I ...?

edebiyat literature

efendi 'gentleman', 'master' – formerly respectful way of addressing social superiors; now used in a derogatory way

efendim sir; madam efendim? pardon (me)?, sorry?

Efes Ephesus

eflatun purple

Ege [egeh] the Aegean

egzos exhaust (pipe)

eğer [eh-er] if

eğlenmek [eh-lenmek] to enjoy oneself, to have fun eğlendik [eh-lendeek] it was fun

eh [eH] enough; come on; well; all right

ehliyet [ehlee-yet] licence

ekim October

ekip team

ekonomi sınıfı [sühnuhfuh] economy class

eksik missing; lacking

ekspres express (train)

ekspresyol motorway, freeway, highway

ekspresyol kavşağı [kavsha-uh] motorway junction

ekspresyolun sonu end of motorway/freeway/highway

ekşi [ekshee] sour

ek ücret [ewjret] supplement, extra charge

el hand

el arabası [arabasuh] trolley; wheelbarrow

el bagajı [bagaJuh] hand luggage, hand baggage

elbette [elbetteh] of course, certainly

elbezi dishcloth

elbise [elbeeseh] clothes

elbiseler clothes

el çantası [chantas**uh**] handbag, (US) purse

elçilik [elcheel**eek**] embassy

elden düşme [dewshm**eh**] second-hand

elde yıkanabilir can be handwashed

eldiven gloves

elektrik electricity

elektrikçi [elektreekch**ee**] electrician

elektrik düğmesi [dewmes**ee**] switch

elektrik kesilmesi power cut

elektrikli electric

elektrikli aletler electrical appliances

elektrikli tıraş makinesi [tuhr**ash**] electric shaver

elektrik sobası [sobas**uh**] electric fire

elektrik süpürgesi [sewpewrges**ee**] vacuum cleaner

el feneri torch

el freni handbrake

eline sağlık! [eleen**eh** sa-lu**hk**] well done!

elle yıkayınız wash by hand

elli fifty

elmas diamond

el sanatları [sanatlar**uh**] crafts

el sanatları dükkanı [dewk-kan**uh**] craft shop

elverişsiz [elvereesh-s**eez**] inconvenient

emanet left luggage office, baggage check

emanet kasası [kasas**uh**] left luggage locker

emek work

emekli retired; pensioner

-emem I can't

emin safe; sure

emin misiniz? are you sure?

emniyet kemeri seatbelt

emniyet kemerlerinizi bağlayınız fasten seat belts

emniyetli safe (not dangerous)

emniyette [emnee-yett**eh**] safe (not in danger)

emzik dummy

en most; width

enayi [enī-ee] idiot, fool

en azından [azuhnd**an**] at least

en çok [chok] mostly; at the most

ender rare

endişe etmek [endeesh**eh**] to worry about

enfeksiyon infection

enformasyon information

enişte [eneesht**eh**] brother-in-law (sister's husband); aunt's husband

en iyi best

enjeksiyon [enJeksee-y**on**] injection

en kötü [kurt**ew**] worst

en son latest

en sonunda eventually

epey [epay] rather; pretty well

erkek arkadaş [arkad**ash**] boyfriend

erkek çocuk [choj**ook**] boy

erkek giyim eşyası [esh-ya**suh**] menswear

erkek gömleği [gurmleh-**ee**]
men's shirts

erkek iç çamaşırı [eech
chamashuhr**uh**] men's
underwear

erkek kardeş [kard**esh**] brother

erkek konfeksiyon(u) menswear

erkekler men

erkekler tuvaleti gents' toilets,
men's room

erkeklik organı [organ**uh**] penis

erkek tuvaleti gents' toilet

erken(den) early

Ermeni Armenian

Ermenistan Armenia

ertelemek to postpone

ertesi next; following
ertesi gün [gewn] the
following day, the next day

esas main; basic

eski ancient; old; former

eskimo® ice lolly

eski moda old-fashioned

eski şehir [sheh-h**ee**r] old town

esnasında [esnashund**a**] during

esnek elastic

estağfurullah [esta-fooroolla**H**]
don't mention it; don't say
so

eş [esh] wife; husband

eşarp [esh**a**rp] scarf (for head)

eşek [esh**e**k] donkey

eşek arısı [aruhs**uh**] wasp

eşlik etmek [eshl**ee**k] to
accompany

eşofman [eshofm**an**] tracksuit

eşşoğlu eşek [eshshol**oo** eshek]
ass; lout

eşya [esh-y**a**] furniture; things

eşya arabası [arabas**uh**]
luggage trolley, baggage
trolley

eteğinde [eteh-eend**eh**] bottom
(of hill)

etek skirt

etiket label

etkileyici [etkeelay-eej**ee**]
impressive

etmek to do (used in compounds)

et pazarı [pazar**uh**] meat
market

etyemez vegetarian

ev house; home
evde [evd**eh**] at home
evde mi? is he/she in?

eve gitmek [ev**eh**] to go
home

evet yes

evlenmek to get married

evlenme yıldönümü [evlenm**eh**
yuhl-durnewm-**ew**] wedding
anniversary

evli married

evrak çantası [chantas**uh**]
briefcase

evvel first; before
-den evvel before

evvelki the previous; the ...
before last
evvelki gün [gewn] the day
before; the day before
yesterday

evvelsi the previous; the ...
before
evvelsi gün [gewn] the day
before yesterday

evye [**e**v-yeh] sink

eyer [ay-**e**r] saddle

eylemek [aylemek] to do; to
make (used in compounds)
eylül [aylewl] September
eyvah! [ayvaH] alas!
eyvallah! [ayvallaH] cheerio!;
thanks!
ezan Muslim call to prayer

F

fabrika factory
Fahrenheit Fahrenheit
faiz [fa-eez] interest
fakat but
fakir poor
faks çekmek [chekmek] to send
a fax
fakslamak to fax
falan and so on; about
fanila vest (under shirt)
far (head)light; eye shadow
fare [fareh] mouse; rat
fark difference
farlar headlights
fatura invoice
favori favourite
fayda [fida] use; advantage
fazla too (excessively); more than
fazla bagaj [bagaJ] excess
baggage
fazla pişmiş [peeshmeesh]
overdone
felaket disaster
fen science
fena nasty, bad
fener lamp
fenni scientific
feribot ferry
fermuar [fermoo-ar] zip

fes fez
fevkalade [fevkaladeh]
extraordinary, unusual;
super
Fırat [Fuhrat] the Euphrates
fırça [fuhrcha] brush
fırın [fuhruhn] oven; bakery
fırtına [fuhrtuhna] storm
fikir idea
film banyo etmek to develop
film banyosu film processing
film yıldızı [yuhlduhzuh] film
star, movie star
filtre kağıdı [feeltreh ka-uhduh]
filter papers
fincan [feenjan] cup
fincan tabağı [taba-uh] saucer
fiş [feesh] slip of paper; card;
plug (electrical)
fiyat price
flaş [flash] flash
flaster plaster
fondöten [fondurten]
foundation cream
formda fit
formüler [formewler] form
fotoğraf [foto-raf] photo
fotoğraf çekmek [chekmek] to
photograph
fotoğrafçı [foto-rafchuh]
photographer; camera shop
fotoğraf makinesi camera
fön [furn] blow-dry
fönle kurutma [furnleh] blow dry
Fransa [fransa] France
Fransız [fransuhz] French (adj)
Fransızca [fransuhzja] French
(language)
fren brakes

fren yapmak to brake
fuar [fwar] trade fair
fuaye [fwī-eh] foyer
futbol football, soccer
futbol maçı [machuh] football
   match

G

galeri upper circle
galiba presumably
Galler Wales
Galli Welsh
gar terminus
garaj [garaɪ] garage
garip strange; peculiar; poor;
   lonely; stranger
garson waiter
garson kız [kuhz] waitress
gayet [gī-et] very
gaz gas
gazete [gazeteh] newspaper
gazete bayii [bī-ee-ee]
   newsagent's
gazete satıcısı [satuhjuhsuh]
   newspaper kiosk; news
   vendor
gaz geçirgen lensler [gecheergen]
   gas permeable lenses
gazi war veteran
gazino open-air restaurant,
   nightclub
gaz pedalı [pedaluh]
   accelerator
gaz tüpü [tewpew] gas cylinder
gaz vermek to accelerate
gebe [gebeh] pregnant
gebeliği önleyici [gebelee-ee
   urnleh-yeejee] contraceptive

gece [gejeh] night; a.m. (from
   midnight to 4 a.m.); overnight
   geceleyin [gejelay-een] at
   night
gece bekçisi [bekcheesee] night
   porter
gecekondu [gejekondoo] shanty
gecekondu bölgesi [burlgesee]
   shanty town
gece kulübü [koolewbew]
   nightclub
gecelik [gejeleek] nightdress
gece yarısı [yaruhsuh] midnight
gecikme [gejeekmeh] delay
gecikmeli [gejeekmelee]
   delayed
geç [gech] late; cross
geçe [gecheh] past
geçen [gechen] past; last
   geçen hafta last week
   geçen yıl [yuhl] last year
geçerli [gecherlee] valid
geçici güzergah [gecheejee
   gewzergah] diversion, detour
geçin: ...-i geçin [gecheen] go
   past the ...
geçiş [gecheesh] crossing
geçit [gecheet] pass (in
   mountains)
geç kalmak to arrive late, to be
   late
geçmek [gechmek] to pass; to
   overtake; to go through; to
   cross
geçme yasağı no overtaking
geçmiş olsun! [gechmeesh] get
   well soon!
geçmişte [gechmeeshteh] in the
   past

geldiği ülke country of departure
gelecek [gelejek] future
gelecekte [gelejekteh] in future
gelecek hafta next week
gelecek yıl [yuhl] next year
gelen bagaj [bagaɹ] baggage claim
gelenek custom; tradition
geleneksel traditional
gel-git tide
gel-git olayı [olī-**uh**] tide
Gelibolu Gallipoli
gelin daughter-in-law; bride
geliş [gel**ee**sh] arrival
geliş nedeni reason for arrival
geliştirmek [gel**ee**shteerm**ek**] to improve
gelmek to come; to arrive
gemi boat; ship
gemiyle [gemee-il**eh**] by ship
genç [gench] young; young person
genç kız [kuhz] teenager (female)
gençler [gench**le**r] young people
gençlik hosteli [genchl**ee**k] youth hostel
gene [gen**eh**] again; still
genel general (adj)
genellikle [genelleekl**eh**] usually, generally
genel olarak generally
geniş [gen**ee**sh] wide
gerçek [gerch**e**k] real, genuine; true
gerçekten [g**e**rchekten] really

gerçekten üzgünüm [gerchekt**e**n ewzgewn**ew**m] I'm really sorry
gerçi [gerch**ee**] although
gerek(li) necessary
gerekmek to be necessary
geri back, rear; backwards; reverse
geride [gereed**eh**] at the back
geri aramak (telefonla) to ring back
geri dönülmez no U-turns
geri gelmek to come back
geri geri gitmek to reverse
geri gidin go back
gerinmek to stretch
geri ödeme [urdem**eh**] refund
geri vites reverse gear
germek to stretch
getirmek to get, to fetch; to bring
gevşek malzeme loose chippings
gevşek şev falling rock
gevşemiş [gevshem**ee**sh] loose
gezi trip
gezinti trip; outing
gezmek to walk about/around; to stroll; to go out; to tour; to look round
gıda zehirlenmesi [guhd**a**] food poisoning
gibi as; like
gideceği yer [geedejeh-**ee**] destination
giden yolcular salonu [yoljool**a**r] departure lounge
gidermek to remove

gidilecek yer [geedeelejek] destination

gidip getirmek: -i gidip getirmek to fetch

gidiş [geedeesh] single, one-way

gidiş bileti single ticket, one-way ticket

gidiş dönüş bileti [durnewsh] return ticket, round trip ticket

girilmez no entry

girin enter, come in

giriniz enter, come in

giriş [geereesh] way-in, entrance; admission charge

giriş holü [holew] foyer

giriş ücreti [ewjretee] admission fee

giriş ücretledir admission fee charged

giriş ücretsizdir free entrance

Girit Crete

girmek to go in, to enter, to come in

girmek yasaktır no entry, keep out

girmeyiniz do not enter

gişe [geesheh] counter; ticket window

git! [geet] go away!

gitar guitar

gitmek to go

gitti he/she's gone

gittikçe [geetteekcheh] gradually

giydirmek [gee-ideermek] to dress

giyim eşyası [esh-yasuh] clothing

giyinmek to get dressed

giyip denemek to try on

giymek [gee-imek] to wear

gizli secret

golf sahası [sahasuh] golf course

göğüs [gur-ews] chest; breast; bust

göğüsleri açık [gur-ewsleree achuhk] topless

gök [gurk] sky

gök gürültüsü [gewrewltewsew] thunder

göl [gurl] lake

... Gölü [gurlew] Lake ...

gölge [gurlgeh] shade; shadow

gölgede [gurlgedeh] in the shade

gölgede kurutunuz dry away from direct sunlight

gömlek [gurmlek] shirt

gönderen [gurnderen] sender

gönderilecek adres [gurndereelejek] forwarding address

göndermek [gurndermek] to send

göre: -e göre [-eh gureh] according to

görevli [gurevlee] official; officer

görmek [gurmek] to see

gör(ül)meye değer yerler [gur(ewl)mayeh deh-er] (the) sights

görümce [gurewmjeh] sister-in-law (husband's sister)

görünmek [gurewnmek] to seem;
to look

görüşmek üzere [gurewshmek
ewzereh] see you later

görüşürüz! [gurewshewrewz] see
you!

gösteri [gursteree] show (in
theatre)

göstermek [gurstermek] to
show

götürmek [gurtewrmek] to take
(away); to carry

göz [gurz] eye; drawer

göz boyası [boyasuh] eye
shadow

göz damlası [damlasuh] eye
drops

gözde [gurzdeh] favourite

göz doktoru optician

gözlük [gurzlewk] glasses,
spectacles, (US) eyeglasses

gözlükçü [gurzlewkchew]
optician

göz makyajı çıkarıcısı [makyaJuh
chuhkaruh-juhsuh] eye make-
up remover

gramer grammar

gri grey

grip [greep] flu

grup group; party

gururlu proud

gücendirmek [gewjendeermek] to
offend

güçlü [gewchlew] strong

güçsüz [gewchsewz] weak,
feeble

gül [gewl] rose

güle güle [gewleh] goodbye
(said to person leaving)

güle güle giy! [gee-i] literally:
'wear it happily!' – said to
someone who has bought
new clothes

güle güle kullan! literally: 'use
it happily!' – said to
someone who has bought
something new

gülmek [gewlmek] to laugh

gülümsemek [gewlewm-semek] to
smile

gülünç [gewlewnch]
ridiculous

Gümrük [gewmrewk] Customs

gümrük beyannámesi Customs
declaration

gümrüksüz [gewmrewksewz]
duty-free

gümüş [gewmewsh] silver;
silverware

gümüş yaprak silver foil

gün [gewn] day

gün ağanrken [a-aruhrken] at
dawn

günaydın [gewnīduhn] good
morning

günbatımı [gewn-batuhmuh]
sunset

günce [gewnjeh] diary

günde bir/iki/üç defa once/
twice/three times a day

günde üç defa ikişer tablet alınız
take two tablets three times
a day

gündüz [gewndewz] daytime;
by day

güneş [gewnesh] sun

güneşte [gewneshteh] in the
sun

güneş banyosu yapmak to
sunbathe
güneş çarpması [charpmas**uh**]
sunstroke
güneş gözlüğü [gurzlew-**ew**]
sunglasses
güneş ışığı [uhsh**uh**-uh]
sunshine
güneşli [gewneshl**ee**] sunny
güneşlik [gewneshl**ee**k]
sunshade
güneş losyonu suntan lotion
güneş merhemi sunblock
güneşte yanmak [gewnesht**eh**] to
get a tan
güneş yanmış [yanm**uh**sh]
sunburnt, tanned
güneş yağı [ya-**uh**] suntan oil
güneş yanığı [yanuh-**uh**]
sunburn
güney [gewn**ay**] south
güneyde [gewnayd**eh**] in the
south
...-in güneyi [gewnay-**ee**] south
of ...
güney batı [bat**uh**] southwest
güney doğu [d**oh**-oo] southeast
günlük [gewnl**ew**k] day; daily
günlük bilet day ticket
günlük gezi day trip
günü [gewn**ew**] on
Gürcistan [gewrjeest**an**] Georgia
Gürcü [gewrj**ew**] Georgian
gürültü [gewrewl-t**ew**] noise
gürültülü [gewrewl-tewl**ew**] loud;
noisy
gürültü yapmayın! [y**a**pmī-uhn]
quiet!
güverte [g**ew**verteh] deck

güzel [gewz**e**l] beautiful; nice;
pretty; fine; attractive
güzergah [gewzerg**a**H] route

H

haber news (on radio, TV etc)
ne haber? how are things?
hacı [haj**uh**] literally: 'pilgrim'
– respectful way of
addressing someone who
has made the pilgrimage to
Mecca
hafif light (not heavy); mild
hafif koşu [kosh**oo**] jogging
hafif müzik [mewz**ee**k] light
music
hafif rüzgar [rewzg**a**r] breeze
hafta week
haftaya bugün [haftī-**a**
boog**ew**n] a week (from)
today
haftaya yarın [yar**uh**n] a week
(from) tomorrow
haftada per week
haftalık bilet [haftal**uh**k] weekly
ticket
hafta sonu weekend
hafta sonunda at the weekend
hakikaten really, truly
hakiki true; real, genuine
hakkında [hakk**uh**nda]
concerning
hakkıyla [hakk**uh**-ila] properly
haklı [hakl**uh**] right, justified
hala aunt (paternal)
hâlâ still
halat rope
halı [hal**uh**] carpet

halıcı [haluhjuh] carpet seller

halı kaplama fitted carpet

halılar [haluhlar] carpets

Haliç [haleech] the Golden Horn

haliç inlet; bay

halk people

halka açık [achuhk] public; open to the public

halk dansları [danslaruh] folk dancing

halk müziği [mewzee-ee] folk music

halk oyunları [oyoonlaruh] folk dances

halletmek: -i halletmek to fix, to arrange

hamal porter

hamam Turkish bath

hamamböceği [–burjeh-ee] cockroach

hamile [hameeleh] pregnant

han tradesmen's hall; inn; caravanserai; office block
... Hanı [hanuh] ...
tradesmen's hall; ... inn; ... office block

hangi? which?

hangisi? which one?

hanım [hanuhm] lady; wife
... hanım Mrs ...

hap pill(s); contraceptive pill(s)

hapis(hane) [hapees(haneh)] prison

hapşırık [hapshuhruhk] sneeze

hapşırmak [hapshuhrmak] to sneeze

harabe [harabeh] ruin

harabeler ruins

harcamak [harjamak] to spend

hareket etmek to move

hareket saati [sa-atee] time of departure

hariç [hareech] except; external; abroad

harika! great!

harikulade [hareekooladeh] wonderful

harita [hareeta] map

hasar görmüş [gurmewsh] damaged

hassas sensitive

hasta sick, ill

hastabakıcı [–bakuhjuh] nurse

hastalık [hastaluhk] illness; disease

hastalık sigortası [seegortasuh] health insurance

hastane [hastaneh] hospital
... Hastanesi ... Hospital

hat route; line

hata mistake; fault

hatıra [hatuhra] souvenir

hatırlamak [hatuhrlamak] to remember

hatırlıyorum [hatuhrluh-yoroom] I remember

hatta even

hava air; weather

hava soğuk [soh-ook] it's cold

havaalanı [hava-alanuh] airport

hava basıncı [basuhnjuh] air pressure

hava cereyanı [jereh-yanuh] draught

havai fişek [feeshek] fireworks

havale [havaleh] money order

havalimanı [havaleeman**uh**]
airport
havalimanı otobüsü [otob**ew**sew]
airport bus
hava tahmini weather
forecast
havayolu [havĭ-ol**oo**] airline
havlu bath towel
havuz pond; pool
hay Allah! [hĭ] damn!
hayat [hĭ-at] life
haydi! [hĭdee] come on!
haydi gidelim! [hĭdee] let's go!
hayhay! [hĭ-hĭ] certainly!, by all
means!
hayır [hĭ-uhr] no; goodness
hayran [hĭran] fan; admirer
hayret! [hĭret] well well!
hayvan [hĭvan] animal
hayvanat bahçesi [hĭvanat
ba**H**ches**ee**] zoo
hayvanlara yiyecek vermeyiniz
do not feed the animals
hazımsızlık [hazuhm-suhzl**uh**k]
indigestion
hazır [haz**uh**r] ready
hazırlamak [hazuhrlam**a**k] to
prepare
haziran June
hediye [hedee-y**eh**] present,
gift
hediyelik eşya dükkanı [esh-ya
dewkkan**uh**] gift shop
hekim doctor
hela W.C., toilet, restroom
hem moreover, besides; both
... and
hemen immediately; almost
hemen hemen almost

hemen hemen hiç [heech]
hardly ever
hemen şimdi [sh**ee**mdee]
straight away
hemşire [hemsheer**eh**] nurse;
sister
hemzemin geçit [gech**ee**t] level
crossing
henüz [hen**ew**z] yet; just now;
a minute ago
henüz değil [deh-**ee**l] not yet
hep always; the whole
hep birden altogether
hepimiz all of us
hepsi all of it/them, the whole
lot
hepsi bu kadar that's all
hepsi o kadar nothing else
her each; every
her gün [gewn] every day;
daily
her defasında [defasuhnd**a**]
every time
herif bloke, guy
her iki ... de [deh] both ...
her ikisi de both of them
herkes everyone
her neyse [nays**eh**] anyway
her şey [shay] everything
her şey dahil all-inclusive
her şeyden önce [shayd**e**n
u**r**njeh] first of all
her yer everywhere
her yerde [yerd**eh**]
everywhere
her zaman always
hesap bill, (US) check;
account
hesap makinesi calculator

heyecan verici [hayejan vereejee] exciting

Heyelan! landslides!

heykel [haykel] statue

hırdavatçı [huhrdavatchuh] hardware store

Hıristiyan [huhreestee-yan] Christian

hırka [huhrka] cardigan

hırsız [huhrsuhz] thief

hırsızlık [huhrsuhzluhk] burglary; theft

hıyar [huh-yar] lout; cucumber

hız [huhz] speed

hız kısıtlaması sonu end of speed restriction

hızla [huhzla] quickly

hızlı [huhzluh] fast; quickly

hicri [heejree] Muslim system of dates

hiç [heech] none; nothing; never; ever
  hiç de değil [deh deh-eel] not in the least
  hiç ... iz mi? have you ever ...?
  hiç ... yok I don't have any ...; there isn't any ...
  hiç bir ... no ... at all
  hiç biri neither of them
  hiç kalmadı [kalmaduh] there's none left

hiçbir şey [heechbeer shay] nothing

hiçbir yerde [yerdeh] nowhere

hiçbir zaman never

hiç kimse [keemseh] nobody, no-one

hidrofil pamuk cotton wool, absorbent cotton

hikâye [heekī-eh] story

his feeling

hisar fortress, castle

hissetmek to feel

hitap ekmek to call

Hititler the Hittites

hizmet etmek to serve

hoca [hoja] teacher; teacher in charge of religious instruction

hol entrance hall, lobby
  ... holü [holew] ... hall

horlamak to snore

hostes stewardess

hoş [hosh] nice, pleasant; fine

hoş bulduk! it's nice to be here! – usual response to 'hoş geldiniz'

hoşça kal [hosh-cha] bye (said by person leaving)

hoşça kalın [kaluhn] goodbye

hoş geldiniz! welcome!

hoşlanmak [hoshlanmak] to like

hükümet [hewkewmet] government

hür [hewr] free

hürriyet [hewr-ree-yet] freedom

I

-ı [-uh] his; her; its; accusative noun ending

ılıca [uhluhja] hot spring

ılık [uhluhk] lukewarm

ılık ütü warm iron

ılımlı [uhluhmluh] mild; moderate

-ım [-uhm] my; I am

-ımız [-uhmuhz] our

-ın [-uhn] of; your
-ınız [-uhnuhz] your
 ...-ınız var mı? [muh] have you
 got ...?
Iraklı [uhrakluh] Iraqi
ırmak [uhrmak] river
ırza geçme [uhrza gechmeh]
 rape
ısırık [uhsuhruhk] bite, sting
ısırma [uhsuhrma] bite
ısırmak [uhsuhrmak] to bite
ısıtma [uhsuhtma] heating
ıslak [uhslak] wet
ısmarlamak [uhsmarlamak] to
 order
ışık [uhshuhk] light
-ız [-uhz] we are
ızdıraplı [uhzduhrapluh] painful

İ

-i his; her; its; the
iade [ee-adeh] refund
iade etmek to give back
iç [eech] interior, inside
iç çamaşırı [chamashuhruh]
 underwear
içerde [eecherdeh] indoors,
 inside
içeri [eecheree] inside
içeride [eechereedeh] indoors,
 inside
içeri kilitlemek [eecheree] to
 lock in
içerisi [eechereesee] inside
içermek [eechermek] to contain
iç hastalıkları mütehassısı
 [hastaluhklaruh
 mewteHassuhsuh] specialist in

internal diseases
iç hatlar [eech] domestic flights
iç hat seferi domestic flight
içilmez [eecheelmez] not for
 drinking
için [eecheen] for; as
içinde [eecheendeh] in;
 included
 iki gün içinde [gewn] in two
 days from now
içinden [eecheenden] through
içine [eecheeneh] into
iç kale [kaleh] citadel
içki [eechkee] alcoholic drinks
içkili olarak araba sürmek
 [sewrmek] drunken driving
içkisiz no drinks allowed
iç lastik inner tube
içmek [eechmek] to drink
içme suyu [eechmeh] drinking
 water
içten [eechten] sincere
idi it was
iğne [ee-neh] needle; injection
iğrenç [ee-rench] disgusting,
 revolting; obnoxious
... ihtiyacında [eeHtee-yajuhnda]
 in need of ...
ihtiyaç [eeHtee-yach] need
ihtiyaç duymak [doo-imak] to
 need
ihtiyar [eeHtee-yar] old; old
 person
ikamet stay
ikamet adresi domicile
iken while
iki two
iki hafta fortnight
iki kere [kereh] twice

iki kişilik oda [keesheel**ee**k] double room

iki kişilik yatak double bed

iki misli twice as much

ikinci [eekeen**jee**] second (adj)

ikinci kat second floor, (US) third floor

ikinci sınıf [suhn**uhf**] second class

ikisi: ikisi de [deh] both ikisinden biri either of them

iki tane tek kişilik yatak [t**a**neh tek keesheel**ee**k] twin beds

iki yol ağzı [**a**-zuh] fork (in road)

iki yönlü trafik two-way traffic

ikizler twins

iklim climate

il province; county ... **l**li Province of ..., County of ...

ilaç [eel**a**ch] medicine

ilan yapıştırmak yasaktır stick no bills

ilçe [eelch**eh**] administrative district

ile [eel**eh**] with; and; by otobüs ile [otob**ew**s] by bus

ileri front part; forward

-ileri the

ileride [ilereed**eh**] further (on); in future

ilerleyelim lütfen! please move forward!

iletmek to forward; to pass on

ilgilenmek to be interested in; to show interest in; to take care of

ilginç [eelg**ee**nch] interesting

ilim science

ilişki kurmak [eeleeshk**ee**] to contact

ilişkin: -e ilişkin [eeleeshk**ee**n] relating to

ilk first ilk önce [**u**rnjeh] at first ilk kez the first time

ilkbahar spring (season)

ilk hareket first departure

ilk olarak first

ilk yardım [yard**uh**m] first aid

ilk yardım çantası [chantas**uh**] first aid kit

iltihap inflammation

-im my; I am

imam prayer leader in a Mosque

imaret soup kitchen and hostel

imdat emergency

imdat! help!

imdat freni emergency brake

-imiz our

imkansız [eemkans**uh**z] impossible

imza signature

imza etmek to sign

-in of; your

inanılmaz [eenanuhlm**a**z] incredible, amazing

inanmak to believe

ince [eenj**eh**] thin

incitmek [eenjeetm**e**k] to hurt

inç [eench] inch

indirimli satış [sat**uh**sh] sale

inek cow

İngiliz [**ee**ngeeleez] English; British; Englishman

İngiliz anahtarı [anaнtar**uh**] wrench

İngilizce [eengeeleezjeh] English (language); in English

İngiliz kadın [kaduhn] English woman

İngilizler the English

İngiliz sterlini pound sterling

İngiltere [eengeeltereh] England; the UK

inik lastik flat tyre

inilir get off here

-iniz your

inmek to get off; to get out; to go down; to land; to fly in

insan person; man

insanlar people

inşallah [eenshal-lah] I hope so; hopefully; God willing

inşallah öyle değildir [urleh deheeldeer] I hope not; God forbid

ip string; rope

ipek silk

iple çekmek [eepleh chekmek] to look forward to

iplik thread

iptal edildi cancelled

iptal etmek to cancel

İranlı [eeranluh] Iranian

iri big

İrlanda [eerlanda] Ireland; Irish

İrlandalı [eerlandaluh] Irishman; Irishwoman

İsa [eesha] Jesus

ishal [ees-hal] diarrhoea

isilik rash (on skin)

isim name

iskele [eeskeleh] jetty; quay; ferry terminal

... İskelesi ... Jetty; ... Docks; ... Terminal

iskemle [eeskemleh] chair

İskoç [eeskoch] Scottish

İskoçya [eeskochya] Scotland

iskonto discount

İslami [eeslamee] Islamic

İspanya [eespanya] Spain

İspanyol [eespanyol] Spanish (adj)

İspanyolca [eespanyolja] Spanish (language)

ısrar ediyorum I insist

ısrar etmek: -de ısrar etmek to insist on

İstanbul Boğazı [eestanbool boazuh] the Bosphorus

istasyon station

istasyonda at the station

istemek to want; to wish; to ask for

istemiyorum I don't want

isterim I want

... ister misiniz? do you want ...?

istiyor he/she wants

... istiyor musunuz? do you want ...?

istiyor(d)um I would like

istiyorsunuz: ne istiyorsunuz? [neh] what do you want?

istiyorum I want

İsveç [eesvech] Sweden; Swedish (adj)

İsveççe [eesvech-cheh] Swedish (language)

İsviçre [eesveechreh] Switzerland

iş [eesh] work; job; business; deal

işaret levhası [eesharet levhasuh]
  signpost
işe: bu işe yaramaz [eesheh] it's
  no good
iş günü [eesh gewnew]
  weekdays
işitme cihazı [eesheetmeh
  jeehazuh] hearing aid
işitmek [eesheetmek] to hear
işkembeci [eeshkembejee] tripe
  restaurant
işkembe salonu [eeshkembeh]
  tripe shop
işlek [eeshlek] busy
işleme günleri ferry timetable
iş seyahati [eesh sayahatee]
  business trip
işsiz [eeshseez] unemployed
iştah [eeshtaH] appetite
işte [eeshteh] here is/are; there
  is/are; here it is; her; him
İtalya [etalya] Italy
İtalyan [eetalyan] Italian (adj)
itfaiye [eetfa-ee-yeh] fire
  brigade
itiniz push
itmek to push; push
iyi good; well; kind
  iyi misin? are you OK?
iyi akşamlar [akshamlar] good
  evening
iyice [ee-yeejeh] properly
iyi geceler [gejeler] good night
iyi günler [gewnler] hello
  (literally: good day); have a
  nice day
iyilik sağlık [sa-luhk] I'm fine
iyimser optimistic
iyi şanslar! [shanslar] good luck!

iyiyim I'm all right, I'm fine
iyi yolculuklar! [yoljoolooklar]
  have a good journey!
-iz we are
izin holiday, vacation; permit
izin belgesi licence
izin vermek to let, to allow
izlemek to follow

J

jaluzi [Jaloozee] blinds
jant [Jant] rim; spoke
jarse [Jarseh] jersey (cloth)
jel [Jel] jelly; hair gel
jeton [Jeton] telephone token
jikle [Jeekleh] choke
jilet [Jeelet] razor blade
jinekolog [Jeenekolog]
  gynaecologist
jogging yapmak to go jogging
jöle [Jurleh] hair gel

K

kaba rude; rough; vulgar
kabaca [kabaja] roughly,
  approximately
kabadayı [kabadī-uh] macho
kabak bald; pumpkin;
  marrow; courgette, zucchini
kabakulak mumps
kabarcık [kabarjuhk] blister
kabız [kabuhz] constipated
kabızlık [kabuhzluhk]
  constipation
kabin cabin; changing
  cubicle
kabin memuru steward

kablo lead; wire

kabul etmek to accept

kaburga rib

kaç? [kach] how many?; how much?

  kaç kişilik [keesheeleek] for how many people?

  kaç tane? [taneh] how many?

  kaç yaşındasınız? [yashuhnda-suhnuhz] how old are you?

  kaç gecelik? [kach gejeleek] for how many nights?

kaçak [kachak] leak; fugitive; contraband

kaçık [kachuhk] weirdo

kaçırmak [kachuhrmak] to miss (bus etc)

kadar until; about; as much as; as many as

  kadar ...-e kadar [-eh] as ... as; until; as much as; as far as

  ne kadar? [neh] how much?

  ne kadar iyi! how nice!; it's so good!

kadın [kaduhn] woman; lady

kadın bağı [ba-uh] sanitary towel

kadın giyim eşyası [esh-yasuh] ladies' wear

kadınlar [kaduhnlar] women

kadın polis policewoman

kadran dial

kafa head

kafatası [kafatasuh] skull

kafeterya cafeteria

kâğıt [ka-uht] paper

kâğıt çocuk bezi [chojook] disposable nappies/diapers

kâğıt mendil tissues, Kleenex®

kâğıt para banknote, (US) bill

kahvaltı [kaHvaltuh] breakfast

kahvaltı dahil breakfast included

kahve [kaHveh] coffee; coffee shop (usually for men only)

kahvehane [kaHveh-Haneh] café (usually for men only)

kahverengi [kaHverengee] brown

kala: -e ... kala [-eh] to; remaining

  beşe on kala [besheh] ten to five

kalabalık [kalabaluhk] crowd; crowded, busy

kalabalık saatler [sa-atler] rush hour

kalacak yer [kalajak] accommodation

kalan the rest (of)

kalça [kalcha] hip

kaldırım [kalduhruhm] pavement, sidewalk

kaldırınız lift (the receiver)

kaldırmak [kalduhrmak] to raise; to lift; to remove

kale [kaleh] castle, fort

  ... Kalesi ... Castle, Fort ...

kalem pencil

kalın [kaluhn] thick

kalın kafa thickhead

kalite [kaleeteh] quality

kaliteli high quality

kalkış [kalkuhsh] departure

kalkmak to stand up; to get up; to take off; to leave

kalmak to stay, to remain

kalorifer (central) heating; heater

kalp heart
kalp krizi heart attack
kamara cabin
kambiyo bureau de change
kamp ateşi [ateshee] campfire
kamping campsite; caravan
  site, trailer park
kamp yapmak to camp
kamp yapmak yasaktır no
  camping
kamp yeri campsite
kamu the public
kamyon lorry
kamyonet van
kan blood
Kanada Canada; Canadian (adj)
Kanadalı [kanadaluh]
  Canadian (person)
kanamak to bleed
kanat wing
kan grubu blood group
kano canoe
kano kullanmak canoeing
kanun law
kapa çeneni! [chenenee] shut
  up!
Kapadokya Cappadocia
kapak cap; lid
kapalı [kapaluh] closed; off;
  covered
kapalı çarşı [charshuh] covered
  bazaar
kapalı havuz indoor pool
kapalı yüzme havuzu
  [yewzmeh] indoor swimming
  pool
kapamak to switch off; to
  close; to shut
kapatmak to close, to shut

kapı [kapuh] door; gate
kapıcı [kapuhjuh] caretaker;
  doorman; porter
kapı kolu [kapuh] door handle
kap kacak [kajak] cooking
  utensils, pots and pans
kaplıca [kapluhja] thermal
  spring
kaporta bonnet, (US) hood
kapsamak to include
kaptan captain
kaput bonnet, (US) hood
kar snow
kâr profit, benefit
kara black
karabasan nightmare
karaciğer [karajee-er] liver (in
  body)
Karadeniz the Black Sea
karakol police station
karanlık [karanluhk] dark;
  darkness
karantina quarantine
karar decision
  (-e) karar vermek [-eh] to
  decide (on)
karayolu [karı-oloo] highway
karayolu haritası [hareetasuh]
  road map
karbüratör [karbewratur]
  carburettor
kardeş [kardesh] brother; sister
karı [karuh] wife
karın ağrısı [karuhn a-ruhsuh]
  stomachache
karınca [karuhnja] ant
karışıklık [karuhshuhkluhk] mess
karıştırmak [karuhshtuhrmak] to
  mix

karmaşık [karmashuhk]
complicated
karşı: -e karşı [-eh karshuh]
across; against; towards;
contrary
karşıda [karshuhda] opposite
karşıdan gelen taşıtlara öncelik
oncoming traffic has right
of way
karşılaşmak [karshuhlashmak] to
meet
karşın: -e karşın [-eh karshuhn]
in spite of
karşısında [karshuhsuhnda]
opposite
karşıt [karshuht] opposite;
contrary; anti-; counter-
kart card
kartlı telefon [kartluh]
cardphone
karton cardboard; box
kartpostal postcard
kartvizit business card
kas muscle
kasa till, cash desk;
cashier
kasaba small town
kasadan fiş alınız please obtain
ticket from the till
kasap butcher's
kasap dükkanı [dewkkanuh]
butcher's shop
kase [kaseh] bowl
kasetli teyp [tayp] cassette
recorder
kasım [kasuhm] November
kasis uneven road surface
kasiyer cashier
kask helmet

kasket cap
kasten deliberately
kaş [kash] eyebrow
kaşık [kashuhk] spoon
kaşıntı [kashuhntuh] itch
kaş kalemi [kash] eyebrow
pencil
kat floor, storey
katakomp catacomb
katedral cathedral
katiyen olmaz! no way!
Katma Değer Vergisi [deh-er]
VAT
Katolik Catholic
kavanoz jar
kavga fight
kavga etmek to fight
kavim people; tribe
kavşak [kavshak] crossroads,
intersection; junction
kaya [kī-a] rock
kayak skiing
kayak pisti ski slope
kayak yapmak to ski
kaybetmek [kībetmek] to lose
kaybolmak [kībolmak] to
disappear
kaygan [kīgan] slippery
kaygan yol slippery road
kaygı [kīguh] worry
kaygılanmak [kīguhlanmak] to
worry about
kayık [kī-uhk] small boat;
rowing boat
kayınbirader [kī-uhn-beerader]
brother-in-law (husband's/wife's
brother)
kayınpeder [kī-uhnpeder] father-
in-law

kayınvalide [kī-uhnvaleed**eh**] mother-in-law

kayıp eşya [kī-**uh**p esh-y**a**] lost property

kayıp eşya bürosu [bewros**oo**] lost property office

kayış [kī-**uh**sh] strap

kayıt numarası [kī-**uh**t noomaras**uh**] registration number

kaymak [kīm**a**k] to skid; cream

kaynak [kīn**a**k] spring, source

kaynana [kīn**a**na] mother-in-law

kaza accident

kazak jumper, sweater

kazan boiler

kazanmak to earn; to win

kazık [kaz**uh**k] rip-off; tent peg

KDV [ka deh veh] VAT

kebapçı [kebapch**uh**] meat restaurant

keçe uçlu kalem [kech**eh** oochl**oo**] felt-tip pen

keçi [kech**ee**] goat

kederli depressed

kedi cat

kel bald

kelebek butterfly

kelime [keleem**eh**] word

kemençe [kemench**eh**] small violin with three strings

kemer belt

kemik bone

-ken while

kenar edge
deniz kenarında [kenar**uh**nda] by the sea

kenar mahalle poor quarters near the edge of the town, slum

kenar şeridi [shereed**ee**] hard shoulder

kendi himself; herself; itself; oneself; his/her/its own

kendileri themselves

kendim myself

kendimiz ourselves

kendin yourself

kendiniz yourselves

kent town

kepenk shutter

kere [ker**eh**] time; occasion

kerpeten pliers

kervansaray [kervansar**ī**] inn, caravanserai

kes (artık)! [art**uh**k] stop it!

kesici platinler [keseej**ee**] points

kesik cut

kesinlikle [keseenl**ee**kleh] definitely; certainly
kesinlikle! absolutely!
kesinlikle (öyle) değil [(url**eh**) deh-**ee**l] definitely not, certainly not

keskin sharp

kesmece word used by street vendors meaning that melons can be cut open and examined before you buy

kesmek to cut

kestirme [kesteerm**eh**] shortcut

keten cotton

keyif [kay**ee**f] pleasure; disposition

kez time

Kıbrıs [**kuh**bruhs] Cyprus;
Cypriot (adj)
Kıbrıslı [**kuh**bruhsluh] Cypriot
(person)
Kıbrıslı Rum Greek Cypriot
(person)
Kıbrıs Rum Greek Cypriot (adj)
Kıbrıs Türk [tewrk] Turkish
Cypriot (adj)
kılavuz [kuhlav**ooz**] guide;
leader
kılık [kuhl**uh**k] appearance;
costume
kına [kuhn**a**] henna
kır [kuhr] countryside
kırık [kuhr**uh**k] broken;
fracture
kırk [kuhrk] forty
kırmak [kuhrm**a**k] to break; to
offend
kırmızı [kuhrmuhz**uh**] red
kırsal alanlar [kuhrs**a**l]
countryside
kırtasiye [kuhrtasee-y**eh**]
stationery
kırtasiyeci [kuhrtasee-yej**ee**]
stationer's
kısa [kuhs**a**] short; brief
en kısa zamanda [k**uh**sa] as
soon as possible
kısa yolculuk [yoljool**oo**k] short
journey
kısım [kuhs**uh**m] part, portion
kıskanç [kuhsk**a**nch] jealous
kış [kuhsh] winter
kışın [kuhsh**uh**n] in the
winter
kış tatili winter holiday, winter
vacation

kıvırcık [kuhvuhrj**uh**k] curly;
lettuce
kıyafet [kuh-yaf**e**t] dress, attire;
general appearance and
dress
kıyı [kuh-y**uh**] coast
kıymık [kuh-im**uh**k] splinter
kız [kuhz] girl; daughter
kızaklı tekne [kuhzakl**uh** tekn**eh**]
hydrofoil
kızamık [kuhzam**uh**k] measles
kızamıkçık [kuhzamuhkch**uh**k]
German measles
kız arkadaş [arkad**a**sh] girlfriend
kızarmak [kuhzarm**a**k] to be
fried; to be roasted; to be
toasted; to blush
kızartmak [kuhzartm**a**k] to fry;
to roast; to toast
kız(evlat) [kuhz(evl**a**t)] daughter
kızgın [kuhzg**uh**n] angry;
furious
Kızılay [kuhzuhl**ī**] Red Crescent
– Turkish Red Cross
Kızılhaç [kuhz**uh**lhach] Red
Cross
kızıl saçlı [kuhz**uh**l sachl**uh**] red-
headed
kız kardeş [kard**e**sh] sister
kızlık adı [kuhzl**uh**k ad**uh**]
maiden name
kızmak [kuhzm**a**k] to get angry
ki that; who; which; so that;
seeing that
kibrit matches
kilidi açmak [ach**a**k] to unlock
kilim rug
kilise [keelees**eh**] church
... Kilisesi Church of ...

kilit lock

kilitlemek to lock

kilitli locked

kilometre kısıtlaması yok
[keelom**e**treh kuhsuhtlamas**uh**]
unlimited mileage

kim? who?

kimi some

kimin? whose?

kimlik identification

kimlik kartı [kart**uh**] ID card

kimse [k**ee**mseh] anybody;
nobody

kira rent; rental

kiralamak to rent, to hire

kiralık [keeral**uh**k] for rent, for
hire

kiralık bisiklet bicycle hire

kiralık kayık [kī-**uh**k] boat hire

kiralık otomobil [keeral**uh**k] car
rental; rented car

kira ücreti [ewjret**ee**] hire
charge

kirli dirty; polluted

kişi [keesh**ee**] person

kitabevi bookshop, bookstore

kitap book

kitapçı [keet**a**p-chuh] bookshop,
bookstore

kitaplık [keetapl**uh**k] library

KKTC Turkish Republic of
Northern Cyprus

klakson horn

Klasik Batı müziği [bat**uh**
mewzee-**ee**] Western classical
music

klima air-conditioning

klimalı [kleemal**uh**] air-
conditioned

koca [koj**a**] husband; large;
great; old; huge

kod numarası [noomaras**uh**]
dialling code

koğuş [ko-**oo**sh] ward

koklamak to smell

kokmak to smell; to stink

koku smell

kol arm; handle

kolay [ko-l**ī**] easy

kolej [kolе**ј**] college

koleksiyon collection

koli [k**o**lee] parcel(s)

koli gişesi [geeshes**ee**] parcels
counter

kolonya eau de cologne

kol saati [sa-at**ee**] watch

koltuk armchair; seat; stalls

kolye [k**o**l-yeh] necklace

kombinezon slip (garment)

komik funny

kompartıman [kompartuhm**a**n]
compartment

kompartıman sigara içmeyenlere
mahsus [eechmayenler**eh**
maнs**oo**s] nonsmoking
compartment

komple kahvaltı [kompl**eh**
kahvalt**uh**] full breakfast

komşu [komsh**oo**] neighbour

konak large private
residence

konaklamak to stay the night

konfeksiyon off-the-peg
clothes

konferans conference

konser concert

konserve açacağı [kons**e**rveh
achaj**a**-uh] can-opener

konserve kutusu tin, can
konsolosluk consulate
kontak ignition
kontak lensleri contact lenses
kontrol check, inspection
kontrol etmek to check
konu subject, topic
konuk guest
konukseverlik [konookseverleek] hospitality
konuşma [konooshma] speech, talk; conversation; call
konuşmak [konooshmak] to talk; to speak
konut residence; house
koridor yanı [yanuh] aisle seat
korkmak: ...-den korkmak to be afraid (of) ...
korku fear
korkunç [korkoonch] appalling; shocking; horrible
korna horn
koruma faktörü [fakturew] protection factor
korumak to protect
koruma kremi aftersun cream
koruyucu gözlük [koroo-yoojoo gurzlewk] goggles
koruyucu sıvı [suhvuh] soaking solution
kostüm [kostewm] dress; costume
koşmak [koshmak] to run
koşu [koshoo] race; jogging
koşu yapmak to race; to go jogging
kova bucket

koy bay
koymak to put
koyu dark
koyun sheep
köpek [kurpek] dog
köpek var beware of the dog
köprü [kurprew] bridge
kör [kur] blind
körfez [kurfez] gulf; bay
köşe [kursheh] corner
köşede [kurshedeh] on the corner; in the corner
köşk [kurshk] lodge; pavilion, gazebo; villa
kötü [kurtew] bad; nasty; badly
kötü kalite [kaleeteh] poor quality
köy [kuh-i] village
köylü [kurlew] villager; peasant
köy yolu country road
kral king
kraliçe [kraleecheh] queen
krank mili crankshaft
kravat tie, necktie
kredi kartı [kartuh] credit card
kredi kartı kabul edilmez credit cards not accepted
krem cream, lotion
krema cream
krem rengi cream (colour)
kreş [kresh] creche
kriko jack
kuaför [kwafur] hairdresser's (women's)
kubbe [koobbeh] dome
kuduz rabies; rabid

kulak ear

kulak, burun ve boğaz [veh boh-**az**] ear, nose and throat

kulaklıklar [koolakluhkl**ar**] headphones

kule [kool**eh**] tower

kullanım [koollan**uhm**] use

kullanmak to use

kulübe [koolewb**eh**] kiosk; hut; booth

kulüp [kool**ewp**] club

kum sand

kumanda tablosu dashboard

kumanya packed lunch

kumaş [koom**ash**] cloth, fabric, material

kumullar sand dunes

kundura shoes

kunduracı [koondooraj**uh**] shoe shop

kundura tamircisi [tameerjees**ee**] shoe repairer's

kupa mug; cup (sporting)

kupür bilet [koop**ewr**] book of bus tickets

kur rate

kuron crown

kurşun kalem [koorsh**oon**] pencil

kurşunsuz benzin [koorshoons**ooz**] unleaded petrol

kuru dry

kurukahveci [koorookahvej**ee**] coffee seller

kurulama bezi tea towel

kurum society; institution

kurumak to dry oneself

kuru temizleme [temeezlem**eh**] dry clean

kuru temizleyici [temeezl**ay**eejee] dry-cleaner's

kurutmak to dry

kuru yemişçi [yemeeshch**ee**] seller of dried fruit and nuts

kurye [koor-y**eh**] courier

kusmak to vomit

kusura bakmayın [bakmī-**uhn**] pardon me

kuş [koosh] bird

kuş beyinli [bayeenl**ee**] stupid, bird-brained

kuşet [koosh**et**] couchette

kutu box; carton

kuyruk [koo-ir**ook**] queue; tail

kuyruk olmak to queue

kuytu [koo-it**oo**] secluded

kuyu well

kuyumcu [koo-yoomj**oo**] jeweller's

kuzen cousin (male)

kuzey [kooz**ay**] north; northern

kuzeyi north of

kuzey yönünde [yurnewnd**eh**] to the north

kuzeyde [koozayd**eh**] in the north

kuzeybatı [bat**uh**] northwest

kuzeydoğu [koozaydoh-**oo**] northeast

Kuzey İrlanda [eerl**a**nda] Northern Ireland

Kuzey Kıbrıs Türk Cumhuriyeti [kuhbr**uh**s tewrk joomHooree-yet**ee**] Turkish Republic of Northern Cyrprus kuzin cousin (female)

küçük [kewchewk] little; small

küçük jeton [Jeton] small
  token

küçük paket small packet

küfür [kewfewr] swearword

külliye [kewllee-yeh] complex of
  buildings attached to a
  mosque

külot [kewlot] pants, briefs,
  panties

külotlu çorap [kewlotloo chorap]
  tights, pantyhose

kül tablası [kewl tablasuh]
  ashtray

kültür [kewltewr] culture

kültür merkezi cultural centre

küpe [kewpeh] earring(s)

kürek çekmek [kewrek chekmek]
  to row (boat)

kürk [kewrk] fur

Kürt [kewrt] Kurdish; Kurd

küsmek: -e küsmek [-eh
  kewsmek] to be in a huff
  with

kütüphane [kewtewp-haneh]
  library

küvet [kewvet] bathtub

L

lacivert [lajeevert] navy blue

lağım [la-uhm] drain; sewer

lamba lamp

-lar they are; -s, -es (plural
  endings)

-ları [-laruh] their

lastik rubber; elastic; tyre

lastik bant rubber band

lastik basıncı [basuhnjuh] tyre
  pressure

lastik patlaması [patlamasuh]
  puncture

lavabo washhand basin

lazım [lazuhm] necessary;
  must; should
  bana ... lazım I need ...

-le [-leh] by; with

Lefkoşa [lefkosha] Nicosia

lehçe [leHcheh] dialect

leke [lekeh] spot

-ler they are; -s, -es (plural
  endings)

-leri their

libre [leebreh] pound (weight)

liman harbour; port

lira Turkish unit of currency

lisan okulu language school

lise [leeseh] high school,
  secondary school

...-'liyim I am from ...

lokanta restaurant

lokum Turkish delight

Londra London
  Londra'da in London

losyon lotion

-lu with

Lübnan [lewbnan] Lebanon

lügat [lewgat] dictionary;
  word

lüks [lewks] luxury; luxurious;
  posh

lütfen [lewtfen] please

lütfen ayakkabılarınızı çıkarınız
  please take off your shoes

lütfen bozuk para veriniz small
  change please

M

-m my

maalesef [ma-alesef]
  unfortunately

maç [mach] game, match

madem since, seeing that

madeni para coin

Magosa Famagusta

mağara [ma-ara] cave
  ... Mağarası [ma-arasuh] ...
  Cave

mağaza [ma-aza] store

mahalle [mahalleh] quarter;
  area of city

mahallesi district;
  neighbourhood

mahsus deliberately

mahzen cellar

makas scissors

makbuz receipt

makina/makine [makeeneh]
  machine

makinist mechanic; engine
  driver

makul reasonable

makyaj [makyaɹ] make-up

makyaj malzemesi cosmetics

Malazgirt Manzikert

...-malı [-maluh] he/she has
  to ...

...-malıyım [maluh-yuhm] I have
  to ...

mallar goods

mal olmak to cost

mal sahibi owner

manastır [manastuhr]
  monastery

manav greengrocer's

mandal hook; clothes peg

manifatura drapery; textiles

manivela lever

mankafa thick, stupid

mantar mushroom(s); cork

manto coat (woman's)

manzara view; scenery

marka make, brand name

Marmara Denizi the Sea of
  Marmara

marş [marsh] starter

mart March

martı [martuh] seagull

masa table

masaj [masaɹ] massage

masa örtüsü [urtewsew]
  tablecloth

masatopu table tennis

masum innocent

maşallah! [mashallah]
  wonderful! – used to express
  admiration and wonder and
  to avert the evil eye

matbua printed matter

matine [mateeneh] matinée

mavi blue

Mavi Tren blue train – Ankara-
  Istanbul train

mayıs [mī-uhs] May

mayo [mī-o] swimming
  costume; swimming trunks

mazot diesel

mecburi [mejbooree]
  compulsory

mecburi iniş emergency
  landing

mecburi trafik sigortası
  [seegortasuh] third party
  insurance

meç [mech] highlights

medeni hali marital status

medrese [medreseh]
theological school
... Medresesi ... Theological
School

mefruşat [mefrooshat] fabrics
and furnishings

mektup letter

mektup arkadaşı [arkadashuh]
penfriend

mektup kutusu letterbox

...-meli he/she must ...

...-meliyim I must ...

...-mem I won't ...; I don't ...

meme vermek [memeh] to
breastfeed

memleket (home) country

memnun glad, pleased

memnun oldum I am
pleased; pleased to meet
you

memur official

memur bey [bay] officer

mendil handkerchief

mensup: -e mensup [-eh]
belonging to, connected
with

merak hobby

mercek [merjek] lens

merdiven ladder; stairs

merhaba! hello!, hi!

merhem ointment

merkez centre

merkezi central

merkez postanesi main post
office

mersi thank you

Meryemana Virgin Mary

mesai saatleri [mesa-ee sa-
aatleree] opening hours

mesaj [mesaJ] message

mescit [mesjeet] small mosque

mesela for example

mesele [meseleh] question,
problem

mesleği [mesleh-ee]
(applicant's) occupation

meslek profession;
occupation

meşgul [meshgool] busy;
engaged, occupied

meteliksiz broke, penniless

meteliksizim I'm broke

metro underground (railway),
(US) subway

mevsim season

meydan [maydan] square

meyhane [mayhaneh] tavern
serving alcohol and food,
usually frequented by men
only

mezar grave, tomb
... mezarı [mezaruh] ... grave,
... tomb

mezarlık [mezarluhk] cemetery

mı? [muh] question particle
... mı? is it ...?, is that ...?

-mız [-muhz] our

mi? question particle
... mi? is it ...?, is that ...?

mide [meedeh] stomach
midem bulanıyor [boolanuh-
yor] I feel sick

mide ağrısı [a-ruhsuh]
stomachache

mide bozukluğu [bozookloo-oo]
upset stomach

mide bulantısı [boolantuhs**uh**] nausea

midilli pony

mihrap [meeH**r**ap] niche in a mosque indicating the direction of Mecca

mikro dalga microwave (oven)

mikroplu septic

miktar amount

mil mile

milâdi Christian year-numbering system

millet nation

milletlerarası [meelletleraras**uh**] international

milli national

milli park national park

milliyet nationality

milyar one thousand million, (US) one billion

milyon million

minare [meenar**eh**] minaret

minibüs [meeneeb**ews**] minibus

minik tiny

minnettar grateful

misafir [mees**a**feer] guest

misiniz: bana ... verebilir misiniz? can I have ...?

miyim: ...-ebilir miyim? can I ....?, may I ...?

miyop shortsighted

-miz our

mizah humour

mizanpli set

mobilya furniture

mocamp caravan site, trailer park

moda fashion; fashionable, trendy

modaya uygun [m**o**dī-a/oo-ig**oo**n] trendy, fashionable

mola pause; rest

mor purple

motor motorboat; engine

motor kapak contası [jontas**uh**] cylinder head gasket

motosiklet motorbike

mozaik [moza-**ee**k] mosaic

M.Ö. B.C.

M.S. A.D.

mu? question particle ... mu? is it ...?, is that ...?

muavin assistant; driver's assistant on intercity coaches

muayene [moo-ī-en**eh**] examination

muayenehane [moo-ī-enehan**eh**] surgery

muazzam [moo-azz**a**m] tremendous

muhafaza etmek to keep

muhallebici [mooHallebeej**ee**] pudding shop

muhtar [mooHt**a**r] village headman

muhtemelen [mooHt**e**melen] probably

mum [moom] candle

musluk tap, faucet

muslukçu [mooslookch**oo**] plumber

mutfak kitchen

mutfak eşyası [esh-yas**uh**] pots and pans

mutlu happy

-muz our
mü? [mew] question particle
... mü? is it '...?, is that ...?
mücevherat [mew-jevherat]
jewellery
müddet [mewddet] period (of
time)
müdür [mewdewr] manager;
director
müdür muavini assistant
director
müezzin [mew-ezzeen] muezzin
– man who pronounces call
to prayer from the minaret
of a mosque
mükemmel [mewkemmel]
excellent; perfect
mükemmel! that's great!
mümkün [mewmkewn]
possible
mümkün olduğu kadar çabuk
[oldoo-oo – chabook] as soon
as possible
mürekkepli kalem [mewrek-
keplee] pen
mürettebat [mewrettebat] crew
müsaade etmek [mewsa-adeh]
to allow
müshil [mews-heel] laxative
Müslüman [mewslewman]
Muslim
müteakip boşaltma [mewteh-
akeep boshaltma] next
collection
mütehassıs [mewtehassuhs]
specialist
mütevazı [mewtevazuh]
downmarket; modest,
humble

müthiş [mewt-heesh] terrific
-müz [-mewz] our
müze [mewzeh] museum
müzik [mewzeek] music
müzik aleti musical
instrument
müzisyen [mewzees-yen]
musician

N

-n your
nadide [nadeedeh] rare
nadiren not often
nahoş [nahosh] unpleasant
nakil transfer; transmission;
transport
nakit: nakit ödemek [urdemek]
to pay cash
nakit para cash
nalbur hardware shop
namaz Muslim prayer
performed five times a day
nane şekeri [naneh shekeree]
peppermints
nargile [nargeeleh] hookah,
water pipe
nasıl? [nasuhl] how?
nasılsın? [nasuhlsuhn] how are
you?
nasılsınız? [nasuhl-suhnuhz] how
are you?; how do you do?
naylon torba [nîlon] plastic
bag; carrier bag
naylon yağmurluk [ya-moorlook]
cagoule
nazik polite; nice; kind,
generous
ne? [neh] what?

ne ...! what a ...!
ne var? what is it?; what's the matter?
ne kadar? how much?
neden cause
neden? why?
nedeniyle [nedenee-ileh] because of
nedir: o nedir? what's that?
nefes almak to breathe
nefis delicious; lovely
nefret etmek to hate
nehir [neh-Heer] river
... Nehri [neHree] River ...
nemlendirici (krem) [–deereejee] moisturizer
nemli damp; humid
ne ... ne ... [neh] neither ... nor ...
ne oldu? what's up?, what's wrong?; what's happened?
ne oluyor? what's happening?
nerede? [neredeh] where?; where is it?
neredeyse [neredayseh] nearly; almost; soon
ne var ki but; only; however
ney [nay] reed flute
ne yazık ki unfortunately
ne zaman? when?
-nın [-nuhn] of
-nız [-nuhz] your
niçin? [neecheen] why?; why not?
nihayet [nee-Hİ-et] end; at last
-nin of
nisan April

nişanlı [neeshanluh] engaged (to be married); fiancé; fiancée
niye? [nee-yeh] why?
-niz your
Noel Christmas
Noel Gecesi [gejesee] Christmas Eve
Noeliniz kutlu olsun! Merry Christmas!
normal [normahl] normal; 2/3 star petrol, regular gas
Norveç [norvech] Norway; Norwegian (adj)
not defteri notebook
nöbet [nurbet] fit (attack); turn of duty, watch
nöbetçi doktor [nurbetchee] duty doctor
nöbetçi eczane [ejzaneh] duty chemist's
numara number
-nun of
-nuz your
nüfus [newfoos] population
-nün [-newn] of
-nüz [-newz] your

O

o that; those; he; she; it; it is
o işte [eeshteh] that's him/her/it
o ...-dir it is ...
o nedir? what's that?
obdüratör [obdewratur] shutter
objektif [obJekteef] lens
ocak [ojak] January; home; cooker; fireplace

oda room
oda hizmetçisi [heezmetcheesee] maid, chambermaid
oda numarası [noomarasuh] room number
oda servisi room service
o dö tuvalet [dur] eau de toilette
ofis office
oğlan [oh-lahn] boy
oğul [oh-ool] son
oje [oJeh] nail varnish
okul school
okumak to read; to study
olağan [ola-an] ordinary; usual
olamaz impossible; impractical
olay event
oldu OK; alright
ne oldu? [neh] what's up?, what's wrong?; what's happened?
olduğunca ... [oldoo-oonja] as ... as possible
oldukça [oldookcha] fairly, quite, rather
oldukça çok [chok] quite a lot
oldu mu? OK?; is it OK?
olgun ripe; mature
olmak to be; to happen; to become
olmaz it won't do; it's not possible
olur all right; I agree
oluyor: ne oluyor? [neh] what's happening?
omuz shoulder
on ten
ona him; her; it; to him/

her/it
on altı [altuh] sixteen
on beş [besh] fifteen
on beş gün [gewn] fortnight
on bir eleven
onda on/in him; on/in her; on/in it
ondan from him/her/it
ondan sonra then, after that
on dokuz nineteen
on dört [durt] fourteen
on iki twelve
onlar they; those; them
onlara them; to them
onlarda on/in them
onlardan from them
onları [onlaruh] them
onların [onlaruhn] their; theirs
onlarınki [onlaruhnkee] theirs
onlarla with them
on sekiz eighteen
onu him; her; it
onun his; her; hers; its
onuncu [onoonjoo] tenth
onun için [eecheen] for him/her/it; therefore
onunki his; hers
on üç [ewch] thirteen
on yedi seventeen
ora that place
orada over there
orası [orasuh] there
oraya [ori-a] there
orda over there
ordu army
orijinal [oreeJeenal] original; unusual; original soundtrack

orman woods, forest

orta middle; medium; mean· average

ortada in the middle

orta büyüklükte [bewyewklewkt**eh**] medium-sized

orta jeton [Jet**o**n] medium token

ortalama olarak on average

ortopedi uzmanı [oozman**uh**] orthopaedist

Osmanlı [osmanl**uh**] Ottoman

ot grass

otel hotel

otel odası [od**a**suh] hotel room

otobüs [otob**ew**s] bus, coach

otobüs ile [eel**eh**] by bus

otobüs bileti bus ticket

otobüs durağı [doora-**uh**] bus stop

otobüs garajı [gara**ʃuh**] bus station

otobüsle gezi [otob**ew**sleh] coach trip

otobüs terminali bus station

otogar bus terminal, bus station

otomat vending machine

otomatik automatic

otomatik arama direct dialling

otomatik para çekme makinesi [chekm**eh**] cash dispenser, automatic teller

otomatik vitesli automatic (car)

otomatlı çamaşırhane [otomatl**uh**

chamash**uhr**-haneh] launderette

otomobil car

otomobil ile [eel**eh**] by car

otomobil kiralama (servisi) car rental (service)

otomobil yıkama yeri [yuhkam**a**] carwash

otopark car park, parking lot

otostop hitchhiking

otostop yapmak to hitch-hike

otoyol motorway, freeway, highway

oturacak yer [ot**oo**rajak] seat

oturmak to live; to sit down

oturma odası [odas**uh**] living room

oturun! sit down!

otuz thirty

ova plain; plateau

... Ovası [ovas**uh**] ... Plain

oynamak to play; to folkdance

oynatmak to move

oysa but; yet; whereas

oyun play; folkdancing; game

oyuncak [oyoonj**a**k] toy

oyuncu [oyoonj**oo**] actor; actress

o zaman then, at that time

Ö

öbür [urb**ew**r] the other

öbür gün [gewn] the day after tomorrow

öbür türlü [tewrl**ew**] otherwise

öbürü [urbewr**ew**] the other one

ödemek [urdem**e**k] to pay

ödemeli [urdemelee] reverse charge call, collect call

ödemeli konuşma [konooshma] reverse charge call, collect call

ödeyiniz [urdayeeneez] pay

ödünç almak [urdewnch] to borrow

ödünç vermek to lend

öfkeli [urfkelee] angry

öğle [ur-leh] midday, noon

öğleden sonra [urleden] afternoon; p.m.

öğle yemeği [urleh yemeh-ee] lunch

öğleyin [ur-layeen] midday, noon

öğrenci [ur-renjee] student

öğrenci kartı [kartuh] student card

öğrenci yurdu student hostel

öğrenmek [ur-renmek] to learn

öğretmek [ur-retmek] to teach

öğretmen [ur-retmen] teacher

öksürük [urksew-rewk] cough

öksürük şurubu [shoorooboo] cough medicine

ölçek [urlchek] scale

öldürmek [urldewrmek] to kill

ölmek [urlmek] to die

ölü [urlew] dead

Ölü Deniz the Dead Sea

ölüm [urlewm] death

ön [urn] front

ön tarafta at the front

ön cam [jam] windscreen, windshield

önce [urnjeh] before; ago; first; at first

-den önce before

önceden [urnjeden] in advance

öncelik [urnjeleek] priority

öncelikle [urnjeleekleh] first of all

önce siz (buyrun) [urnjeh – (booiroon)] after you

önde [urndeh] in front

önden [urnden] at the front

önden binilir entry at front

önem [urnem] importance

önemi yok it doesn't matter

önemli [urnemlee] important

önermek [urnermek] to advise; to suggest

önünde: ...-in önünde [urnewndeh] in front of ...

öpmek [urpmek] to kiss

öpücük [urpewjewk] kiss

ören [uren] ruin

ören yeri ruins

örgü [urgew] knitwear

örnek [urnek] example; pattern

örneğin [urneh-een] for example

örümcek [urewmjek] spider

övgü [urvgew] compliment

öyle [ur-ileh] so, thus

öyle yapmayın! [yapmī-uhn] stop it!

öyleyse [ur-ilayseh] then, in that case

özel [urzel] private; special

özel bakım ünitesi [bakuhm ewneetesee] special care unit

özel fiyat special price

özel hasta private patient

özel indirim special offer

özellikle [urzelleekl**eh**]
especially
özel ulak special delivery;
express mail
özür [urz**ewr**] apology; excuse;
defect
özür dilemek to apologize
özür dilerim I'm sorry; excuse
me
özürlü [urzewrl**ew**] disabled;
defective
özürlü kişiler handicapped
people, the disabled

P

padişah [padeesha**H**] Sultan;
ruler
pahalı [pa**H**alu**h**] expensive
paket packet, package
paketlemek to pack
paket tur package holiday
paletler flippers
palto coat
pamuk cotton
pamukçuk [pamookch**oo**k]
mouth ulcer
panayır [pan**ī**-**uh**r] fair, funfair
pansiyon guesthouse
pansuman dressing
pantolon trousers, (US) pants
para money
para almak to charge
para cüzdanı [jewzdan**uh**] wallet
para çantası [chantas**uh**] purse
paraya çevirmek [par**ī**-**a**
cheveerm**ek**) to cash
parayı geri vermek [par**ī**-**uh**] to
refund

parça [parch**a**] part; piece
bir parça ... a piece of ...
büyük bir parça [bew-yew**k**] a
big bit
pardon pardon; excuse me
parfüm [parfew**m**] perfume
parfümeri [parfewmer**ee**]
perfumes
park edilir parking
park edilmez no parking
park etmek to park
park lambaları [lambalar**uh**]
sidelights
park yapılmaz no parking
parlak brilliant
parmak finger
parmaklık [parmakl**uh**k] fence
parti party
pasaport passport
pasaport kontrolü [kontrol**ew**]
passport control
Paskalya Easter
pastane [past**a**neh] cake shop;
café
pasta ve şekerlemeler [veh
shekerlemel**er**]
confectionery
pastil pastilles; lozenges
patika path
patiska cambric
patlak burst; punctured
patlak lastik puncture
patron boss
pavyon cheap nightclub, joint;
pavilion; stand
paylaşmak [p**ī**lashm**a**k] to share
pazar Sunday; market
pazar çantası [chantas**uh**]
shopping bag

pazar günleri dışında except
  Sundays
pazarlık [pazarl**uh**k] bargaining
pazarlık edilmez no bargaining
pazarlık etmek to bargain
pazartesi Monday
pazen brushed cotton
peçete [pech**eteh**] napkin
pek very; extremely; a great
  deal; firm; strong
  pek (fazla) değil [deh-**eel**] not
  too much
pekâlâ all right; very well
pek az few
peki all right
pembe [pemb**eh**] pink
pencere [pen**je**reh] window
pencere yanı [yan**uh**] window
  seat
perçem [perch**em**] fringe; tuft
  of hair
perde [perd**eh**] curtain; act
perdeler curtains
perhiz diet
peron platform, (US) track
perşembe [persh**em**beh]
  Thursday
peşin [pesh**een**] in advance
pezevenk pimp
piç [peech] bastard
pijama [peej**a**ma] pyjamas
pikap record player
piknik yemeği [yemeh-**ee**]
  packed lunch
pil battery
pipo [peer**eh**] pipe (for smoking)
pire [peer**eh**] flea
pis [pees] filthy
pislik dirt

pişirmek [peesheerm**ek**] to cook
piyes play
PK P.O. box
plaj [plaɹ] beach
  plajda on the beach
plaj şemsiyesi [shemsee-yes**ee**]
  beach umbrella
plaj yaygısı [yīguhs**uh**] beach
  mat
plak record
plaka number plate
plaster plaster(s), (US)
  Bandaid
poliklinik out-patients clinic
polis police; policeman
polis karakolu police station
polis memuru policeman,
  officer
pompa pump
pop müzik [mewz**ee**k] pop
  music
popo bottom (of person)
pop şarkıcısı [sharkuhjuhs**uh**]
  pop singer
porselen china
porsiyon portion
portatif yatak campbed
portbebe [portbeb**eh**] carry-cot
portre [p**o**rtreh] portrait
posta post, mail
postacı [postaj**uh**] postman
posta kartı [kart**uh**] postcard
posta kodu postcode, zip code
posta kutusu postbox,
  mailbox
postalamak to post, to mail
postane [post**a**neh] post office
Posta Telgraf Telefon post and
  telephone office

pozometre [pozometreh] light meter

pratik practical

prens prince

prenses princess

prezervatif condom

priz socket, power point

protez dentures

prova etmek to try on

PTT [peh teh teh] post and telephone office

pul stamp(s)

puro cigar

puset pushchair, buggy

pusula compass

R

radyatör [radyatur] radiator; heater

radyo radio
  radyoda on the radio

raf shelf

rahat comfortable

rahatsız etmek [rahatsuhz] to disturb

rahip priest

Ramazan Ramadan – the Muslim month of fasting and prayer

randevu appointment

ranza bunk; berth; couchette

ray [rī] track; rail

razıyım [razuh-yuhm] I agree; I accept

rebap three-stringed violin

reçete [recheteh] prescription

reçete ile satılır prescription only

reçete yazmak to prescribe

rehber [reHber] guide; guidebook

rehberli tur [reHberlee] guided tour

renk colour

renkli colour

renkliler colours

resepsiyon reception
  resepsiyonda at reception

resepsiyoncu [resepsee-yonjoo] receptionist

resepsiyon masası [masasuh] reception desk

resepsiyon memuru receptionist

resim picture; painting

resmi formal

resmi tatil public holiday

restoran restaurant

reyon [rayon] department

rezervasyon reservation

rıhtım [ruhHtuhm] quay
  rıhtımda on the quayside

rica ederim [reeja] my pleasure, don't mention it

rica etmek to request

rimel mascara

rizikolu risky

robdöşambr [robdurshambr] man's dressing gown

rock müziği [mewzee-ee] rock (music)

Rodos Rhodes

roman novel

Romanya Rumania

romatizma rheumatism

rondela washer

rota route

römork [rurmork] trailer

röntgen [ru̇rntgen] X-ray
ruh durumu mood
ruj [rooJ] lipstick
Rum [room] ethnic Greek
Rumca [roomja] Greek
(language)
Rum kadını [kaduhn**uh**] ethnic
Greek (woman)
Rum Ortodoks Greek Orthodox
Rus Russian
rüya [rew-**ya**] dream
rüzgâr [rewzgar] wind
rüzgârlı [rewzgarl**uh**] windy

S

saat [sa-**at**] hour; o'clock;
clock; wristwatch
saat kaç? [kach] what time is
it?
saat kayışı [kī-uhsh**uh**] watch
strap
sabah [saba**H**] morning; a.m.
(from 4 a.m. to noon)
bu sabah this morning
sabahleyin [saba**H**layeen] in the
morning
sabahlık [saba**H**l**uh**k] woman's
dressing gown
sabun soap
sabun tozu soap powder
saç [sach] hair
saç fırçası [fuhrchas**uh**]
hairbrush
saç kesme [kesm**eh**] haircut
saç kurutma makinesi
hairdryer
saçma [sachma] silly
saçma! rubbish!, nonsense!

saç spreyi [sach spray-**ee**]
hairspray
saç tıraşı [tuhr**a**shuh] haircut
saç tokası [tokas**uh**] hairgrip(s)
sade [sa-d**eh**] plain, simple
sadece [sa-dejeh] only, just
sağ [sa] alive; right (not left)
sağa dön [sa-**a** durn] turn right
sağa dönülmez no right turn
sağa dönün [durn**ewn**] turn
right
sağanak [sa-anak] shower
sağa sapın [sap**uh**n] turn right
sağa viraj bend to right
sağda [sa-d**a**] on the right
sağdan direksiyonlu [sa-d**a**n]
right-hand drive
sağdan gidiniz keep to the
right
sağında [sa-**uh**nda] on the right
sağır [sa-**uh**r] deaf
sağlığınıza! [sa-luh-uhnuhz**a**]
your health!
sağlıklı [sa-luhkl**uh**] healthy
sağol [sa-**ol**] bless you; thanks
saha field; area
sahil coast; shore, seafront
sahilde [sa**H**eeld**eh**] on the
coast
sahil yolu coast road
sahi mi? really?
sahip owner
sahip olmak to have; to own
sahne [sa**H**neh] stage
sahte [sa**H**teh] false;
counterfeit
sakal beard
sakal tıraşı [tuhrash**uh**] shave
sakın! [sak**uh**n] beware!; don't!

sakin quiet; peaceful
sakız [sakuhz] chewing gum
saklamak to hide
saklanmak to hide
saldırgan [salduhrgan] aggressive
saldırı [salduhruh] attack
salı [saluh] Tuesday
salık vermek [saluhk] to recommend
salon lounge; hall
saman nezlesi hay fever
sana you; to you
sanat art
sanatçı [sanatchuh] artist
sanat galerisi art gallery
sanayi [sani-ee] industry
sandal sandal(s); dinghy
sandık [sanduhk] box; chest; coffer
saniye [sanee-yeh] second (in time)
  bir saniye! just a second!
sanki as if
sanmak to suppose; to think
santigrat centigrade
santimetre [santeemetreh] centimetre
santral memuru operator
santrifüjlü kurutma makinesi [santreefewJlew] spindryer
sap stem; stalk; handle
sapak turning
saray [sarī] palace
  ... Sarayı [sarī-uh] ... Palace
sargı [sarguh] bandage
sarhoş [sarhosh] drunk
sarı [saruh] yellow
sarışın [saruh-shuhn] blond

sarmak to wrap
satılan mal geri alınmaz goods cannot be exchanged
satılık [satuhluhk] for sale
satın alma [satuhn] purchase
satın almak to buy
satış [satuhsh] sale; selling
satış kuru selling rate
satışlarımız peşindir no credit allowed
satmak to sell
satranç [satranch] chess
savaş [savash] war
sayfa [sīfa] page
sayı [sī-uh] number
sayın ... [sī-uhn] esteemed ... – formal way of addressing people followed by surname
saymak [sīmak] to count; to value; to consider
saz oriental music; reed; Turkish string instrument
seans [seh-ans] performance
sebep cause
sebil public drinking fountain
seçmek [sechmek] to choose
sefer journey; flight; voyage; time; occasion
  bu sefer this time
  geçen sefer [gechen] last time
  gelecek sefer [gelejek] next time
seferden kaldırıldı [kalduhruhlduh] flight/ departure cancelled
sefer numarası [noomarasuh] flight number

sefer sayısı [sī-uhs**uh**] flight
number
sekiz eight
sekizinci [sekeez**ee**njee] eighth
seks sex
seksen eighty
sel flood
Selçuklular [selchooklool**a**r]
Selchuks
sele [sel**eh**] saddle
seloteyp [sel**o**tayp] Sellotape®,
Scotch tape®
sema dervish ceremony
sempatik nice
semt area, district,
neighbourhood
sen you
sende [send**eh**] you; on/in you
senden (from) you
sene [sen**eh**] year
seni you
senin your; yours
seninki yours
sepet basket
serbest vacant; free,
independent; allowed
sergi exhibition; trade fair
serin cool; fresh
sersem silly; fool
serseri tramp, vagabond
sert hard; strong; stern
sert dönüş sharp turn
sert lensler hard lenses
sert viraj sharp bend
servis dahildir service charge
included
servis istasyonu service station
servis otobüsü [otobews**ew**]
shuttle bus

servis ücreti [ewjret**ee**] service
charge
ses voice
sessizlik silence
sever:... sever misiniz? do you
like ...?
sevgi love
sevici [seveej**ee**] lesbian
sevilen popular
sevişmek [seveeshm**e**k] to make
love
sevmek to love
seyahat [sayah**a**t] travel;
journey
seyahat acentası [ajentas**uh**]
travel agency
seyahat çeki [chek**ee**]
travellers' cheque
seyahat çekleri [chekler**ee**]
travellers' cheques
seyahat etmek to travel
seyirci [sayeerj**ee**] audience
seyretmek [sayretm**e**k] to watch
-sı [-suh] his; her; its
sıcak [suhj**a**k] hot; warm
hava sıcak it's hot
sıcaklık [suhjakl**uh**k] heat;
temperature
sıcak su [suhj**a**k] hot water
sıçan [suhch**a**n] rat
sıfır [suhf**uh**r] zero
sığ [suh] shallow
sıhhat [suh-h**a**t] health
sık [suhk] frequent; dense;
thick
sıkıcı [suhkuh-j**uh**] boring
sıkıntılı [suhkuhn-tuhl**uh**] dull
sıkışmış [suhkuhsh-m**uh**sh] stuck
sıkmayınız do not wring

sık sık [suhk] often
-sın [-suhn] you are
sınav [suhnav] exam
sınıf [suhnuhf] class; sort, kind
sınır [suhnuhr] border
-sınız [-suhnuhz] you are
sırasında [suhra-suhnda] during
sırf [suhrf] only
sırf gidiş [geedeesh] single
   ticket, one-way ticket
sırt [suhrt] back (of body)
sırt ağrısı [a-ruhsuh] backache
sırt çantası [chantasuh]
   rucksack
sıska [suhska] skinny
sızıntı [suhzuhntuh] leak
-si his; her; its
sigara cigarette
sigara içenler [eechenler]
   smokers
sigara içilen [eecheelen]
   smoking
sigara içilmez no smoking
sigara içmek [eechmek] to
   smoke
sigara içmek yasaktır no
   smoking
sigara içmeyenler [eechmayenler]
   nonsmokers
sigara içmeyenlere mahsus
   bölüm/kısım [eechmayenlereh
   maHsoos burlewm/kuhsuhm]
   nonsmoking section
sigara içmeyenlere mahsus
   (kompartıman) [kompartuhman]
   nonsmoking (compartment)
sigara içmeyiniz do not smoke
sigorta insurance; fuse
sigorta kutusu fuse box

sigorta teli fuse wire
silah weapon
silecekler [seelejekler]
   windscreen wipers
silgi rubber, eraser
-sin you are
sinek fly
sinema cinema, movie theatre
sinir hastası [hastasuh] neurotic
sinirli nervous
-siniz you are
sinyal indicator
sipariş [seepareesh] order
sis fog; mist
sisli foggy
site [seeteh] estate
sivil civilian
sivilce [seeveeljeh] pimple
sivrisinek mosquito
sivrisinek ilacı [eelajuh]
   mosquito repellent
siyah black
   siyah beyaz [bayaz] black and
   white
siz you; one
-siz without
sizde [seezdeh] on/in you
sizde kalsın [kalsuhn] please
   keep it
sizden from you
size [seezeh] to you
sizi you
sizin your; yours
sizinki yours
sizinle [seezeenleh] with you
sizlerin your
ski yapmak skiing
slayt [slīt] slide
sofa hall

soğuk [so-**oo**k] cold

soğuk aldım [ald**uh**m] I have a
  cold

soğuk algınlığı [alguhnluh-**uh**]
  cold

soğuk su cold water

Sok. St

sokak street; road

sokma insect bite

sokmak to sting; to bite; to
  thrust into; to insert

sokulgan friendly

sol left

sola to the left

sola dön [durn] turn left

sola dönülmez no left turn

sola dönün [durn**ew**n] turn left

solak left-handed

sola sapın [sap**uh**n] turn left

sola viraj bend to left

solda on the left

solgun pale

solunda on the left of

somun nut (for bolt); loaf

somun anahtarı [ana**H**tar**uh**]
  spanner

son end; last; final
  yolun sonunda at the end of
  the street

sona erdi it's over

sonbahar autumn, (US) fall
  sonbaharda in the autumn, in
  the fall

son derece [derej**eh**] extremely

son durak terminus

son hareket last train; last bus

son istasyon rail terminus

son kullanma tarihi ... use
  before ...

son moda trendy

sonra next; after; afterwards;
  later
  -den sonra after
  daha sonra later; later on

sonradan afterwards

sormak to ask

soru question

sorumlu responsible

sorun problem
  hiç sorun değil! [heech – deh-
  eel] no problem!
  sorun nedir? what's wrong?

sorup öğrenmek [ur-renm**ek**] to
  find out

soyadı [soyad**uh**] surname

soyunma odası [odas**uh**] fitting
  room; changing room

sömestr [surm**e**str] term

söndürmek [surndewrm**ek**] to
  put out, to extinguish

sönük [surn**ew**k] off; dim;
  lacklustre; extinguished

sörf [surf] surf

sörf tahtası [ta**H**tas**uh**]
  surfboard

sörf yapmak to surf

söylemek [sur-ilem**ek**] to say; to
  tell

sözcük [surzj**ew**k] word

sözlük [surzl**ew**k] dictionary

söz vermek [surz] to promise

spiral [spee-r**a**l] IUD; spiral

spor sport

spor malzemeleri sports goods

spor salonu gym

spor tesisleri sporting facilities

stabilize yol macadam road

su water; river; stream

-su his; her; its

suçiçeği [soochech**eh**-ee] chickenpox

sufi dervish; mystic

su geçirmez [gecheerm**e**z] waterproof

su kayağı [kī-a-**uh**] waterski; water-skiing

Sultan Ahmet Camii [aнmet jamee-**ee**] Blue Mosque

-sun you are

suni artificial; false; affected

-sunuz you are

Suriye [s**oo**ree-yeh] Syria

Suriyeli Syrian

sus! shut up!

susadım [soosad**uh**m] I'm thirsty

susamak to be thirsty

su sporları [sporlar**uh**] water sports

suyla [soo-il**a**] with water

-suz without

-sü [-sew] his; her; its

süet [sew-et] suede

sükseli [sewksel**ee**] fashionable

-sün [-sewn] you are

sünger [sewn**g**er] sponge

sünnet [sewnnet] circumcision

-sünüz [-sewn**ew**z] you are

süper [sewper] 4-star petrol, premium gas

süpürge [sewpewrg**eh**] broom

sürahi [sewra**h**ee] jug; carafe

sürat tahdidi speed limit

süre [sewr**eh**] period (of time)

sürgülemek [sewrgewlemek] to bolt

sürmek [sewrmek] to drive; to rub on; to smear; to continue

sürpriz [sewrpre**e**z] surprise

sürücü [sewrewj**ew**] driver

sütlü çikolata [sewtl**ew** cheekolat**a**] milk chocolate

sütsüz çikolata [sewts**ew**z] plain chocolate

sütun [sewt**oo**n] column

sütyen [sewt-y**en**] bra

svetşört [svet-sh**u**rt] sweatshirt

Ş

şadırvan [shaduhrv**a**n] fountain attached to mosque for ritual ablutions

şafak [shafak] dawn

şahane [shaнane**h**] wonderful, amazing, very good

şair [sha-**ee**r] poet

şaka [shak**a**] joke

şal [shal] shawl

şalter [shalter] mains switch

şamandıra buoy

şampuan [shampoo-**an**] shampoo

şampuan ve mizanpli [veh] shampoo and set

şans [shans] luck

şapka [sh**a**pka] hat

şarkı [shark**uh**] song

şarkıcı [sharkuhj**uh**] singer

şarkı söylemek [shark**uh** sur-ilem**e**k] to sing

şarküteri [sharkewter**ee**] delicatessen

şart [shart] essential

... şarttır [sharttuhr] it is
essential that ...
şaşılacak [shashuhlajak]
amazing, surprising
şaşırtıcı [shashuhr-tuhjuh]
surprising, astonishing
şato [shatoh] castle
şayet [shī-et] if
şebeke planı [shebekeh planuh]
network map
şef [shef] boss
şehir [sheh-heer] city
şehirde [sheh-heerdeh] in
town
şehiriçi [sheh-heereechee] local;
local mail
şehir kodu area code
şehirlerarası konuşma [sheh-
heerler-arasuh konooshma]
long-distance call
şehirlerarası otobüs işletmesi
[otobews eeshletmesee] long-
distance coach service
şehir merkezi city centre
şehir planı [planuh] streetmap
şehir turu city tour
şehzade [sheHzadeh] prince;
heir apparent
şeker [sheker] sugar; sweet,
candy
şeker hastası [hastasuh]
diabetic
şemsiye [shemsee-yeh]
umbrella
şenlik [shenleek] carnival;
amusement
şerefe [sherefeh] balcony of
minaret
şerefe! cheers!

şerit [shereet] motorway lane
şerit metre [metreh] tape
measure
şey [shay] thing
şeyh [shayH] sheikh – head of a
religious order
şezlong [shezlong] deckchair;
sun lounger
şık [shuhk] trendy
şiddetli [sheeddetlee] sharp
şikayet [sheekī-et] complaint
şikayet etmek to complain
şilebezi [sheelebezee]
cheesecloth
şilte [sheelteh] mattress
şimdi [sheemdee] now
şimdi değil [deh-eel] not just
now
şimdi anladım [anladuhm] I see,
I understand now
şimdiden [sheemdeeden]
already
şimşek [sheemshek] lightning
şirket [sheerket] company, firm
şişe [sheesheh] bottle
şişe açacağı [achaja-uh] bottle-
opener
şişlik [sheeshleek] swelling
şişman [sheeshman] fat
şişmiş [sheeshmeesh] swollen
şofben [shofben] water
heater
şoför [shofur] driver
şoför ehliyeti driver's licence
şok [shok] shock
şort [short] shorts
şöyle [shuh-ileh] thus, such
şöyle böyle [buh-ileh] so-so
şu [shoo] this; that

şubat [shoobat] February
şube [shoobeh] branch
şu ...-lar those ...
şunlar [shoonlar] those
şura [shoora] that place
şurada [shoorada] over there
şurda [shoorda] there
şurup [shooroop] cough
  syrup

T

-ta in
taahhütlü [ta-ah-hewtlew] by
  registered mail
taahhütlü mektup registered
  mail
tabak plate; dish
taban floor; base; sole
tabanca [tabanja] gun, pistol
tabii! [tabee-ee] sure!; of
  course!
  tabii değil [deh-eel] of course
  not
tabla ashtray
tablet çikolata [cheekolata] bar
  of chocolate
tahta [taHta] wood (material)
takıldı [takuhlduh] jammed
takım [takuhm] set; team
takım elbise [elbeeseh] suit
  (man's)
takıp denemek [takuhp] to try
  on
takip etmek to follow
taklit imitation, fake
takma ad nickname
takma diş [deesh] dentures
taksi taxi

taksi durağı [doora-uh] taxi
  rank
taksimetre [takseemetreh]
  taximeter
taksi şoförü [shofurew] taxi-
  driver
taksitler instalments
takunya pattens, clogs – worn
  in Turkish baths
takvim calendar
talep etmek to demand
tali secondary
talihin açık olsun! [achuhk]
  good luck!
tali yol kavşağı secondary
  junction
talk pudrası [tahlk poodrasuh]
  talcum powder
tam quite; exact; complete,
  entire; perfect
tamam OK, all right;
  complete, finished; perfect
tamam! right!
  (böyle) tamam [buh-ileh]
  that'll do nicely
  ...-in tamamı [tamamuh] the
  whole of ...
tamamen completely
tamamlamak to finish
tam bilet full-price ticket
tamirci [tameerjee] mechanic
tamir etmek to mend, to
  repair
tamirhane [tameerhaneh] garage
  (for repairs)
tam pansiyon full board
tampon bumper, fender;
  tampon
tam ücret [ewjret] exact fare

tam zamanında [zamanuhnda] on time

tanbur long-necked stringed instrument like a lute

tane [taneh] item; piece

tanık [tanuhk] witness

tanım [tanuhm] description

tanımak [tanuhmak] to know; to recognize

tanıştığımıza memnun oldum! [tanuhshtuh-uhmuhza] pleased to meet you!

tanıştırmak [tanuhshtuhrmak] to introduce

tanıtmak [tanuhtmak] to introduce

Tanrı [tanruh] God

tanrıça [tanruhcha] goddess

tanrılar [tanruhlar] gods

tansiyon blood pressure

tapınak [tapuhnak] temple

taraf side; part

... tarafından yazılan [tarafuhndan yazuhlan] written by ...

tarafta: bu tarafta this way
o tarafta that way

taraftar fan (sports etc)

tarak comb

taramak to comb

tarife [tareefeh] charges, price list; timetable, (US) schedule

tarifeli sefer scheduled flight

tarih [tareeH] date (time); history

tarihi yerler [tareeHee] historical places

tarla field

tas bowl

taş [tash] stone, rock

taşımak [tashuhmak] to carry

taşıma ücreti [tashuhma ewj-retee] fare

taşıt [tashuht] vehicle

taşıt giremez no entry for vehicles

taşıt trafiğine kapalı yol closed to all vehicles

tat taste; flavour

tatil holiday, vacation
tatilde [tateeldeh] on holiday, on vacation

tatil köyü [kur-yew] holiday village

tatil sitesi holiday village

tatmak to taste

tava frying pan

tavan ceiling

tavla backgammon

tavsiye etmek [tavsee-yeh] to recommend

tayyör [tī-ur] suit (woman's)

taze [tazeh] fresh

taze boya wet paint

TC [teh jeh] Republic of Turkey

TCDD [teh jeh deh deh] Turkish State Railways

-te [teh] in

tebrikler! congratulations!

tecrübeli [tejrewbelee] experienced

tedavi treatment

tedavi etmek to cure

tedricen [tedreejen] gradually

tehlike [tehleekeh] danger

tehlike çıkışı [chuhkuhshuh] emergency exit

tehlikeli dangerous

tehlikeli akıntı dangerous
current

tehlikeli eğim steep gradient

tek one, sole, single

tekel government monopoly
on alcohol and tobacco

Tekel bayii [bī-ee-ee] off-
licence, liquor store

tekerlek wheel

tekerlekli araba trolley

tekerlekli sandalye [sandalyeh]
wheelchair

tek gidiş bilet [geedeesh] single
ticket, one-way ticket

tekke [tekkeh] dervish
convent; lodge

tek kişilik (bir) oda [keesheeleek]
single room

tek kişilik yatak single bed

teklif etmek to offer; to
propose

tekrar again

tekrar gelmek to come back

tekrarlamak to repeat

tek yön [yurn] one-way street

tek yönlü yol [yurnlew] one-way
street

tel wire

teleferik cable car

telefon phone

telefon etmek to phone, to call

telefon kabini telephone box/
cubicle

telefon kartı [kartuh]
phonecard

telefon kodu dialling code

telefon konuşması
[konooshmasuh] phone call;
phone conversation

telefon kulübesi [koolewbesee]
phone box

telefonla uyandırma [oo-
yanduhrma] wake-up call

telefon numarası [noomarasuh]
phone number

telefon rehberi [reнberee] phone
book

teleks telex

telesiyej [telesee-yeJ] chairlift

televizyon television

telgraf telegram

tembel lazy

temiz clean

temizlemek to clean

temizleme kremi [temeezlemeh]
cleansing lotion

temizleme losyonu cleansing
lotion

temizleme sıvısı [suhvuhsuh]
cleaning solution

temizleyici krem [temeezlayeejee]
cleansing lotion

temmuz July

temsilci [temseeljee] agent;
representative

tencere [tenjereh] pan,
saucepan

teneke kutu [tenekeh] can, tin

tenis kortu tennis court

tepe [tepeh] hill

tepsi tray

terbiyesiz rude, ill-mannered

tercih etmek to prefer

tercüman [terjewman]
translator; interpreter

tercüme [terjewmeh] translation

tercüme etmek to translate; to
interpret

terlemek to sweat
terlik slipper(s)
termometre [termom**e**treh] thermometer
termos vacuum flask
tersane [tersan**eh**] shipyard
... Tersanesi ... Shipyard
terzi tailor's
tesadüfen [tesadewf**e**n] by chance
tesisatçı [teseesatch**uh**] plumber
teslim delivery
teslim etmek to deliver
teşekkür (ederim) [teshekk**e**wr] thanks, thank you
çok teşekkür ederim [chok] thank you very much
teşekkür etmek to thank
teyp [tayp] tape, cassette; tape recorder
teyze [tayz**eh**] aunt (maternal)
THT [teh ha teh] domestic air service
THY [teh ha yeh] Turkish Airlines
tıkaç [tuhk**a**ch] plug (in sink)
tıkalı [tuhkal**uh**] blocked
TIR [tuhr] international road haulage
tıraş fırçası [tuhr**a**sh fuhrchas**uh**] shaving brush
tıraş köpüğü [kurpew-**ew**] shaving foam
tıraş losyonu aftershave
tıraş makinesi electric shaver
tıraş makinesi prizi shaving point
tıraş olmak to shave
tıraş sabunu shaving soap

tırnak [tuhrn**a**k] fingernail
tırnak cilası [jeelas**uh**] nail polish
tırnak fırçası [fuhrchas**uh**] nailbrush
tırnak makası [makas**uh**] nail clippers
tırnak törpüsü [turpews**ew**] nailfile
tiksindirici [–reej**ee**] disgusting
tip [teep] sort, type
tipi blizzard
tipik typical
tirbuşon [teerboosh**o**n] corkscrew
tişört [tee-sh**u**rt] T-shirt
tiyatro theatre
TL [teh leh] Turkish Lira
tok full; thick
ton vermek tint
top ball
toplam total
toplamak to collect
toplantı [toplant**uh**] meeting
toplu iğne [ee-n**eh**] pin
toprak earth
toprak eşya [esh-y**a**] pottery
topuk heel
tornavida screwdriver
Toros Taurus
torun grandchild
toz dust; powder
tozlu dusty
trafik ışıkları [uhshuhk-lar**uh**] traffic lights
trafik kanunu traffic laws
trafik kazası [kazas**uh**] road accident
Trafik Kuralları Highway Code

trafik lambaları [–laruh] traffic lights

trafik tıkanıklığı [tuhkanuhkluh-uh] traffic jam

Trakya Thrace

tramplen diving board

tramvay [tramvī] tram

tren train

trenle [trenleh] by train

tren bileti train ticket

tren istasyonu railway station

tren yolu geçidi [gecheedee] level crossing

triko knitwear

troleybüs [trolaybews] trolleybus

TRT [teh reh teh] Turkish Radio and Television

Truva Troy

tuğla [too-la] brick

tuhaf weird

tuhafiyeci [toohafee-yejee] haberdasher's

tur tour

turist tourist

turistik otel tourist hotel

turizm tourism

turizm bürosu [bewrosoo] tourist office

turnike [toorneekeh] turnstile

tur operatörü [operaturew] tour operator

turuncu [tooroonjoo] orange (colour)

tutar amount

tutmak to take, to accept; to hold; to hire, to rent; to support

tutuklamak to arrest

tutuşmak [tootooshmak] to catch fire

tutuşturmak [tootooshtoormak] to set on fire, to ignite

tuvalet toilet

tuvalet kağıdı [ka-uhduh] toilet paper

tuvalet temizleyicisi [temeezlay-eejeesee] bleach

tuzlu salty

tüfek [tewfek] rifle

tüh! [tewH] oh no!

tükendi [tewkendee] sold out

tükenmez (kalem) [tewkenmez] ballpoint (pen)

tüm [tewm] whole

tümüyle [tewmewleh] altogether

Tünel [tewnel] Istanbul underground/subway

tünel tunnel

tüpgaz [tewpgaz] camping gas

tür [tewr] kind, sort, type

ne tür ...? [neh] what sort of ...?

türbe [tewrbeh] tomb

... Türbesi [tewrbesee] Tomb of ...

Türk [tewrk] Turk; Turkish (adj)

Türkçe [tewrkcheh] Turkish (language); in Turkish

Türk Hava Yolları [yollaruh] Turkish Airlines

Türkiye [tewrkee-yeh] Turkey

Türkiye Cumhuriyeti [tewrkee-yeh joomHooree-yetee] Republic of Turkey

Türkiye Cumhuriyeti Devlet
  Demiryolları Turkish State
  Railways
Türkiye Radyo Televizyon
  Kurumu Turkish Radio and
  Television Corporation
Türkiye'ye giriş tarihi date of
  entry to Turkey
Türk Lirası [leerasuh] Turkish
  Lira
Türk sanat müziği [mewzee-ee]
  Turkish classical music
türkü [tewrkew] folk song
türlü [tewrlew] sort, kind,
  variety
tütün [tewtewn] tobacco

U

-u his; her; its; accusative
  noun ending
ucuz [oojooz] cheap,
  inexpensive
uçak [oochak] aeroplane
uçakla by air; airmail
uçak postası [postasuh] airmail
uçak postasıyla [postasuh-ila]
  by airmail
uçak seferi flight
uçak zarfı [zarfuh] airmail
  envelope
uçmak [oochmak] to fly
uçuk [oochook] pale
uğramak: -e uğramak [-eh oo-
  ramak] to drop by, to drop
  in, to stop by
ulus nation
uluslararası [oolooslararasuh]
  international

-um my; I am
ummak to hope
umumi general; common;
  public
umumi hela public
  convenience
umumi tatil public holiday
umumi telefon payphone
umut hope; expectation
-umuz our
-un of; your
unutmak to forget
unuttum I forget, I've
  forgotten
-unuz your
unvanı [oonvanuh] title
usta skilful; clever; foreman;
  master craftsman – often
  used respectfully/ironically
  to address master
  craftsman
ustura razor
utanç [ootanch] shame
utanç içinde [eecheendeh]
  ashamed
utandırıcı [ootanduhruhjuh]
  embarrassing; disgraceful
utangaç [ootangach] shy
uyandırmak [oo-yanduhrmak] to
  wake
uyanık [oo-yanuhk] awake;
  vigilant; sharp; smart
uyanmak to wake up
uydurma şeyler [oo-idoorma
  shayler] rubbish
uygun [oo-igoon] convenient;
  appropriate; reasonable;
  just right
uykuda [oo-ikooda] asleep

uyku ilacı [oo-ikoo eelajuh] sleeping pill

uykulu [oo-ikooloo] sleepy

uykusu gelmiş [oo-ikoosoo gelmeesh] sleepy

uykusuzluk [oo-ikoosoozlook] insomnia

uyku tulumu [oo-ikoo] sleeping bag

uyluk [oo-ilook] thigh

uyruk [oo-irook] nationality

... uyruğu [oo-iroo-oo] ... nationality

uyudunuz: iyi uyudunuz mu? [oo-yoodoonooz] did you sleep well?

uyumak [oo-yoomak] to sleep

uyuşturucu [oo-yooshtooroojoo] drug, narcotics

-uz we are

uzak far

uzakta in the distance

uzak dur keep out; keep away

uzaklık [oozakluhk] distance

uzanmak to lie down

uzatma kablosu extension lead

uzun long

uzun boylu tall

uzunluk length

uzun süre [sewreh] a long time

Ü

-ü [-ew] accusative noun ending

ücret [ewjret] cost; pay; fee; wage

ücretler [ewjretler] charges; wages

ücretsiz giriş admission free

üç [ewch] three

üçüncü [ewchewnjew] third

üçüncü kat third floor, (US) fourth floor

ülke [ewlkeh] country, nation

ülser [ewlser] ulcer

-üm [-ewm] my; I am

-ümüz [-ewmewz] our

-ün [-ewn] of; your

üniversite [ewnee-verseeteh] university

ünlü [ewnlew] famous

-ünüz [-ewnewz] your

üst [ewst] top

üst bagaj yeri [bagaɹ] roof rack

üst kat upper floor; upstairs; top floor

üstte [ewstteh] at the top

üstünde [ewstewndeh] on; above; over

...-in üstünde on top of ...

üstünü değiştirmek [ewstewnew deh-eeshteermek] to get changed

üşümek [ewshewmek] to feel cold

üşütmek [ewsewtmek] to catch cold

ütü [ewtew] iron

ütülemek [ewtewlemek] to iron

üvey anne [ewvay anneh] stepmother

üvey baba stepfather

-üz [-ewz] we are

üzere [ewzereh] in order to;

just about to

üzerinden [ewzereenden] via; from the top of

üzgün [ewzgewn] sad

üzgünüm [ewzgewnewm] I'm sorry

V

vadi valley

vagon carriage, coach

vagon restoran dining car

vajina [vaʒeena] vagina

vakıf [vakuhf] Islamic religious foundation

vakit time

vali governor

valide sultan [valeedeh] Sultan's mother

valiz suitcase

vana valve

Van Gölü [gurlew] Lake Van

vantilatör [vanteelatur] fan (electrical)

vantilatör kayışı [kī-uhshuh] fanbelt

vapur steamer; passenger ferry

vapur gezisi cruise

var there is, there are

... var mı? [muh] is there/are there ...?; do you have...?

ne var? [neh] what is it?; what's the matter?

varış [varuhsh] arrival

varış istasyonu destination

varış saati [sa-atee] time of arrival

varmak: -e varmak [-eh] to arrive

varyete [var-yeteh] floor show, variety show

vatan motherland

vay anası! [vī anasuhnuh] I'll be damned!

vay canına! [vī januhna] I'll be damned!

vazo vase

ve [veh] and

vejetaryen [veʒetar-yen] vegetarian

veresiye verilmez no credit allowed

vergi tax

vermek to give

vestiyer cloakroom

veteriner vet

veya [vay-a] or

vezne [vezneh] cash desk, till; cashier

veznedar cashier

vida screw

video (aleti) video recorder

video kamera camcorder

vilayet [veelī-et] province

... Vilayeti Province of ...

vilayet konağı [kona-uh] provincial headquarters building

viraj [veeraʒ] bend

vites gears

vites kolu gear lever

vites kutusu gearbox

vitrin shop window

vitrinde [veetreendeh] in the window

vize [veezeh] visa

vizör [veezur] viewfinder
voltaj [voltaɹ] voltage
vurmak to knock; to hit; to
  shoot
vurunuz knock
vücut [vewjoot] body

Y

ya or
  ya! oh!; really?
-ya to
-'ya to
yabanarısı [yabanaruhsuh]
  wasp
yabancı [yabanjuh] foreign;
  foreigner; stranger
yabancı dil kılavuzu
  [kuhlavoozoo] phrasebook
yabani wild
yafta placard; label; poster
yağ [ya] fat; oil
yağlı [ya-luh] greasy
yağlı güreş [gewresh] Turkish
  wrestling
yağmak [ya-mak] to rain
yağmur [ya-moor] rain
  yağmurda in the rain
  yağmur yağıyor [ya-uh-yor] it's
  raining
yağmurluk [ya-moorlook]
  raincoat
yağ seviyesi oil level
Yahudi Jew; Jewish
yaka collar
yakalamak to catch; to arrest
yakın [yakuhn] near
  ...-e yakın [-eh] near to ...
  en yakın ... the nearest ...

yakında [yakuhnda] soon;
  nearby; recently
yakınında [yakuhnuhnda] near
yakışıklı [yakuh-shuhkluh]
  handsome
yakıt deposu [yakuht] tank
yaklaşık [yaklashuhk] about,
  approximately
yaklaşmak: -e yaklaşmak
  [-eh yaklashmak] to
  approach
yakmak to burn
yalanlamak to deny
yalan söylemek [suh-ilemek] to
  lie, to tell a lie
yalı [yaluh] waterside
  residence
yalnız [yalnuhz] just, only;
  alone
  yalnız biraz just a little
  yalnız burada just here
  yalnız başıma [bashuhma] by
  myself
  yalnız başına [bashuhna] by
  yourself
yalnız gidiş [geedeesh] single
  journey
yan side
yanak cheek
yangın [yanguhn] fire
  yangın var! fire!
yangın alarmı [alarmuh] fire
  alarm
yangın çıkışı [chuhkuhshuh]
  emergency exit; fire exit
yangın merdiveni fire escape
yangın söndürme cihazı
  [surndewrmeh jeehazuh] fire
  extinguisher

yanık [yanuhk] (switched) on;
  burn
yanında [yanuhnda] beside
yanıt [yanuht] answer
yanıtlamak [yanuhtlamak] to
  answer
yanıyor [yanuh-yor] it's on fire
yani that is to say
yankesici [yankeseejee]
  pickpocket
yanlış [yanluhsh] wrong;
  mistake
yanlış anlama
  misunderstanding
yanlış numara wrong number
yanmak to burn
yanmış [yanmuhsh] burnt
yapı [yapuh] building
yapma artificial
  yapma! don't!
  yapma be!? [beh] really?
yapmak to do; to make
yaprak leaf
yar cliff
yara wound
yaralı [yaraluh] injured
yararlı [yararluh] useful; helpful
yardım [yarduhm] help
yardım etmek to help
yarı [yaruh] half
yarı fiyat half-price
yarım [yaruhm] half
  yarım düzine [dewzeeneh] half
  a dozen
  yarım saat [sa-at] half an
  hour
yarım pansiyon half board
yarım tarife [tareefeh] half fare
yarın [yaruhn] tomorrow

yarın sabah [sabaH] tomorrow
  morning
yarın görüşürüz
  [gurewshewrewz] see you
  tomorrow
yarış [yaruhsh] race (competition)
yasa law
yasak forbidden
yasak bölge restricted zone
yasaktır not allowed
yastık [yastuhk] pillow; cushion
yastık kılıfı [kuhluhfuh] pillow
  case
yaş [yash] age
yaşamak [yashamak] to live
yaşlı [yashluh] old
yaşlılar [yashluhlar] old people
yat yacht
yatak bed
yatakhane [yatakhaneh]
  dormitory
yataklı vagon [yatakluh]
  sleeping car
yatak odası [odasuh] bedroom
yatak takımı [takuhmuh] bed
  linen
yatmak to lie down; to go to
  bed
yavaş [yavash] slow; quiet
  yavaş! slow down!
  çok yavaş [chok] very slowly
yavaşça [yavash-cha] slowly
yavaş git go slow
yavaş vasıta şeridi crawler lane
yay [yī] spring
ya ... ya ... either ... or ...
yaya [yī-a] pedestrian; on foot
yaya geçidi [gecheedee]
  pedestrian crossing

yaya giremez no entry for
pedestrians
yayalar pedestrians
yayalara mahsus bölge [yī-al**ar**a
– burlg**eh**] pedestrian
precinct
yayan [yī-**a**n] on foot
yaz summer
yazın [yaz**uh**n] in the summer
yazık [yaz**uh**k] pity; it's a pity
ne yazık! [neh] what a shame!
yazı kâğıdı [yaz**uh** ka-uhd**uh**]
writing paper
yazı makinesi typewriter
yazmak to write
-ye [-yeh] to
-'ye to
yedek spare; reserve; standby
yedek depo spare tank
yedek lastik spare tyre
yedek parça [parch**a**] spare part
yedi seven
yedinci [yed**ee**njee] seventh
yeğen [yeh-**e**n] nephew; niece
yelek waistcoat
yelken sail
yelkencilik [yelkenjee**lee**k]
sailing
yelkenli sailing boat
yelkenli sörf [surf] windsurfing;
sailboard
yelkenliyle gezmek [yelkenl**ee**-
ileh] to sail
yelpaze [yelpaz**eh**] fan (handheld)
yemek to eat; meal; dish;
food
yemeklerden önce [urnj**eh**]
before meals
yemeklerden sonra after meals

yemekli vagon buffet car,
restaurant car
yemek salonu dining room
yemek takımları [takuhmlar**uh**]
crockery
yemek tarifi recipe
yen sleeve
yenge [yeng**eh**] sister-in-law
(brother's wife); uncle's wife
yeni new
Yeni Yıl [yuhl] New Year
Yeni Yılınız Kutlu Olsun!
[yuhluhn**uh**z] Happy New
Year!
Yeni Zelanda New Zealand
Yeni Zelandalı [zelandal**uh**] New
Zealander
yepyeni brand new
yer place; seat; ground; floor
yerde [yerd**eh**] on the floor;
on the ground
yeraltı şehri [shehr**ee**]
underground city
yer ayırtmak [ī-uhrtm**a**k] to
book, to reserve
yerel local
yerel konuşma [konoo**shma**]
local call
yerfıstığı [yerfuhstuh-**uh**]
peanuts
yerine [yeree**neh**] instead of
yerleşmek [yerleshm**e**k] to check
in; to settle
yesaltı mezarı [yesalt**uh**
mezar**uh**] catacomb
yeşil [yesh**ee**l] green
yeşil kart [yesh**ee**l] green card
yeter enough, sufficient
bu kadar yeter that's enough

yeterince [yetereenjeh] enough; sufficiently
yetişkin [yeteesh-keen] adult
yetişkinler [yeteeshkeenler] adults
yetmez insufficient
yetmiş [yetmeesh] seventy
-yı [-yuh] accusative noun ending
yıkamak [yuhkamak] to wash
yıkama ve mizanpli [yuhkama veh] wash and set
yıkanmak [yuhkanmak] to have a wash, to get washed
yıl [yuhl] year
yılan [yuhlan] snake
Yılbaşı (Gecesi) [yuhlbashuh (gejesee)] New Year's Eve
yıldırım telgraf [yuhlduhruhm] express telegram
yıldız [yuhlduhz] star
yıldönümü [yuhldurnewmew] anniversary
-yım [-yuhm] I am
-yız [-yuhz] we are
-yi accusative noun ending
-yim I am
yine [yeeneh] (once) again; still
yirmi twenty
yitirmek to lose
yiyecek [yee-yejek] food
-yiz we are
yoğun bakım ünitesi [yo-oon bakuhm ewneetesee] intensive care unit
yok no; there isn't; there's none (left)
... yok there isn't any ...

yok be! [beh] really!
yok canım? [januhm] really?
yoksa otherwise
yol road; route; path; way
yolcu [yoljoo] passenger
yolcular passengers
yolculuk [yoljoolook] trip; journey
yolcu otobüsü [yoljoo otobewsew] coach
yolcu salonu passenger lounge
yolda çalışma roadworks
yol hakkı right of way
yol inşaatı roadworks
yol kapalı road closed
yollamak to send
yol ver give way
yorgan duvet; quilt
yorgun tired
yorgunluktan bitmiş [beetmeesh] very tired, shattered
yosun seaweed
yön [yurn] direction
yönetici [yurneteejee] manager
yönetici bayan [bī-an] manageress
-yu accusative noun ending
yukarı [yookaruh] up
yukarıda [yookaruhda] at the top; above; upstairs; up there
-yum I am
yumuşak [yoomooshak] soft
yumuşak kontak lensleri soft lenses
Yunan Greek (adj)
Yunanistan Greece
Yunanca [yoonanja] Ancient Greek

Yunanlı [yoonanl**uh**] Greek (man)

Yunanlı kadın [kad**uh**n] Greek (woman)

yurdumda at home (in my country)

yurt home; homeland; student housing; hostel

yurtdışı [yoortduhsh**uh**] abroad

yurt dışında [duh-shuhnd**a**] abroad

yurtdışı posta ücretleri [yoortduhsh**uh** – ewjretler**ee**] overseas postage rates

yurtiçi [yoorteech**ee**] inland

yurtiçi posta ücretleri [ewjretler**ee**] inland postal rates

yutmak to swallow

yuvarlak round

-yuz we are

-yü [-yew] accusative noun ending

yüksek [yewks**ek**] tall, high

yükseklik [yewksekl**eek**] height

yüksek sesle [sesl**eh**] loud

yüksek tansiyon high blood pressure

-yüm [-yewm] I am

yün [yewn] wool

yünlü [yewnl**ew**] woollen

yürümek [yewrewm**ek**] to walk

yürüyüş [yewrew-y**ew**sh] walk; walking

yürüyüşe çıkmak [yewrew-yewsh**eh** chuhm**a**k] to go for a walk

yüz [yewz] face; surface; hundred

-yüz [-yewz] we are

yüzde [yewzd**eh**] per cent

yüzde yüz 100 per cent

yüz kremi cold cream

yüz losyonu toner

yüzme [yewzm**eh**] swimming

yüzmeye gitmek [yewzmay**eh**] to go swimming

yüzme havuzu swimming pool

yüzmek [yewzm**ek**] to swim

yüzmek yasaktır no swimming

yüz numara toilet

yüzük [yewz**ewk**] ring

yüzyıl [yewz-y**uh**l] century

Z

zam increase

zaman time; when

zaman? when?

o zaman then, at that time

zaman zaman from time to time

zamk glue

zarar damage

zararı yok [zarar**uh**] never mind

zarar vermek to damage

zarf envelope

zarif elegant

zaruri essential, necessary

zaten anyway

zatürree [zatewrr**eh**] pneumonia

zaviye [zavee-y**eh**] lodge for dervishes

zayıf [zī-**uh**f] slim; thin; weak

zehir poison

zehirli poisonous

zeki intelligent

zemin kat ground floor, (US) first floor

zengin rich
zevkli enjoyable; pleasant;
  amusing
zil bell
zincir [zeenjeer] chain
ziyan loss; damage; harm
ziyaret visit
ziyaret etmek to visit
zor hard, difficult
zorluk difficulty
zurna reed instrument like an
  oboe
zücaciye [zewjajee-yeh]
  glassware

Menu Reader:

Food

ESSENTIAL TERMS

appetizers meze [mezeh]
cup fincan [feenjan]
dessert tatlı [tatluh]
fork çatal [chatal]
glass (tumbler) bardak
 (wine glass) kadeh
knife bıçak [buhchak]
meat dishes et yemekleri
menu yemek listesi
pepper biber
plate tabak
salad salata
salt tuz
set menu tabldot [tabldot]
soup çorba [chorba]
spoon kaşık [kashuhk]
starter (food) ordövr [ordurvr], meze [mezeh]
table masa

another ... başka bir ... [bashka]
excuse me! (to call waiter/waitress) bakar mısınız! [muhsuhnuhz]
could I have the bill, please? hesap, lütfen [lewtfen]

acı biber [ajuh] hot chillies
Adana kebabı [kebabuh] spicy
  meatballs
ahtapot [aHtapot] octopus
ahtapot salatası [salatasuh]
  octopus salad
ahududu [aHoodoodoo]
  raspberries
akıtma [akuhtma] pancake
akşam yemeği [aksham yemeh-
  ee] evening meal
alabalık [alabaluhk] trout
ananas pineapple
ançüez [anchew-ez]
  anchovies
armut pear
Arnavut ciğeri [jee-eree] spicy
  fried liver with onions
aşure [ashooreh] 'Noah's
  pudding' – a dessert made
  from wheat grains, nuts and
  dried fruit
av eti game
ayşekadın fasulyesi [īshekaduhn]
  French beans
ayva [īva] quince
ayva laabı [la-abuh] quince
  jelly
ayva reçeli [rechelee] quince
  jam
az pişmiş [peeshmeesh] rare;
  underdone

badem almond(s)
badem kurabiyesi macaroons;
  giant almond biscuits/
  cookies
badempare [–pareh] almond
  cakes in syrup

badem tatlısı [tatluhsuh]
  almond cakes
baharat spice
baharatlı [baharatluh] spicy
bakla broad beans
baklava pastry filled with nuts
  and syrup
bal honey
balık [baluhk] fish
balık buğulaması [boo-
  oolamasuh] fish baked with
  tomatoes
balık çorbası [chorbasuh] fish
  and lemon soup
balık köftesi [kurftesee] fish
  balls
balık pane [paneh] fish coated
  in breadcrumbs and fried
balık plaki fish baked with
  potatoes, carrots, celery
  and onions
bamya okra, ladies' fingers
barbunya red mullet; a type of
  red bean
barbunya pilakisi beans cooked
  in olive oil and served hot or
  cold
barbunya tava fried red mullet
bazlama flat bread cooked on
  a hotplate
beyaz peynir [bayaz payneer]
  white sheep's cheese,
  similar to Greek feta
beyaz peynirli makarna noodles
  with sheep's cheese
beyin salatası [bayeen salatasuh]
  brain salad
beyin tava brain slices in
  batter

beykın [baykuhn] bacon

bezelye [bezelyeh] peas

bıldırcın ızgara [buhlduhrjuhn uhzgara] grilled quail

bıldırcın yahni quail stew with onions

biber pepper(s), capsicum(s)

biber dolması [dolmasuh] stuffed green peppers/ capsicums

biftek steak

bir buçuk [boochook] a portion and a half

bisküvi [beeskew-vee] biscuits, cookies

bonfile [bonfeeleh] fillet steak

böbrek [burbrek] kidneys

böbrek ızgara [uhzgara] grilled kidneys

böbrek sote [soteh] sautéed kidneys

böğürtlen [bur-ewrtlen] blackberries

börek [bur-rek] layered pastry with cheese, meat or spinach filling

börülce [burewljeh] black-eyed beans

Brüksel lahanası [brewksel laHanasuh] Brussels sprouts

buğulama [boo-oolama] steamed; poached

bulgur bulgur wheat, cracked wheat

bulgur pilavı [peelavuh] bulgur wheat cooked with tomatoes

Bursa kebabı [kebabuh] grilled lamb kebab on pitta bread

with tomato sauce and yoghurt

bülbül yuvası [bewlbewl yoovasuh] dessert with nuts and syrup

cacık [jajuhk] cucumber, garlic and yoghurt dip

caneriği [janeree-ee] greengage

ceviz [jeveez] walnuts

cezeriye [jezeree-yeh] carrot, honey and nut bar

ciğer [jee-er] liver

ciğer sarması [sarmasuh] minced liver wrapped in lamb's fat

ciğer tava fried liver

çam fıstığı [cham fuhstuh-uh] pine nuts

çavdar ekmeği [chavdar ekmeh-ee] rye bread

çerez [cherez] pumpkin seeds, chickpeas, almonds etc served in bars

Çerkez peyniri [cherkez payneeree] cheese similar to Edam

Çerkez tavuğu [tavoo-oo] cold chicken in walnut sauce with garlic

çeşni veren otlar [cheshnee] herbs

çevirme [cheveermeh] spit-roasted

çılbır [chuhlbuhr] poached eggs with yoghurt

çift porsiyon [cheeft] double portion

çiğ köfte [chee kurfteh] raw

meatballs made from
minced meat, bulgur wheat
and chilli powder

çikolata [cheekolata] chocolate

çikolatalı [cheekolataluh] with
chocolate

çikolatalı dondurma chocolate
ice cream

çikolatalı pasta chocolate cake

çilek [cheelek] strawberry

çilekli dondurma [cheeleklee]
strawberry ice cream

çilek reçeli [rechelee]
strawberry jam

çips [cheeps] crisps, (US)
potato chips

çipura [cheepoora] gilt-headed
bream

çiroz [cheeroz] salted dried
mackerel

çoban salatası [choban
salatasuh] mixed tomatoes,
peppers/capsicums,
cucumbers and onion salad

çocuk porsiyonu [chojook]
children's portion

çorba [chorba] soup

çöp kebabı [churp kebabuh]
small pieces of lamb or offal
grilled on wooden skewers

çörek [chur-rek] sweet or
savoury bun

çulluk [choollook] woodcock

dana eti veal

dana rozbif roast veal

deniz ürünleri [ewrewnleree]
seafood

dereotu [dereh-otoo] dill

dil tongue

dil balığı [baluh-uh] sole

dilber dudağı [dooda-uh] sweet
pastry with nut filling

dil peyniri [payneeree] cheese
similar to mozzarella

dolma stuffed vegetables

domates tomato(es)

domatesli with tomatoes

domatesli pilav rice cooked
with tomatoes

domatesli pirinç çorbası
[peereench chorbasuh] rice
and tomato soup

domates salatası [salatasuh]
tomato salad

domates salçalı patlıcan
kızartması [salchaluh patluhjan
kuhzartmasuh] fried
aubergines/eggplants with
tomato and garlic sauce

domates salçası [salchasuh]
tomato purée

domuz eti pork

dondurma ice cream

döner kebap [durner] lamb
grilled on a spit and served
in thin slices, usually served
with rice and salad

dövme dondurma [durvmeh] ice
cream made according to
the Kahraman Maraş
tradition

dut [doot] mulberries

düğün çorbası [dew-ewn
chorbasuh] 'wedding soup'
made from meat stock,
yoghurt and egg

ekmek bread
ekmek kadayıfı [kadī-uhf**uh**] sweet pastry
ekşi [eksh**ee**] sour
elma apple(s)
elmalı tart [elmal**uh**] apple pie
elma tatlısı [tatluhs**uh**] dessert made with apples
enginar [engeen**a**r] artichoke(s)
erik plum(s)
erişte [ereesht**eh**] homemade noodles
et meat
etli with meat
etli ayşekadın [īshehkad**uh**n] meat with green beans
etli bezelye [b**e**zelyeh] pea and meat stew
etli biber dolması [dolmas**uh**] peppers/capsicums stuffed with rice and meat
etli börek [bur-rek] meat pie
etli bulgur pilavı [peelav**uh**] bulgur wheat with meat
etli domates dolması [dolmas**uh**] tomatoes stuffed with meat and rice
etli kabak dolması marrows stuffed with meat and rice
etli kapuska cabbage and meat stew
etli kuru fasulye [fas**oo**lyeh] lamb and haricot beans in tomato sauce
etli lahana dolması [laH**a**na dolmas**uh**] cabbage leaves stuffed with meat and rice
etli nohut chickpea and meat stew

etli taze fasulye [taz**eh** fas**oo**lyeh] stew of meat, runner beans, tomatoes and onions
etli yaprak dolması [dolmas**uh**] vine leaves stuffed with rice and meat
et sote [sot**eh**] sautéed meat
et suyu meat stock
ezme [ezm**eh**] purée
ezo gelin çorbası [chorbas**uh**] lentil and rice soup

fasulye [fas**oo**lyeh] haricot beans
fasulye pilaki(si) haricot beans cooked in olive oil
fasulye piyazı [pee-yaz**uh**] haricot bean and onion salad
fava broad bean purée
fındık [fuhnd**uh**k] nuts; hazelnuts
fındık fıstık [fuhst**uh**k] nuts
fırın [fuhr**uh**n] baked; oven-roasted
fırında [fuhruhnda] baked; oven-roasted
fırın sütlaç [sewtl**a**ch] baked rice pudding
fıstık [fuhst**uh**k] peanuts; pine nuts
fıstıklı [fuhstuhkl**uh**] with pistachio nuts
fıstıklı dondurma [fuhstuhkl**uh**] pistachio ice cream
fıstıklı muhallebi rice flour and rosewater pudding with pistachio nuts

fileto fillet
füme [fewm**eh**] smoked

garnitür salata [garneet**ewr**] side
salad
gözleme [gurzlem**eh**] crêpe-like
bread with various
toppings; pancake
greyfrut grapefruit
güllaç [gewll**ach**] rice wafers
filled with nuts, cooked in
rose-flavoured milky syrup
gümüş balığı [gew-m**ew**sh baluh-
uh] silverfish
güveç [gew-v**ech**] meat and
vegetable casserole
güvercin [gew-verj**een**] pigeon

hamsi anchovy
hanım parmağı [han**uh**m parma-
uh] 'Lady's Fingers' – finger-
shaped pastry sticks in
syrup
hardal mustard
has ekmek white bread
haşlama [hashlam**a**] boiled;
stewed
haşlanmış yumurta
[hashlanm**uh**sh] boiled egg
havuç [hav**ooch**] carrot(s)
havuç salatası [sal**a**tasuh]
grated carrot salad
havyar caviar
haydari [h**ī**dar**ee**] thick garlic
dip with parsley or spinach
hazır yemek [haz**uh**r] ready-to-
eat food
helva baked flour, butter,
sugar and flavoured water
with various fillings like

tahini paste
hesap bill, (US) check
hıyar [huh-y**a**r] cucumber
hindi turkey
hindiba wild chicory
hindi dolması [dolmas**uh**]
stuffed turkey
hindistan cevizi [jeveez**ee**]
coconut
hoşaf [hosh**af**] stewed fruit
höşmerim [hurshmer**ee**m]
cheese helva
hurma dates
hünkar beğendi [hewnk**a**r beh-
end**ee**] 'Sultan's Delight' –
lamb served with aubergine/
eggplant purée

ıspanak [uhspan**a**k] spinach
ıspanaklı börek [uhspanakl**uh**
bur-r**e**k] pastry filled with
spinach
ıspanaklı yumurta eggs with
spinach
ıstakoz [uhstak**o**z] lobster;
crayfish
ızgara [uhzg**a**ra] grilled
ızgara balık [bal**uh**k] grilled fish
ızgarada grilled
ızgara köfte [kurft**eh**] grilled
meatballs
... ızgarası [uhzgaras**uh**]
grilled ...
ızgara tavuk [uhzg**a**ra] grilled
chicken
ızgara yemek meat dishes
grilled to order

iç [eech] filling
içecek [eechej**e**k] beverage

içli köfte [eechl**ee** kurft**eh**]
   meatballs stuffed with
   bulgur wheat
iç pilav [eech] rice with
   currants, pine nuts and
   onions
imam bayıldı [bī-uhld**uh**] 'Imam
   Swoons' – aubergine/
   eggplant with tomatoes and
   onions, cooked with olive
   oil and eaten cold
incir [eenj**eer**] figs
irmik helvası [helvas**uh**]
   semolina helva – sweet
   made from semolina, nuts,
   butter and sugar
islim kebabı [kebab**uh**] steamed
   kebab
istavrit horse mackerel
istiridye [eesteer**ee**d-yeh]
   oyster(s)
işkembe çorbası [eeshkembeh
   chorbas**uh**] tripe soup
İskender kebabı [eeshkender
   kebab**uh**] döner kebab on
   pitta bread with tomato
   sauce and yoghurt
iyi pişmiş [peeshm**ee**sh] well-
   done; well-cooked

jambon [Jamb**o**n] ham
jelatin [Jelat**ee**n] gelatin

kabak courgette, zucchini;
   pumpkin; marrow
kabak dolması [dolmas**uh**]
   stuffed courgettes/
   zucchini
kabak kızartması [kuhzartmas**uh**]
   fried marrows

kabak reçeli [rechel**ee**] marrow
   jam
kabak tatlısı [tatluhs**uh**]
   pumpkin with syrup and
   walnuts
kabuklu deniz ürünleri
   [ewrewnler**ee**] shellfish
kadayıf [kada-y**uh**f] shredded
   wheat-type dessert in syrup
kadın budu köfte [kad**uh**n –
   kurft**eh**] 'Lady's Thighs' –
   meat and rice croquettes
kadın göbeği [gurb**eh**-ee]
   'Lady's Navel' – a ring-
   shaped pastry with syrup
kağıt kebabı [ka-**uh**t kebab**uh**]
   lamb and vegetables baked
   in paper
kağıtta barbunya [ka-**uh**tta] red
   mullet baked in paper
kağıtta pişmiş [peeshm**ee**sh]
   baked in paper
kahvaltı [kahvalt**uh**] breakfast
kalamar squid
kalamar tava fried squid
kalkan turbot
kara biber black pepper
karadut black mulberries
kara ekmek brown bread
karagöz [karag**ur**z] black bream
kara turp horseradish
kara zeytin [zayt**ee**n] black
   olives
karışık [karuhsh**uh**k] mixed
karışık dondurma [karuhsh**uh**k]
   mixed ice cream
karışık ızgara [uhzg**a**ra] mixed
   grill
karışık salata mixed salad

karides prawns
karides güveç [gewvech] prawn
  stew
karides kokteyl [koktayl] prawn
  cocktail
karides tava prawns in batter
karides tavası [tavasuh] prawns
  in batter
karnabahar cauliflower
karnabahar tavası [tavasuh]
  fried cauliflower
karnıyarık [karnuh-yaruhk] split
  aubergine/eggplant with
  meat filling
karper peyniri [payneeree]
  processed cheese, cheese
  spread
karpuz water melon
kaşar (peyniri) [kashar
  payneeree] mild yellow
  cheese
kaşar peynirli makarna noodles
  with kaşar
kavun honeydew melon
kavunlu dondurma melon ice
  cream
kayısı [kī-uhsuh] apricot(s)
kayısı reçeli [rechelee] apricot
  jam
kaymak [kī-mak] clotted cream
kaymaklı [kīmakluh] with
  clotted cream
kaymaklı dondurma dairy ice
  cream
kaynamış yumurta [kīnamuhsh]
  boiled egg
kaz goose
kazan dibi pudding with a
  caramel base

kebap roast meat, kebab
keçi eti [kechee] goat's meat
keçi peyniri [payneeree] goat's
  cheese
kefal grey mullet
kefal pilakisi mullet cooked in
  olive oil with vegetables
kek cake
keklik partridge
Kemalpaşa [kemalpasha] syrup-
  soaked dumpling
kepekli ekmek bread made
  from whole bran
kerevit crayfish
kereviz celery
kestane [kestaneh] chestnut(s)
kestane şekeri [shekeree]
  marrons glacés, candied
  chestnuts
keş [kesh] dry curd cheese
keşkek [keshkek] lamb with
  bulgur wheat
keşkül [keshkewl] almond
  pudding
ketçap [ketchap] tomato
  ketchup
kılıç (balığı) [kuhluhch (baluh-
  uh)] swordfish
kılıç ızgara [uhzgara] grilled
  swordfish
kılıç şiş [sheesh] swordfish on
  skewers
kırmızı biber [kuhrmuhzuh]
  paprika; red pepper,
  capsicum
kırmızı mercimek çorbası
  [merjeemek chorbasuh] red
  lentil soup
kırmızı turp radish

kısır [kuhs**uhr**] bulgur wheat salad with spring onions, green pepper/capsicum and tomatoes

kış türlüsü [kuhsh tewrlews**ew**] stewed winter vegetables

kıvırcık salata [kuhvuhrj**uhk**] lettuce

kıyma [kuh-ima] minced meat

kıymalı [kuh-imal**uh**] with minced meat

kıymalı bamya okra with minced meat

kıymalı ıspanak [uhspan**a**k] spinach with minced meat

kıymalı karnabahar cauliflower with minced meat

kıymalı makarna noodles with minced meat

kıymalı mercimek [merjeem**e**k] minced meat and lentils

kıymalı pide [peed**e**h] flat bread with minced meat topping

kıymalı yumurta eggs with minced meat

kızarmış [kuhzarm**uh**sh] fried; toasted; grilled

kızarmış ekmek [kuhzarm**uh**sh] toast

kızartma [kuhzartm**a**] fried; broiled

kiraz cherries

kiremitte balık [keeremeett**e**h bal**uh**k] fish baked on a tile

koç yumurtası [koch yoomoortas**uh**] ram's testicles

kokoreç [kokorech] lamb's intestines grilled on a spit

kolyoz chub mackerel

komposto fruit compote

koyun (eti) mutton

köfte [kurft**e**h] meat balls or patties

köpek balığı [kurp**e**k baluh-**uh**] shark

krema cream

kremalı mantar [kr**e**maluh] mushrooms with cream

kremalı pasta cream cake

krem karamel crème caramel

krem şantiye [shantee-y**e**h] whipped cream

krik krak cracker

kupes type of sea bream

kurabiye [koorabee-y**e**h] cake with almonds or nuts

kuru dried

kuru fasulye [fas**oo**lyeh] haricot beans in tomato sauce

kuru köfte [kurft**e**h] fried meatballs

kuru üzüm [ewz**ew**m] raisins

kuru yemiş [yem**ee**sh] dried fruit and nuts

kuskus pilavı [peelav**uh**] couscous – semolina grains with a meat stew

kuşbaşı et [koosh-bash**uh**] small pieces of meat

kuşkonmaz [kooshkonm**a**z] asparagus

kuzu (eti) lamb

kuzu fırında [fuhruhnd**a**] roast leg of lamb

kuzu kapama lamb stew with lettuce and carrots

kuzu pirzolası [peerz**o**lasuh] lamb chops

külbastı grilled cutlet
kümes hayvanları [kewmes
hīvanlaruh] poultry

lahana [laHana] cabbage
lahana dolması [dolmasuh]
stuffed cabbage leaves
lahana turşusu [toorshoosoo]
pickled cabbage
lahmacun [laHmajoon] kind of
pizza with spicy meat
topping
lakerda pickled tuna fish
leblebi roasted chickpeas
levrek sea bass
limon lemon
limonlu dondurma lemon ice
cream
lokum Turkish Delight
lop yumurta hard-boiled egg
lüfer [lewfer] bluefish

makarna macaroni; noodles;
pasta
mama baby food
mandalina tangerine
mantar mushroom(s)
mantarlı omlet [mantarluh]
mushroom omelette
mantı [mantuh] similar to
ravioli
Maraş dondurması [marash
dondurmasuh] type of ice
cream
margarin margarine
marmelat jam
marul cos lettuce
maydanoz [mīdanoz] parsley
mayonez [mī-onez]
mayonnaise

mayonezli balık [baluhk] fish
with mayonnaise
menemen omelette with
tomatoes and peppers/
capsicums
mercan [merjan] bream
mercimek [merjeemek] lentils
mercimek çorbası [chorbasuh]
lentil soup
mersin balığı [baluh-uh]
sturgeon
mevsim salatası [salatasuh]
seasonal salad
meyve [mayveh] fruit
meyveli pay [mayvelee pī] fruit
pie
meze [mezeh] hors d'œuvres,
appetizers
mezgit whitebait
mısır [muhsuhr] corn
midye [meed-yeh] mussels
midye dolması [dolmasuh]
stuffed mussels
midyeli pilav rice with mussels
midye pilakisi mussels cooked
in oil with vegetables
midye tava/tavası [tavasuh]
deep-fried mussels
misket limonu lime
muhallebi pudding made
from rice flour and
rosewater
musakka moussaka
muska böreği [bur-reh-ee]
triangular pastries filled
with cheese and parsley
Mustafakemalpaşa [–pasha]
syrup-soaked dumpling
muz banana

mücver [mewjver] vegetable
patties

nane [naneh] mint

nar pomegranate

nemse böreği [nemseh bur-reh-
ee] meat pie made with puff
pastry

nohut chickpeas

nohutlu paça [pacha] lamb's
trotters with chickpeas

nohutlu yahni lamb stew with
chickpeas

omlet omelette

ordövr [ordurvr] starter, hors
d'œuvre

orfoz giant grouper

orman kebabı [kebabuh] veal or
lamb, fried then cooked
with vegetables

orta pişmiş [peeshmeesh]
medium-rare

otlu peynir [payneer] herb-
flavoured cheese from
around Lake Van

öğle yemeği [urleh yemeh-ee]
lunch

ördek [urdek] duck

paça [pacha] lamb's trotters

paça çorbası [chorbasuh] lamb's
trotter soup

palamut tunny fish

pancar [panjar] beetroot

pancar turşusu [toorshoosoo]
pickled beetroot

pandispanya sponge cake

pane [paneh] coated in
breadcrumbs and fried

papaz eriği [eree-ee] green
plum

parça [parcha] piece, slice

paskalya çöreği [chureh-ee]
'Easter bread' – slightly
sweet plait-shaped bread

pasta cake

pastırma [pastuhrma] cumin-
and garlic-cured beef

pastırmalı yumurta
[pastuhrmaluh] fried eggs
with pastırma

patates potato(es)

patates kızartması
[kuhzartmasuh] chips, French
fries

patates köftesi [kurftesee]
potato and cheese balls

patatesli with potatoes

patates püresi [pewresee]
mashed potatoes

patates salatası [salatasuh]
potato salad

patlıcan [patluhjan]
aubergine(s), eggplant(s)

patlıcan dolma turşusu
[toorshoosoo] pickled
stuffed aubergines/
eggplants

patlıcan ezmesi aubergine/
eggplant pâté

patlıcan kebabı [kebabuh]
pieces of meat wrapped in
aubergine/eggplant and
roasted or baked

patlıcan kızartması
[kuhzartmasuh] fried
aubergines/eggplants with
garlic sauce

patlıcanlı pilav [patluhjanl**uh**]
rice with aubergines/
eggplants

patlıcan salatası [sal**a**tasuh]
aubergine/eggplant purée

pavurya crab

pestil pressed dried fruit

peynir [payn**eer**] cheese

peynirli with cheese

peynirli omlet cheese
omelette

peynirli pide [peed**eh**] flat bread
with cheese topping

peynirli tepsi böreği [bur**eh**-ee]
cheese pie

peynir tatlısı [tatluhs**uh**] small
cheesecakes in syrup

pırasa [puhr**a**sa] leek(s)

pide [peed**eh**] leavened flat
bread

pilaki haricot bean vinaigrette

pilav cooked rice

pilavlı tavuk [peelavl**uh**] chicken
and rice

pil füme [fewm**eh**] smoked
tongue

piliç [peel**ee**ch] young chicken

piliç ızgara(sı) [uhzgara(suh)]
grilled chicken

pirinç [peer**ee**nch] rice (uncooked)

pirzola chop

pisi plaice

pişkin [peeshk**ee**n] well-cooked,
well-done

pişmemiş [peeshmemeesh]
underdone; not cooked

poğaça [po-a**cha**] pastries filled
with meat or cheese

portakal orange(s)

portakallı ördek [portakall**uh**
urd**ek**] duck with orange

portakal reçeli [rechel**ee**]
marmalade, orange jam

puf böreği [bur-r**eh**-ee] cheese
or meat pasties

püre [pewr**eh**] purée

rafadan (yumurta) soft-boiled
egg

reçel [rech**el**] jam

revani sweet semolina pastry

roka rocket

rosto roasted

rozbif roast beef

rus salatası [sal**a**tasuh] Russian
salad – potatoes, peas,
salami and gherkins with
mayonnaise

saç kavurma [sach] Anatolian
speciality made from meat,
vegetables, spices and oil,
fried in a Turkish wok

sade omlet [sa-d**eh**] plain
omelette

sade pilav plain rice pilav

sahanda yumurta fried eggs

salam salami

salata salad

salatalık [salatal**uh**k] cucumber

salata sosu salad dressing

salça [sal**cha**] tomato sauce or
paste

salçalı [salchal**uh**] with tomato
sauce

salçalı köfte [kurft**eh**] meatballs
in tomato sauce

salyongoz snails

sandviç [sandv**ee**ch] sandwich

sandviç ekmeği [ekmeh-**ee**]
roll(s)
sap kerevizi celery
saray lokması [sar**ī** lokmas**uh**]
fried batter in syrup
sardalye [sardal-yeh] sardines
sarıgöz [saruhg**ur**z] black
bream
sarığıburma [saruh-**uh**-boorma]
'Twisted Turban' – turban-
shaped baklava
sarmısak [sarmuhs**ak**] garlic
sazan carp
sazan güveç [gewvech] carp
casserole
sazan kiremit carp baked on a
tile
sebze [sebz**eh**] vegetables
sebze çorbası [chorbas**uh**]
vegetable soup
semizotu purslane – a herb
used in salads and stews
semizotu salatası [sal**a**tasuh]
purslane salad
servis course
servis ücreti service charge
sıcak [suhj**ak**] hot; warm
sığır (eti) [suh-**uhr**] beef
sigara böreği [burr**eh**-ee]
cigarette-shaped filo pastry
filled with cheese and
parsley
simit ring-shaped bread
covered with sesame seeds
sirke [seerk**eh**] vinegar
sivribiber long, thin hot or mild
peppers
siyah zeytin [seeya**H** zayt**ee**n]
black olives

soğan [soh-**a**n] onion(s)
soğan dolması [dolmas**uh**]
stuffed onions
soğuk [soh-**oo**k] cold
soğuk antreler [so-**oo**k] cold
hors d'œuvres
soğuk büfe [bewf**eh**] cold food
som balığı [sohm baluh-**uh**]
salmon
somun loaf
sos sauce; gravy; salad
dressing
sosis sausage
soslu with sauce
sote [sot**eh**] sautéed
söğüş et [so-**ew**sh] cold meat
söğüş salata salad served
without dressing
su böreği [bur-r**eh**-ee] layered
pastry filled with cheese,
parsley and dill
sucuk [sooj**oo**k] spicy Turkish
sausage with garlic
sucuklu with sausage
sucuklu pide [peed**eh**] flat
bread with sausage
sumak sumach – herb eaten
with kebabs
su muhallebisi rice flour
pudding with rosewater
supanglez chocolate pudding
sülün [sewl**ew**n] pheasant
süt [sewt] milk
sütlaç [sewtl**a**ch] rice pudding
sütlü tatlılar [sewtl**ew** tatluhl**a**r]
milk puddings
süzme yoğurt [sewzm**eh** yoh-
oort] strained yoghurt

şalgam [shalgam] turnip
şamfıstığı [shamfuhstuh-uh]
  pistachio nuts
şam tatlısı [sham tatluhsuh]
  dessert with syrup
şeftali [sheftalee] peach(es)
şeftali reçeli [rechelee] peach
  jam
şehriye [sheHree-yeh] vermicelli
şehriye çorbası [chorbasuh]
  vermicelli soup with lemon
şehriyeli with vermicelli
şehriyeli pilav rice with
  vermicelli
şeker [sheker] sugar; sweets,
  candies
şekerpare [shekerpareh] small
  cakes with syrup
şinitzel [sheeneetzel] cutlet, thin
  slice of meat
şiş [sheesh] cooked on a
  skewer
şiş kebabı [kebabuh] small
  pieces of lamb grilled on
  skewers
şiş köfte [kurfteh] grilled
  meatballs on skewers
şöbiyet [surbee-yet] sweet
  pastry
şurup [shooroop] syrup

tabldot set menu
tahin helvası [helvasuh] sesame
  seed paste helva
talaşkebabı [talashkebabuh]
  lamb baked in pastry
tam ekmek wholemeal bread
tarama roe pâté
tarator nut and garlic sauce

taratorlu karnabahar cauliflower
  with nut and garlic sauce
tarhana çorbası [chorbasuh]
  soup made with dried
  yoghurt, tomato and
  pimento
taskebabı [taskebabuh] diced
  lamb with rice
tatar böreği [bur-reh-ee] ravioli
tatlı [tatluh] sweet, dessert
tatlı sucuk [soojook] fruit, nut
  and molasses roll
tava(da) fried
tavşan [tavshan] rabbit
tavuk chicken
tavuk çorbası [chorbasuh]
  chicken soup
tavuk göğsü [gur-sew] chicken
  breast pudding – creamy
  dessert made with rice flour
  and finely shredded chicken
tavuk ızgara(sı) [uhzgara(suh)]
  grilled chicken
tavuklu pilav chicken and rice
tavuk söğüş [sur-ewsh] cold
  chicken
tavuk suyu chicken consommé
taze [tazeh] fresh
taze beyaz peynir [bayaz
  payneer] fresh sheep's
  cheese
taze soğan [soh-an] spring
  onions
tekir striped mullet
tel kadayıf [kadī-uhf] shredded
  wheat-type dessert with nuts
  and syrup
terbiye [terbee-yeh] egg and
  lemon sauce

terbiyeli with egg and lemon
sauce
terbiyeli haşlama [hashlama]
boiled lamb with egg and
lemon sauce
terbiyeli köfte [kurfteh]
meatballs with egg and
lemon sauce
tere [tereh] cress
tereyağı [tereh-ya-uh] butter
ton balığı [baluh-uh] tuna
torik large tunny fish
tost toast; toasted sandwich
tulumba tatlısı [tatluhsuh]
semolina doughnut in
syrup
tulum peyniri [payneeree] dry,
crumbly, parmesan-like
cheese made from goat's
milk in a goatskin
turna pike
turp radish
turşu [toorshoo] pickled
vegetables
turşu suyu juice from pickled
vegetables
turta fruit pie
turunç [tooroonch] Seville
oranges
tuz salt
tuzlama salted; pickled
tükenmez [tewkenmez] eggs
fried with tomatoes and
peppers/capsicums
türlü (sebze) [tewrlew (sebzeh)]
meat and vegetable stew

un flour
un helvası [helvasuh] helva

made from flour, sugar,
milk, butter, and sometimes
with nuts
Urfa kebabı [kebabuh] very
spicy kebab
uskumru mackerel
uskumru dolması [dolmasuh]
stuffed mackerel

üzüm [ewzewm] grapes

vanilya vanilla
vanilyalı dondurma [vaneel-
yaluh] vanilla ice cream
vişne [veeshneh] black
cherries, morello cherries

yağ [ya] oil; fat
yağda yumurta [ya-da] fried egg
yahni meat stew with onions
yalancı dolma [yalanjuh] stuffed
vine leaves
yaprak dolması [dolmasuh]
stuffed vine leaves
yayın sheatfish
yayla çorbası [yīla chorbasuh]
yoghurt soup
yaz türlüsü [tewrlewsew] stewed
summer vegetables
yemek meal; dish
yemek listesi menu
yengeç [yengech] crab
yerfıstığı [yerfuhstuh-uh]
peanuts
yeşil biber [yesheel] green
pepper, capsicum
yeşil mercimek çorbası
[merjeemek chorbasuh] green
lentil soup
yeşil salata green salad

yeşil zeytin [zayteen] green
olives
yiyecek [yee-yejek] food
yoğurt [yoh-oort] yoghurt
yoğurtlu with yoghurt
yoğurtlu kebap kebab with
pitta bread and yoghurt
yoğurtlu paça [pacha] lamb's
trotters with yoghurt and
garlic
yoğurt tatlısı [tatluhsuh]
yoghurt cake with syrup
yufka filo pastry
yufka ekmek thin sheets of
unleavened bread
yumurta egg
yumurtalı [yoomoortaluh] with
egg
yumurtalı pide [peedeh] flat
bread with egg
yürek [yewrek] heart

zerde [zerdeh] saffron rice
dessert
zeytin [zayteen] olive(s)
zeytinyağı [zayteenya-uh] olive
oil
zeytinyağlı [zayteenya-luh]
vegetable dish in olive oil,
served cold
zeytinyağlı biber dolması
[dolmasuh] stuffed peppers/
capsicums cooked with
olive oil
zeytinyağlı enginar artichokes
cooked with olive oil
zeytinyağlı kereviz celery
cooked with olive oil
zeytinyağlı patlıcan pilavı

[patluhjan peelavuh] rice with
aubergines/eggplants
cooked in olive oil
zeytinyağlı pırasa [puhrasa]
leeks cooked with olive oil
zeytinyağlı pilaki red haricot
beans cooked with olive oil
zeytinyağlı taze bakla [tazeh]
fresh broad beans cooked
with olive oil
zeytinyağlı taze fasulye
[fasoolyeh] runner beans
cooked with tomatoes and
olive oil
zeytinyağlı yaprak dolması
[dolmasuh] vine leaves
stuffed with rice, pine nuts
and raisins

Menu Reader:

Drink

ESSENTIAL TERMS

beer bira
bottle şişe [sheesh**eh**]
brandy konyak
coffee kahve [ka**H**ve**h**]
cup fincan [feenj**a**n]
alcoholic drinks içkiler [eechkeel**eer**]
gin cin [jeen]
glass (tumbler) bar**d**ak
   (wine glass) kade**h**
milk süt [sewt]
mineral water maden suy**u**
red wine kırmızı şarap [kuhrmuhz**uh** shar**a**p]
soda (water) maden sodası [sodas**uh**]
soft drinks meşrubat [meshroob**a**t]
sugar şeker [sheker]
tea çay [chī]
tonic (water) toni**k**
vodka v**o**tka
water su
whisky visk**i**
white wine beyaz şarap [bay**a**z shar**a**p]
wine şarap
wine list şarap listes**i**

another ... başka bir ... [bashk**a**]
a glass of tea bir bar**d**ak çay
a gin and tonic bir cintonik [jeenton**eek**]

acıbadem likörü [ajuhbadem leekurew] almond liqueur

açık [achuhk] weak

ada çayı [chī-uh] type of sage infusion

alkol alcohol

alkollü [alkollew] alcoholic

alkolsüz [–sewz] non-alcoholic

alkolsüz içki [eechkee] soft drink

ananas suyu pineapple juice

ayran [īran] yoghurt drink

az şekerli kahve [shekerlee kaHveh] slightly sweetened Turkish coffee

bardak glass

beyaz şarap [bayaz sharap] white wine

bira beer; lager

bitkisel çay [chī] herbal tea

boza thick fermented grain drink

buz [booz] ice

buzlu with ice

buzlu kahve [kaHveh] iced coffee

cin [jeen] gin

cintonik gin and tonic

Çankaya [chankī-a] dry, white wine from Cappadocia

çay [chī] tea

çok şekerli kahve [chok shekerlee kaHveh] very sweet Turkish coffee

demli steeped

domates suyu tomato juice

dömi sek [durmee] medium-dry

Efes Pilsen® type of lager

elma çayı [chī-uh] apple tea

elma suyu apple juice

elma şırası [shuhrasuh] cider

fıçı birası [fuhchuh beerasuh] draught beer

fincan [feenjan] cup

gazlı [gazluh] fizzy

gazoz fizzy drink

greyfrut suyu grapefruit juice

ıhlamur [uh-Hlamoor] lime blossom tea

içecek [eechejek] beverage

içki [eechkee] alcoholic drinks

içkiler [eechkeeleer] alcoholic drinks

içkili [eechkeelee] alcoholic drinks served

ithal imported

kafeinsiz kahve [kafeh-eenseez kaHveh] decaffeinated coffee

kahve [kaHveh] coffee; coffee shop (usually for men only)

kakao [kaka-o] hot chocolate; cocoa

kanyak [kanyak] French brandy

kayısı suyu [ka-yuhsuh] apricot juice

kırmızı şarap [kuhrmuhzuh sharap] red wine

konyak brandy

koyu steeped

köpüklü şarap [kurpewklew sharap] sparkling wine

Lâl dry, rosé wine from
    Denizli
likör [leekur] liqueur
limonata still lemon drink
limonlu çay [chī] lemon tea

maden sodası [sodasuh] soda
    (water)
maden suyu mineral water
Marmara® type of lager
menba suyu spring water
meşrubat [meshroobat] soft
    drinks
meyve suyu [mayveh] fruit
    juice
milkşeyk [meelkshayk]
    milkshake
Mocca® almond liqueur

Narbağ [narba] white, medium-
    dry wine from Central
    Anatolia
neskafe [neskafeh] general
    word for any instant coffee

orta şekerli kahve [shekerlee
    kaHveh] medium sweet
    Turkish coffee

papatya çayı [chī-uh] camomile
    tea
pembe şarap [pembeh sharap]
    rosé
portakal suyu orange juice
porto şarabı [sharabuh] port

rakı [rakuh] spirit distilled
    from grape juice and
    flavoured with aniseed,
    similar to Greek ouzo
rom rum

roze [rozeh] rosé

sade kahve [sadeh kaHveh]
    Turkish coffee without
    sugar
sahlep drink made from
    sahlep root infused in hot
    milk and cinnamon
sek dry; straight (no ice)
sek şarap [sharap] dry wine
sıcak süt [suhjak sewt] hot milk
su water
suyla [soo-ila] with water
suyu juice
süt [sewt] milk
sütlü [sewtlew] with milk
sütlü kahve [kaHveh] coffee
    with milk
süzme kahve [sewzmeh] filter
    coffee

şampanya [shampanya]
    champagne
şarap [sharap] wine
şarap listesi wine list
şaraplar wines
şeftali suyu [sheftalee] peach
    juice
şeker [sheker] sugar
şekerli [shekerlee] with sugar
şerbet [sherbet] sweetened and
    iced fruit juice
şeri [sheree] sherry
şıra [shuhra] grape juice
şişe [sheesheh] bottle

tatlı şarap [tatluh sharap] sweet
    wine
taze portakal suyu [tazeh] fresh
    orange juice

tonik tonic (water)
torba çay [chī] teabags
Tuborg® type of lager
Turasan® dry red or white
  wine from Central Anatolia
Türk kahvesi [tewrk kaнvesee]
  Turkish coffee

Venus® type of lager
viski whisky, scotch
vişne suyu [veeshneh] black
  cherry juice
votka vodka

Yakut dry, red wine
yarım şişe [yaruhm sheesheh]
  half-bottle
Yeni Rakı® [rakuh] brand of
  rakı
yerli Turkish brand